The Search for Equity

The Search for Equity

David Foden and
Peter Morris (editors)

Lawrence & Wishart
LONDON

Lawrence & Wishart Limited
99a Wallis Road
London E9 5LN

First published 1998

© ETUI/UNISON 1998

British Library Cataloguing in Publication data.
A catalogue record for this book is available from the
British Library.

ISBN 0 85315 864 9

Photoset in North Wales by
Derek Doyle & Associates, Mold, Flintshire.
Printed and bound in Great Britain by
Redwood Books, Trowbridge.

Contents

Introduction

David Foden and Peter Morris

The essays and reports contained in this volume represent a stage in a debate which is taking place both between progressives and conservatives, and among progressives. The debate between the 'centre-left' (though the label is inadequate) and conservatives concerns whether or not progressive politics remains a possibility in the era of globalisation. A fine example of the conservative view is given by Robert Reich in his account of his time as President Clinton's Secretary of Labour, 'Locked in the cabinet'. He describes an encounter with Ford chairman, Alex Trottman. Reich asks, 'Suppose you were President. What's the most important thing you'd do to reverse the widening income gap and declining earnings of half the American workforce?' Trottman replies, 'The trend can't be reversed. It's inevitable in a global economy. Some will get richer and richer, some poorer and poorer. Nothing we can do about it.'

The authors in this book all assert that there are things we can do about it, but none of them are likely to be done if we fall into the trap of fatalism set by conservatives. This is at the heart of our debate with conservatives, whether public policy can shape economic and social outcomes – to provide more and better jobs, to combine security with efficiency, to rebuild our welfare systems – or whether such attempts to intervene merely spur market forces to ever more perverse and unequal results.

Those seeking arguments for this debate will find many in this book. Both theoretical and empirical approaches illuminate the progressive case: that we're being posed a false choice between more or better jobs; that high labour standards need not imply rigidity; and that decent welfare states are not an economic burden. It would be foolhardy to predict a final outcome to such a debate as this – the end of history has already, and prematurely, been announced. But there is perhaps a growing optimism that neo-liberalism has, for now at least, run its course. An optimism encouraged by the victories of New Labour in Britain and the socialists in France in 1997.

But this means that the second debate takes on a greater significance. This is the debate amongst those on the centre-left as to what form of intervention in the market is appropriate, by whom and with what purpose? The easiest conclusion is the hardest politically – that our goals cannot be reached by the methods which worked in the past. It is particularly hard to persuade the victims of economic change that the old world cannot be recreated, when right-wing forces are trying to seduce them with the comfort blankets of protectionism and reduced immigration. To succeed in so persuading them, the leaders of the progressive forces, in political parties of the left and trade unions, must be able to show how acceptance of change can lead to a better future. In this respect, merely to spread knowledge of positive experiences through our various networks can be useful.

In addition, however, there are a number of unresolved questions to emerge from the various contributions to this volume, which further debate can help to clarify. Two questions on which significant differences of emphasis (at the least) exist are apparent: international economic policy co-ordination and European EMU; and reduced working time. And there are two further questions where, although there may be some consensus, there is less clarity as to what in practice should be done: negotiating flexibility in the labour market; and building new partnerships.

To take first the questions of continuing controversy: the issues of international economic policy co-ordination and EMU are raised in a number of contributions. There is little dissent that economic co-ordination is desirable, or that the immediate goal should be a downward convergence of interest rates, especially in Europe. The clearest divide concerns whether EMU will lock Europe into permanent deflation, perpetuating inappropriately high real interest rates, while constraining even passive fiscal policy through the stability and growth pact; or whether EMU will represent the decisive move to managing Europe's economy in a coherent manner, thus enabling growth and employment to feature once more among the objectives of macroeconomic policy.

Behind this dispute lie not only differing calculations about the politics of EMU – how strictly will the convergence criteria be interpreted, and what institutions for economic management will be created alongside the European Central Bank, for example – but also different views about the scope for active fiscal policy, and the consequences for long-term interest rates, in a world of liberalised capital movements; different views about the forms of labour market flexibility EMU will demand; and different views about the importance of a better developed European-wide public finance system to a well-functioning EMU. These substantive issues will continue to be debated in the months and years ahead. Perhaps our network can play a part.[1]

The second area where major divergences of view can be seen concerns the role of reduced working time in the fight against unemployment. Many trade unions maintain reduced working time as a key demand, both for its role in improving the quality of working life and for its capacity to assist towards a better distribution of productivity gains among the employed and (actually or potentially) unemployed labour force. However, there are a variety of different positions on the financing of reduced working time. Although very few would insist that no sacrifice on the part of the existing workforce is entailed (even the demand for 'no loss of pay' may implicitly accept 'no, or less, reward for increased productivity'), there are important differences between the degree of acceptance of explicit income and work-sharing among different trade union organisations. Where this comes out most clearly is in attitudes to part-time work, seen by some as an acceptable compromise (under certain conditions) to redistribute work and meet demands for flexibility from both employers and workers, and by others as encouraging poor quality employment, undermining the conditions of full-time workers, promoting a dual labour market and ensuring that productivity gains are distributed primarily to capital.

On this issue too, ongoing debate among the progressive camp would seem fruitful, not least because there are probably important issues on which all can agree. There is the potential to link working time reduction to other demands – for life-long learning through the negotiation of leave for education and training; for more family-friendly employment policies through family leave; and for participation in job design, where there is potential to embrace new technology and innovative policies in pursuit of economic growth based on higher employment intensity.

The more difficult questions which must be faced concern the relationship of working time to the problem (in Europe) of low employment rather than high unemployment. Measures to restrict labour supply risk aggravating the long-term problem of financing our welfare states, and the problem of mismatches between supply and demand in the labour market. Although those working-time reductions which are linked to upgrading the potential of the labour force may be able to overcome these objections, a fuller discussion of the role of working-time reduction and reorganisation would seem appropriate.

As for the questions of negotiating labour market reform and building new partnerships, the central issue would seem to be reaching a position where progressive forces can take the initiative, rather than running behind an agenda set by others. This is, of course, much easier said than done, and our network is hardly the first place to discuss the necessary political strategy. There may, however, remain a role for information exchange and mutual support.

And perhaps this is an appropriate note on which to conclude these introductory remarks, with the hope that the network which produced this volume will continue to operate in the coming years. There is no doubt that conservative forces have drawn considerable sustenance from their international dialogue. We hope that this book will make a modest contribution to performing the same function for those on the centre-left.

Note

1. This book is based on papers given to the third 'International Progressive Policy Conference' (IPPC), which followed earlier meetings in Oxford (1994) and Washington (1995) took place in Brussels in March, 1997, and was organised by the editors of this book. It brought together policy makers in trade unions, research bodies and think tanks with close links to political parties on the centre-left from the USA, Japan, Australia and Western Europe.

Economic globalisation: The need for a social dimension

John Evans

Introduction

This chapter is intended to give an impression of the current debate in OECD countries on the orientation of public policy in response to the increasing integration of economies internationally. It makes some comments on the analysis of 'globalisation' and then examines the 'social' agenda in four areas: trade, investment and labour standards; reconciling equity and efficiency in the labour market; international economic coordination; and policy towards the public sector. These are some of the priority areas that have been identified as comprising part of the 'social dimension' of globalisation. Progress or regression in these areas is measured against OECD policy developments.[1]

Globalisation – myth or reality

Globalisation – the accelerated integration of economic activity across national or regional boundaries – has become the catchword dominating economic and social policy discussion at the end of the twentieth century. Despite the debate between academic economists and commentators as to the extent and effects of globalisation, and as to whether this is a new phenomenon, it is more or less irrefutable that there are a series of interconnected developments at work which are

11

profoundly affecting all OECD economies and societies.[2]

Since the late 1980s *the growth of foreign direct investment* (FDI) has been the main factor driving increased economic interdependence. The focus of this has been regional rather than global. International trade grew twice as fast as GNP during the 1980s, but foreign direct investment grew twice as fast as trade. The growth of FDI slowed in the early 1990s but picked up in 1994 and had risen to record levels in 1995. As a result there has been a significant deepening of international and foreign ownership; in the words of the OECD, 'never before have so many firms from so many industries invested in so many countries'.[3] However, FDI has been concentrated among high and middle income countries.[4] Over the decade of the 1980s, OECD countries were responsible for roughly 95 per cent of FDI outflows and received 75 per cent of inflows. A change had occurred in the mid-1990s and by 1995, the OECD share of outflows and inflows had dropped to 85 per cent and 65 per cent respectively. This was largely due to the growth of FDI in East Asia, including China. (China's share of developing country FDI inflows grew from 10 per cent to 38 per cent between 1989 and 1995.) It appears therefore that, up to 1995 at least, the growth of FDI has been regionally rather than globally driven. Moreover the empirical analysis that has been done on FDI data up to 1993 suggests that, 'International businesses remain heavily "nationally embedded" and remain MNCs rather than TNCs'.[5] This has implications for government policy towards MNCs.

Whilst there may be doubts as to the extent to which manufacturing and service companies have become fully globalised, there are no such doubts about the globalisation of *financial markets*. The appearance of the 'eurodollar market' in the 1960s was followed by the collapse of Bretton Woods in the 1970s and the removal of national capital controls and deregulation of the financial sector in the 1980s. The result has been the explosion of cross-border lending, the appearance of new financial 'products' and the appearance of an oligopolist structure of global financial institutions. Cross-border assets held by banks tripled in the decade up to 1993. Daily foreign exchange transactions amount to more than $1.2 trillion ($1,200 billion). This has reduced national sovereignty and shifted power from governments to financial markets.

There has been a shift in the development and diffusion of *technology* to a global level. Access to 'state of the art' technology has become a key factor in determining competitivity in many of the growth sectors. On the production side, joint ventures, sourcing agreements and other types of inter–company cooperation have become part of this process. On the application side, the integration of information and communications technology (the appearance of a 'global information society') is now having a radical effect on the organisation of the production of goods and services. Related to this has been the decline of Taylorist systems of mass production and the appearance of 'post fordist' and 'flexible' forms of organisation. This has implications both for the 'competitive strategies' to be adopted by OECD countries and the feasibility or desirability of pursuing a national approach to managing trade.

Alongside technological change, the policy shift to *deregulation* in the late 1970s and 1980s has clearly been both a stimulant of the globalisation process and a policy reaction to it. In the late 1990s the 'regulatory reform' debate appears at a cross-roads.

There has been an *opening of non OECD countries* to this 'global market system'. The formerly centrally planned countries of Central and Eastern Europe and the former Soviet Union are to varying degrees privatising, liberalising and deregulating their economies. The Asian NICs (Newly Industrialised Countries) have succeeded in pursuing an export–orientated growth strategy, but are now on the threshold of having to open their own economies. Developing countries in general, some under the pressure of the structural adjustment programmes of the IMF and World Bank, are all seeking more reliance on and exposure to world markets. However, despite the emergence of 'new players' the bulk of trade, investment and GNP remains concentrated in the 'TRIAD'.

The political economy of globalisation

Whatever the macroeconomic significance of the 'globalisation' process, it has penetrated very extensively the micro-level relations between trade unions and employers. Increasingly trade unions are finding that international factors arise as a constraint in their relations with governments and in their relations with the employers.

Government action, whether it be in setting tax rates, economic policy management, interest rate policy or exchange rate policy, faces international constraints, which are increasingly cited as reasons for the inability of government to fulfil the tasks that they are elected in democracies to fulfil. The attitudes of employers towards labour unions generally, including attitudes to union recognition, their policy towards labour costs and their attitude to technological change and work organisation, are, again, increasingly dictated by international competitivity and international 'fashions'. The threat of delocation to an offshore site has become the standard play in negotiations and in some cases it has become the reality. These pressures are greatest along the three North/South, East/West 'frontiers' – Mexico/US, Central/Eastern Europe, China/East Asia. The perception is therefore of a footloose international production system where capital is mobile and labour is not. This is contributing to the imbalance of power of unions and employers in the labour market at a time when many of the policies to which we looked to governments to fulfil are being undermined.

For the two ends of the political spectrum this perception may have its advantages. For the 'free market' right this is a wholly desirable situation and it is convenient to exaggerate the loss of local or regional sovereignty. It allows a 'deresponsibilisation' of the elites from the results of their actions. Globalisation is being used as catalyst for a new round of policies to 'roll back the state' at a time when the enthusiasm for the Reagan and Thatcher supply–side revolutions of the 1980s has clearly flagged. It is argued that the full benefits of the 'reforms' of the last two decades will only be felt when all economies and sectors are fully opened up to international competition and 'market contestability'. Thatcher's 'there is no alternative' has now become *'la pensée unique'*. The British government has been most vociferous in arguing for the need to conform to a model of competitiveness existing in some unspecified place in East Asia. Yet, at the same time, the Kim Young Sam government argues that South Korea has to lower its labour standards to stop Korean firms from moving to Scotland and South Wales.

On the other hand, for some on the 'left' globalisation represents a convenient opportunity to rediscover a capitalist conspiracy or reassert the concept of 'socialism in one country' or at least 'protectionism in one country'. But a populist reaction is dangerous terrain. In Europe it is firmly occupied by the National Front in France or by concepts such as the Austrian extreme right's notion of a 'Europe of Fatherlands'.

The real 'conspiracy' is not globalisation, but to argue policy paralysis as a result of it. A spectrum of mechanisms for governance is available as a response to globalisation: with, at one end of the spectrum, a set of 'hard' international regulations covering specific fields (e.g. WTO); in the middle, looser policy coordination (e.g. G7, OECD,

IMF); regional integration (e.g. European Union); continuing national regulation; and, more loosely, regional or district level policies. Binding, 'hard' mechanisms of regulation at a global level will only be able to cover a limited number of areas, and they are therefore not an alternative for the looser forms of coordination and cooperation in other areas.

The social agenda

Trade and investment and core labour standards
Globalisation has drawn dramatic attention to the need to guarantee core workers' rights on a global basis. The regulation of labour standards through the enforcement of certain global minima is not a 'new issue'. It has been part of the response to previous waves of globalisation – the creation of the ILO (International Labour Organisation) after the First World War; the Havana Charter and the attempt to create the International Trade Organisation after the Second World War. The current wave of globalisation and the creation of the World Trade Organisation (WTO) have given the issue new focus. It is perhaps a key area where we need a hard regulation which is internationally binding.

Achieving a 'hard' regulation is still some way off and there is even some criticism[6] from within the labour movement of the single minded pursuit of a 'Social Clause'. Nevertheless, it must be pursued. Achieving other goals will be difficult as long as core labour rights can be easily denied. Functioning civil society is necessary to build up a momentum for satisfactory governance of global markets. Moreover, given the fact that the world trading system has moved to guarantee the rights of intellectual property, investors' rights, and even environmental standards, it will become increasingly difficult to deny human rights.

Over the last three years, there has been perceptible progress in shifting 'conventional economic wisdom' to seeing core labour rights as a 'good thing' economically and socially, as opposed to either an irrelevancy or a market distortion. Focusing on core standards – freedom of association, rights to collective bargaining, freedom from forced labour or prison labour, freedom from child labour exploitation and non–discrimination – has allowed pretty universal acceptance of them as inviolable human rights in a way that the listing of 170 ILO

Conventions would not have done. The empirical and theoretical analysis of the OECD[7] and World Bank[8] now regards core standards – and by virtue of this trade union recognition – as at least neutral in their economic effects, and at best positive. The mainstream thinking of those involved in development assistance has also shifted to see core labour rights as a part of 'participatory development and good governance' strategies.[9]

Five years ago, far more countries and commentators would have argued that authoritarianism and free markets were the necessary routes to achieving economic lift-off. Now such voices tend to remain silent. The fact that in January 1997 the OECD was ready to censure the Republic of Korea – a new member – for not living up to the commitments on freedom of association and collective bargaining given when it joined the organisation, is highly significant. It did not happen in the case of Mexico's membership of the OECD, and would have been unthinkable even five years ago.

The debate has therefore moved on to enforcement mechanisms. At the time of writing this chapter, the 'stand off' on labour standards at the WTO Ministerial Council between the United States and the majority of EU countries on the one hand, and India, ASEAN, the UK, Australia and New Zealand on the other, leaves no one in any doubt about the difficulties of getting the issue into the WTO mechanism. There is visceral hostility from many trade officials about the issue. But despite their efforts to treat it as a 'non-issue', labour standards dominated the media coverage for the whole of the WTO Conference. The 'Singapore declaration' may yet lead to openings in the WTO.

Urgent follow up has to focus on the need to:

strengthen the ILO machinery for the ratification and supervision of core labour standards;

start a dialogue between the WTO and the ILO, raise labour issues in the WTO's Trade Policy Reviews and re-open the whole debate;

ensure the effective treatment of labour issues in the OECD's Multilateral Agreement on Investment through the incorporation of the OECD Guidelines for Multinational Enterprises and the inclusion in the Agreement of a labour clause (along the lines of NAFTA's Article 1114);

continue to use the US and EU GSP labour rights machinery;

integrate obligations for core labour standards into all of the

World Bank's lending policies;
develop targeted consumer boycotts on persistent violations of core standards;
continue to establish codes of conduct with companies or industry associations with effective independent monitoring;
develop the OECD's monitoring and 'peer group pressure plus' system for the respect of core standards in member countries;
extend labour standards clauses in hemispheric and regional trade agreements.

None of these propositions are revolutionary in nature; they are all attainable and their attainment would make a difference. Over time, with productivity growth, it would allow unions to 'bring the bottom up' in the global system.[10]

The process of European political and economic integration has of course allowed cross–frontier regulation of labour standards to move well beyond the guarantee of core workers' rights. For many on the centre-left in Europe, the European Union's 'Social Dimension' is *the* response to globalisation.[11] The European trade union movement has sought: to establish a framework of minimum standards to stop 'social dumping'; to establish consultation, information and negotiation rights with multinational companies at a European level; and to expand the structural funds of the European Community. One of the most significant developments in this process has been the passing of the European 'Works' Council' Directive, requiring multinational companies with more than one thousand employees to establish consultative machinery for their workforces at European level.

It should also be mentioned that, irrespective of mechanisms of global governance, MNCs, given their national characteristics, do still open themselves up to points of leverage. And at the same time, some international trade union company campaigns are becoming more targeted and sophisticated.

A 'socially acceptable' model of competitiveness

Guaranteeing workers' rights in the international system is a necessary but not a sufficient condition for re-establishing social progress in a global system. Moreover, the reappearance of the 'Eurosclerosis' debate against the background of rising European unemployment is in danger of stalling progress on the European Social Dimension. If the 'social agenda' is to progress, the battle of ideas has to be won to show that it is possible to manage change in firms, industries, regions and labour markets in socially equitable ways. A 'model' of industrial organisation has to be developed which is both competitive and socially acceptable. OECD countries have to restructure on the basis of a high set of labour standards not on the basis of a low wage model of development.

Within the OECD, there are two quite divergent analyses of labour markets which have crystallised in the debate over European unemployment. The conventional 'neoclassical' wisdom of the majority of Finance Ministries in OECD countries is that the origin of the problem lies in the inability of the labour market to adapt to macro economic shocks over which governments now have little control. The focus of policy is therefore to reduce 'natural' rates of unemployment through a search for labour market flexibility. This has been behind the recommendations in the OECD Jobs Study[12] to decentralise collective bargaining systems; remove administrative extensions to agreements; weaken minimum wage regulation; and to use competition in product markets to keep downward pressure on nominal wages. Restriction of unemployment benefits goes in the same direction. The UK and New Zealand are praised as successful models for reform and the US held up as being a model of success due to already flexible labour markets.

Few OECD Finance Ministers would strongly dissociate themselves from such a position; it represents '*la pensée unique*'. However, there is strikingly little empirical support for many of the policy elements described, and, short of 'something turning up', little confidence can be given to such policies reducing unemployment through high–quality employment creation. The 'unemployed poor' risk being transferred into 'working poor' with the same social consequences. These doubts were echoed by the OECD itself in the 1996 OECD Employment Outlook which honestly reviewed the evidence on wage dispersion and employment creation.[13] Moreover, countries such as the Netherlands, Ireland and Denmark have all succeeded in combining strong economic performance and equity by not following the 'Anglo-Saxon' model.

A very different view of the policy options emanates from work being carried out in the OECD in a separate, but related, set of issues: technological change; the nature of 'flexible organisations'; skill acquisition and education policy; and corporate governance issues. The changing strategies of firms in response to the global market are seen to be a key factor. One interpretation of this work is that firms in the OECD area are becoming polarised. On the one hand there are those trapped in Taylorist forms of production, having to compete in an ever tougher global market with low wage competition from non-OECD countries. Increasingly, it is not the firms themselves which have to compete but the workers in different countries, bidding for their jobs with the same employers. On the other hand there are firms who have shifted to new forms of work organisation in which a high premium is given to the flow of knowledge and innovation. These 'high skill – high trust' organisations compete in a different and clearly more benign world than their Taylorist rivals.

The policy implications of this are that governments can move their economies onto higher growth paths by encouraging technological diffusion, innovation, 'good practice' management techniques and the development of appropriate infrastructures for the 'information society'. 'Learning societies' and knowledge-based firms are the key to success. In this scenario labour market deregulation is not a central issue. Internal functional flexibility of workers in line with changing work organisation is much more important to firms. Flexibility to 'hire and fire' looks at best irrelevant and at worst could encourage the low wage/low skill route to competitiveness. The challenge for OECD countries is how to move the whole of their societies, and not just an elite, onto a 'high route' to competitiveness.

Many of the same issues arise in the parallel debates taking place on corporate governance around the issue of 'stakeholder capitalism'; on strategies for regional, district or community level development strategies; and on the development of sustainable consumption and production.

Establishing a 'new paradigm' in this area is not a question of 'hard' international regulation; it is a question of shifting attitudes and winning the arguments and shaping the strategies of different levels of government and firms.

International economic coordination

For some time there have been calls, as a necessary condition for fighting unemployment, for a more expansionary macroeconomic strategy, and 'a new international structure' to coordinate policy, built on the existence of the G7.[14]. Progress in this area faces three central problems: diverging analysis and political priorities between North America, Europe and Japan within the G7; the hegemony of Central Banks; and the related globalisation of financial markets.

Diverging priorities in macroeconomic policy have to some extent replaced the supply-side consensus of the 1980s, but they have prevented a coordinated policy response coming from the G7. Despite a differing emphasis within the Clinton administration, the broad approach has been to 'keep growth going' until inflationary constraints really do appear. The success of the fall in measured unemployment in the US, to below previously stated 'natural rates', is marred by the prevalent growth in poverty, declining real wages and insecurity, but nevertheless has reflected an accommodating monetary policy. Japan has also shown itself ready to intervene through traditional public work programmes when faced by genuine recessionary fears. It is in Europe that finance ministers and central banks continue to inflict 'monetary masochism' or more accurately 'monetary sadism' on their populations. The battle is now being fought for the economic architecture, and hence priorities, of the post Economic and Monetary Union period. The central issue must be to shift policy to a less deflationary stance. In most of Europe, real interest rates are still unjustifiably high, and the scenarios for fiscal contraction to meet Maastricht targets are in many cases completely inappropriate given the conjunctural situation. Even the OECD has warned of the dangers of the timing of fiscal restriction, though of course it does not disagree with the goal.[15]

Given the power over monetary policy now vested in independent central banks, it is clear that there is a need to 'reform the objectives of central banks so they will support a pro-growth regime instead of thwarting it'.[16] The one-dimensional pursuit of price stability has now to give way to an approach which allows decisions to be made on the balance of risks and trade-offs between the objectives of employment and inflation. The theoretical battle is also being fought around whether or not monetary policy does affect the real economy in the longer term. Many of the features of this current debate don't look particularly new – they mirror very closely the policy debate of the 1920s in Europe and the United States. It is significant that, by the 1930s, the conventional wisdom had shifted to being concerned at falling prices and deflationary expectations rather than inflationary expectations. Policy shifted to putting floors in markets rather than deregulating them.

The need to 'throw sand in the wheels of international finance' is now recognised not just by Keynesian nobel laureates such as James Tobin,[17] but more dramatically by speculators such as George Soros. Bond market vigilantes contribute to the deflationary overkill of real interest rates, and unwarranted currency fluctuations wipe out years of efforts to manage structural change in the real economy. The unsustainable growth of derivative markets raises major problems concerning the adequacy of prudential rules for dealing with systematic risk. The G7 has asked the Bank of International Settlements (BIS) to monitor these issues. What is needed however is a cooperative framework of action between the BIS, the IMF, the OECD and European Institutions, mixing national and international measures. They should include the following:

National Level Initiatives:
the establishment of effective minimum reserve requirements for the banking system;
the introduction of capital standards for other types of financial activity, particularly securities dealing;
the introduction of more extensive disclosure requirements by financial institutions, so as to increase the transparency of their risk exposure;
the introduction of minimum deposit periods for short–term financial flows;
an increase in the transparency and accountability of the operations of the large institutional investors and notably the reduction of speculative international exposure of pension funds.

International Initiatives:
the progressive removal of structural surpluses and deficits on both trade and capital accounts, most significantly between the two largest contributors, the United States and Japan, together with the lowering of real interest rates through concerted action by monetary authorities;
the introduction of an international tax on foreign exchange transactions;
the certification of financial markets with acceptable risk and prudential controls;
the introduction of more stable parities between the currencies of the European Union, the Yen and the Dollar;

the development in the longer term of an international reserve
currency;
the implementation of international agreements on capital
taxation as recommended in the OECD Jobs Study;
an increase in cooperation between taxation and banking regulatory authorities to eliminate money laundering resulting from
illicit activities;
an increase in international prudential monitoring of financial
markets.

The future of the public sector

The leitmotif of the years 1985–95 was privatisation and deregulation,
and a withdrawal of the state from direct intervention in the economy
or direct ownership. Despite this, 'government' expenditure as a share
of GDP in the OECD has rarely moved from around 40 per cent on
average over the last decade. The state at different levels remains
responsible for administering very substantial proportions of national
income. The challenges ahead will increase the demands on public
finances not to reduce them – the ageing of most OECD populations;
the need to invest in lifelong education; the need to reverse the decline
in infrastructure investment; and the need to counteract the growth in
poverty. The 'governance' debate does provide a framework that
allows a non-ideological debate on the role of the public sector.

A 'social' agenda must espouse the need to change the management
of public services and administration to make them responsive to the
public; the concern cannot be simply to save money; 'partnership'
approaches to change do work. On the other hand, the pressures of
ageing and health care costs, together with the delivery of lifelong
learning, are going to create demands for funds which will inevitably
lead to intense debates on resource allocation at the start of the next
millenium. This will be a global debate (and the US health care reform
stalemate was salutary).

Conclusions

The response of the trade union movement to globalisation cannot be
to bemoan changes or react defensively. It must be to respond and

manage them. To fulfil the legitimate aspirations of consumers, employees and investors, markets require effective governance, whether or not they are organised on a national, regional or global scale. Against a background of globalisation it is the forms of governance that have to change, not the principle of governance itself. The challenge is to shape that debate.

Notes

1. W. Hutton and R. Kuttner 'Full employment in a free society', in S. Pollard (ed) *Jobs and Growth*, A Fabian/Unison Special 1994.
2. C. Oman *Policy Challenges of Globalisation and Regionalisation*, OECD Development Centre Policy Brief, 1996.
3. OECD, *Financial Market Trends*, June 1996.
4. UNCTAD, *World Investment Report*, 1996.
5. P. Hirst and G. Thompson 'Globalisation in Question', Policy Press 1996.
6. P. Evans 'The World Trade Organisation: Challenge to the International Labour Movement', Labour and Society International Discussion Paper, January 1997.
7. OECD, *Trade, Employment and Labour Standards*, 1996.
8. World Bank, *World Development Report*, 1995.
9. OECD, Development Assistance Committee, *Orientations on Participatory Development and Good Governance*, 1996.
10. W. Greider *One World, Ready or Not: The Manic Logic of Global Capitalism*, Simon and Schuster 1997.
11. Guigou, 'L'Europe, une Réponse à la Mondialisation', *CFDT Aujourd'hui*, November–December 1996.
12. OECD, *The OECD Jobs Study – Facts, Analysis, Strategies*, 1996.
13. OECD, *Employment Outlook*, 1996.
14. Pollard, *op.cit.*
15. OECD, *Ecomomic Outlook*, 1996.
16. W. Greider 'Global Warning', *The Nation*, January 1997.
17. M. Ul Haq, I. Kaul, and I. Grunberg *The Tobin Tax: Coping with Financial Volatility*, OUP, Oxford 1996.

Social policy and economic performance

Allan Larsson

This chapter* aims to look at the relationship between social policy and economic performance, a question which is at the heart of European debate. In particular, I will be making a comparison between the European approach to this question and that of the USA. The basic thesis outlined below is that a well-designed social policy is an essential guarantor of a healthy economy. My point of departure here is to pursue that theme by looking, on the one hand, at the strengths and weaknesses of the European and US models, and on the other, at the challenges they have in common.

These common challenges are of great importance. They mean we must adapt our social policies to the realities, and the opportunities, of three key factors: the changing patterns of organisation of work; the changing gender balance in working life; and the ageing of our populations.

Monetary systems, economic regimes and social systems

Let's start with the main differences between the European Union and the United States, in three areas. The first concerns monetary systems, the second, economic regimes, and the third, social and labour market systems.

In terms of monetary systems, the US has had a single currency for more than one hundred years, while Europe has, still, a fragmented

* This article is based on a speech given by Allan Larsson.

24

system, with fifteen different currencies. The difference between the economic regimes is clear also. While the US has had a single market for well over a century, Europe has operated across fifteen sets of national regulatory frameworks, which has hampered trade and investment. This, of course, is beginning to change now. Europe has nearly completed its single market, and is moving towards its single currency. However, it has a long way to go in learning how to understand itself as – and to operate as – an economic entity. There are still fifteen different economic accounts, as opposed to the single economic account which the American President and Congress can plan and act upon. It is important that the European Union does develop this more organic view of itself, because the potential it offers is so great. We have, essentially, two ways of looking at Europe. One is to see it as a series of separate economies and markets. The other is to see Europe as an emerging economic entity.

Figure 1

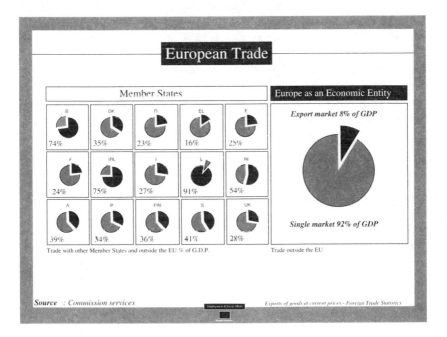

One way of looking at this emerging economic entity is to look at trade. As Figure 1 shows, for individual European member states, trade is a significant factor, ranging from around 25 per cent in the larger member states to 75 per cent or more in the smaller ones. However, since most of this trade is contained within the EU, the scale of extra-EU trade is much smaller, accounting for only 8 per cent of EU GDP. That means, as you can see, that 92 per cent of demand is met by production within Europe, while only 8 per cent is met by imports from countries outside the EU. The fact that – just as in the US – European external trade is small, relative to domestic EU production, demonstrates clearly the degree to which improvements in our living standards already depend, and will depend more and more, on improving productivity and raising employment performance.

The creation of the single market is a huge step in modernising the European economy, with fifteen different sets of rules being replaced with one, broadening markets, increasing competition between enterprises. Europe will soon benefit from the same advantages, of a single market and single currency, that have been crucial to making the US economy the world's most productive, and US enterprises more successful than many others. The fact is that, traditionally, economic policies in Europe have been based on the premise that countries were competing with each other as if they were enterprises, and that growth had to come from export markets. In this mind-set, competitiveness is seen in terms of negative responses, with monetary dumping through devaluations, with social dumping through lowering standards, and fiscal dumping through subsidies, or through other budget manipulations. Can you imagine the US economy, if 50 states were competing against each, while trading in fifty different currencies?

In the European Union, as its economies are becoming more integrated, it is no longer possible to simply export problems. We must learn how to solve problems together. Competitiveness in the EU can only be increased, on a lasting basis, by raising the productivity of companies, and of the people who work in them. Competition is not between countries but between companies, within and across borders. For the EU as an economic entity, the key question is general productivity growth, leading to better real wages and higher profits.

This brings me to the third area of difference of approach between Europe and the USA – the question of social and labour market systems, and the important issues of costs and competitiveness. There are different ways of defining competitiveness, and it is important to the debate to be clear about what is meant by the term.

Being competitive means being able to pay your way in the world, a qualification Europe currently fulfills. The EU has a current account surplus with the rest of the world, of over 1 per cent of GDP. It has surpluses, or balanced trade, with all the main regions – including the Newly Industrialised Countries, Central and Eastern Europe and the US. Being competitive also means being attractive to foreign direct investment. It means being smart enough to invest where we trade. Europe is attractive. Europe is smart. And it is in balance, with similar flows – each of over 20 billion ecus each year – into and out of, the Union.

And, of course, being competitive means keeping costs and prices down, which, again, Europe does. Inflation averages under 3 per cent a year across the Union, with no sign of pressures to increase. And sustained wage moderation over the last decade means Union profitability is back to the levels of the early 1970s.

As is widely acknowledged, real improvements in living standards don't depend on comparative competitiveness. They depend on absolute levels of productivity – producing more output for the capital and labour invested. Europe has a sound record here – producing productivity improvements of 2 per cent over each of the last twenty years, during which time US productivity growth has been more like 0.5 per cent a year. It is often stated that Europe's labour costs are much higher than the United States, but this is not the case. Unit labour costs depend on productivity, not just on wages. If productivity is higher, wages can be higher. And, in measuring trade between countries, unit labour costs in national currencies are adjusted by exchange rates.

These factors equalise comparative labour costs between countries. And it is also true that countries with high wages, high levels of investment, and high living standards perform better than countries with low wages, low investment and low social standards.

These observations on competitiveness underline the importance of rigour in presenting costs, and clarity in defining costs. They do not mean that Europeans can afford to waste money, or be complacent about the effectiveness of expenditure. They do not mean there is no need to change. But they do tell us that we should ensure that our financial decisions – as well as our design decisions - in modernising social policy should be based on the fullest understanding of the present situation.

This is particularly important when we are discussing the question of non-wage labour costs, an important aspect of which is relative costs and relative coverage for a given amount of spending. This matter, of the balance and sourcing of expenditure, across the span of each system's safety nets, between the US and Europe, is illustrated very well in the following tables. They are based on work done by Gosta Esping Andersen, who has compared the social and welfare expenditures for a household in the US and in Sweden.

Figure 2

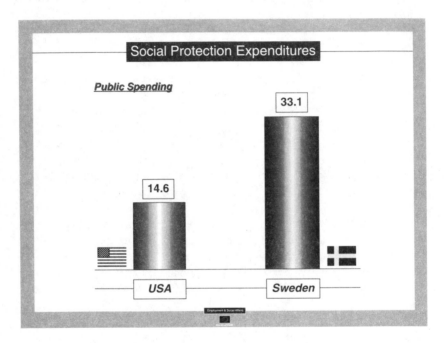

Figure 2 shows the bald facts and argumentation often used when discussing these issues, concerning only public expenditure, with Sweden spending over 33 per cent of public expenditure on social welfare, more than double the spending of the US, at less than 15 per cent. This comparison is stark, and its general message is used often (and often disingenuously presented) to tell us that Europe is uncompetitive. That it cannot afford to carry such a heavy weight of social protection. That Europeans should re-examine their commitment to the European social model because of global competition and high costs.

Figure 3

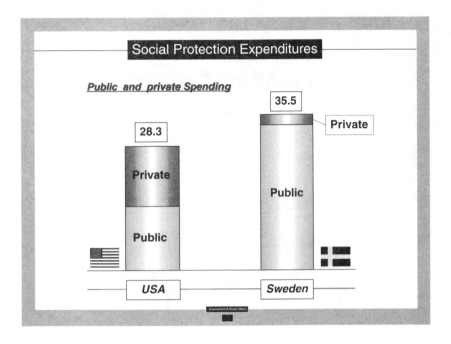

Figure 3 takes us closer to the reality of the investment required to underwrite the two social protection systems. It shows a closer level of financial commitment between the two ends of the spectrum represented by Sweden and the US. It highlights also the difference of culture which has developed in how to meet these needs, between the US model, with its strong degree of private spending, and the European approach, with its much larger proportion of public investment.

Figure 4, however, takes us to the core of the difference between the approaches. It shows that, though Sweden and the USA have very different systems, the burden on the household is remarkably similar, when we look at the bottom line, when we look at the arithmetic, rather than the rhetoric. A household in Sweden spends 41 per cent of its budget on social protection (health, education, pensions, day care and taxes), and a household in the US spends almost 40 per cent. This

tells us that there is, of course, a choice in these matters, but not necessarily the one we are often offered in the public debate. In reality, the
choice is not between high and low costs, but between a more uneven,
or a less uneven, distribution of income and opportunities.

Figure 4

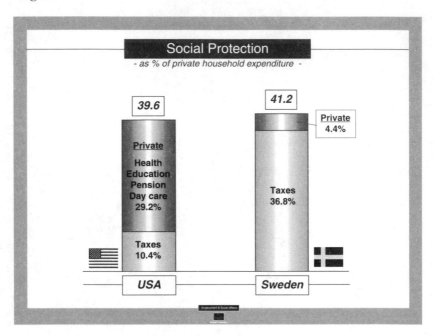

The implications for change

The discussion so far raises a number of questions. The first concerns
monetary and economic systems, and the differences between them.
Just how important has the century and more of a single market and
single currency been for the US? And just how important will the
development of these institutions be for the social and economic
progress of the EU? In terms of social and labour market systems, what
are the pros and cons of public versus private expenditure? And what
are the implications of the messages of the Esping Andersen figures?
And how clear are we that the choices we make in Europe – such as

whether to change the way we pay for social policy, or whether or not to move away from the public approach, and more towards the individualist, rather than collective, approach – are not choices about levels of expenditure? The issues raised are, rather, about breadth of coverage and of access. Moving away from collective provision may offer choice to those who can invest privately, but eliminate opportunity for those who cannot. How far do we understand the ramifications of such distributional decisions for our societies?

Furthermore, if the European approach to social protection is a burden to EU economies, why is European productivity growth significantly above the US performance? And, with Europe, if social policy is such a drag on competitiveness, why are those European economies which have the strongest social provision performing better than those with weaker systems?

This is not to suggest that all is perfect in the European garden. Far from it, unfortunately. Europeans have serious problems to resolve in order to improve and sustain their social policy provision. You only have to look around you to see evidence of the ill-functioning of European employment systems. Change is necessary – but not for the reasons that are usually cited. We do need to reform the European social model, we do need to modernise the European labour market, but not because of global competition. The need for a modernisation of our employment and social protection systems arises from internal, European factors. The problems will, however, be difficult to overcome, and efforts towards their resolution can only profit by a process of drawing lessons from, and sharing common responses with, the experiences in the US, among others.

I now want to look at the need for modernisation in relation to the three areas raised at the beginning of this chapter – the organisation of work, the gender balance in working life, and the ageing of the European population.

The organisation of work

The organisation of work is decisive for social policy. It has, for almost a century, been founded on the same basic principle: a hierarchical, top-down, model of organisation, with a high degree of specialisation, and simple, often repetitive, jobs. This method of organisation was developed as a tool for the emerging industrial society, for the transformation of the economy from handicrafts, via manufacturing, to industrial mass production. During the twentieth century, it spread across the industrialised world. The rebuilding of European industry in the post-war period was based on the concept, developed in the US, of the mass production system.

Europe's present model of social protection was the political response to the risks, insecurity and instability inherent in the new order of mass production. But now, of course, the world is changing again. The mass production system has grown old, and a new system is emerging, based on newer technologies – especially the information technologies – which are changing the nature of work. Europe's social protection system fitted that past model of production, but it does not fit the new patterns of work and, crucially, the evolution of skill demands. In particular, the present system, by offering income support – but only very limited employability support – is no longer providing the oil of change in this new labour market. In some EU member states, for example, 90 per cent of all vacancies are for people with new and higher skills. Yet, in the face of that profile of demand for labour, less than 7 per cent of the unemployed are offered training for new and/or higher skills. The fundamental mistake made throughout the last two decades was the belief that the next recovery would solve the unemployment problem by giving new jobs to people with outdated skills. The message of the fact that only 7 per cent of the unemployed are receiving skills and that, therefore, the other 93 per cent are languishing in de-learning, is that the same mistake is still being made. This must change, especially in the context of the new technologies.

The new technologies are bringing fundamental changes in working life. On average, 80 per cent of existing technologies are expected to be replaced by new technologies in the next ten years. The pace of software development, particularly, means that this turnover may be even faster in the most significant of the new technologies, the information and communication technologies. The changes they are bringing in their train are reshaping work, skill structures and the organisation of enterprises. This represents not simply an adjustment, but a paradigm shift, which social policy must match.

Our economies are being transformed from standardised manual production towards a more diversified, knowledge-based production of goods and services. The organisation of successful 'flexible enterprises' is becoming increasingly based on processes, less on specialised functions. Enterprises are being transformed, from hierarchical and

32

complex organisations with simple jobs, to less hierarchical, more customer-oriented, decentralised and network-oriented organisations, with more complex jobs. There are now clear examples of enterprises turning these developments into new goods and services, into productivity growth. And the organisation of such successful 'flexible enterprises' is becoming more and more based on processes, less and less on specialised functions.

The main policy message from all this is the need for an integrated approach, linking the introduction of ICTs with education and training and with organisational transformation. With such an integrated approach, we can increase our awareness of new and successful forms of work organisation, and we can help to apply these methods more widely. We can also ensure that small and medium-sized enterprises benefit fully from information technology. To achieve this integration, we must modernise labour law, and the agreements governing future working patterns, by finding a new balance between flexibility and security. I will return to this important challenge in a moment.

Figure 5

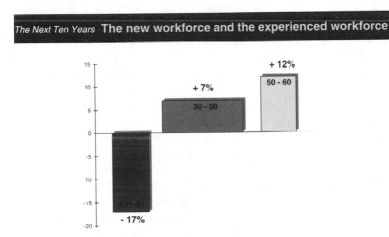

Source: European Commission

A further dimension of working life which must be factored into social policy thinking in Europe, if we are to plan correctly for what is, in reality, the rather short time-span of the next ten years, is the profile of the European Union population, the workforce of the next decade. During the next ten years, the structure and composition of the EU labour force will change dramatically under the influence of demographic trends, as well as continued social changes and new skill demands. Figure 5 illustrates two factors of great importance.

Firstly, some 50 million young people will leave education and training for the labour market in the next decade. In general, they will be better trained than any generation in history, but smaller in numbers than any generation entering the labour market since the Union was created. From 1995 to 2005, the population between twenty and thirty years of age will decrease by 9 million. This smaller, but generally well trained group, will be very attractive to employers.

Secondly, there will be a substantial increase in the population between fifty and sixty years of age. This group will increase by 5.5 million between 1996 and 2005.

I want to look at the implications of putting together the two components we have examined already, those of the new shape of working life and the new profile of the workforce. The introduction of new technologies and the dramatic demographic developments we face, of fewer young people and more older workers, create a huge challenge for economic and social policy in all EU member states. That challenge is shown starkly in Figure 6, with these two elements placed in perspective.

Ten years from now, 80 per cent of the technology we operate today will be obsolete and replaced with new technologies. By that time – on our present human resources investment record – 80 per cent of the workforce will be operating on the basis of formal education and training more than ten years old. The workforce is ageing, the technology is getting younger. That means we must begin to equip the whole of the potential workforce, that we must offer new competences to the unskilled and to those who were last trained some time ago, for function based production. It means we must invest in, rather than discard, older workers. It means we must address the fact that a large proportion of the available workforce, including many of those looking for work, have little grounding in the numeracy and literacy needed to engage in the technologies, and no education and training in informacy – the new basic skill of interaction with the new technologies.

Figure 6

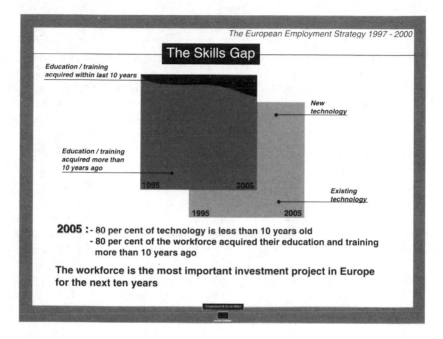

Source: European Commission

These facts highlight one of the central policy challenges of the coming ten years, the need to bridge the 'skills gap'. Heavy investment in human resources is necessary to gain the benefits of the new more knowledge-based production of goods and services. A better distribution of education and training for the new labour market is the best policy approach to overcoming rigidities and to stimulating growth and the flexibility of the labour market. Thus, the task of enabling a broadly-based upgrading of the European labour force is the most crucial investment project of the coming ten years, for governments and for enterprises.

Flexibility and security

Approached correctly, the new shape and pattern of working life now emerging is probably the most promising growth factor for the next ten years in Europe. But it offers us some difficult choices and challenges. Besides the challenge of the 'skills gap', there is the difficult question of the relationship between flexibility and security in the organisation of work and the need for the scope and functioning of labour law to change too, in this new paradigm of working life.

One response to this challenge is to stick to traditional structures and postures in the public debate on labour law, with oversimplified arguments as to whether to regulate or deregulate. But that response leads only to a political impasse, and to a massive loss of productive capacity. The other choice is to re-focus on achieving a new balance between flexibility and security, which must offer recognition, and regularisation, of new forms of employment relationships. It must also offer, not only security against arbitrary dismissals and discrimination, but also the security which can only result from greater influence over one's work and from having the scope and opportunity to enhance skills and employability. The fact is that, in the new, more fluid, labour market, the need for security will not diminish. Far from it, the need for security – the cushion against change it offers people and the flexibility it offers the labour market – will remain just as important as before. But its purpose will be, necessarily, a more dynamic one, to serve, and help create, a more dynamic labour market and economy. It is for reasons of economic success, as well as social justice, that – as enterprises become more flexible – our social protection systems must improve the range, and the reach, of their responsibility to provide stability and security.

An important part of this is, as I have mentioned, a new and stronger focus in the operation of social protection systems on employability and access to skills. Social protection must actively equip people to work, as well as provide basic support. It must not only keep their heads above water, crucial as that is, but also teach them to swim. That means quality and relevance of training and the right range of positive incentives, and positive interaction between parts of our employment systems and their administration. It means mutual rights and responsibilities: in terms of the state, and its responsibility, with the social partners, to ensure the quality and relevance of active measures; and the individual, and his or her responsibility to use the opportunity these measures represent. How can we achieve this, how can we find a new balance, to change the old fashioned approach to the organisation of work, rebalance social protection and bridge the skills gap which threatens the progress and spread of potential benefits of the information society? The process of seeking answers must be open and inclusive, in order to succeed in modernising the labour market, rather than alienating the workforce.

The changing gender balance at work

Figure 7

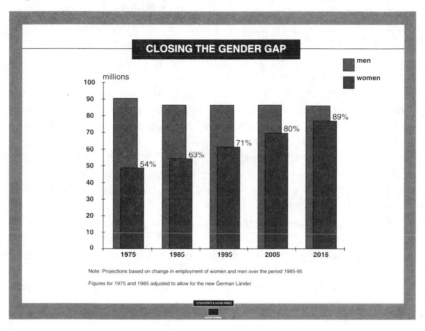

Source: European Commission

The second key factor which is bringing fundamental change to society, across the European Union, is the changing gender balance in working life. Women have accounted for the entire growth of the Union's workforce over the last ten to fifteen years. Women's participation rates have risen steadily, straight through the periods of recovery and downturns, straight through all the structural changes we have experienced. There is great divergence, of course, with, generally, the northern member states, and especially the Scandinavians, having much higher participation rates than the southern member states. But, the trend is Europe-wide, and, as you can see here, is constant. The change over the last twenty years is already very large. In 1975, only 50 per cent of women were represented in the workforce – 91 per cent of men were represented. The gap has steadily narrowed ever since, and in less than ten years, the balance will have changed radically, to around 85 per cent for men and up to 75 per cent for women.

There is still a big gender gap. It can be described with one single figure: 25 million jobs. That is the difference between employment for men and employment for women in the European Union at present. 85 million men are employed, and 60 million women. But the trend is clear. Women's participation in the labour force will continue to grow in the next ten to twenty years, with a strong impact on the economy, on societies and on family life.

We are facing choices and challenges on this issue too. One response is to continue with the social policy approaches of the past in relation to families. We know what this means. It means that society puts a huge burden on families, mainly on women, for childcare. This leads to a further lowering of the birthrate. We can see the reality of this in many member states, especially in the southern countries. It is clear in the stark drop in fertility rates across the Union, from about 3 children per woman in the mid-1960s, to about 1.5 today.

The other choice is a renewal of family policy to enable young parents to combine professional life with responsibility for children. This choice requires a higher and more effective provision of facilities for family support (including both child care and care of the elderly). It also requires a revision of all those regulations which directly or indirectly affect women when interrupting work for childbearing or caring responsibilities. That choice raises great issues in terms of men, their/our reconciliation of working and family life, and the kinds of measures needed to enable this change of balance to develop. The establishment, through the first European collective agreement, of specific leave from work for family reasons is an important step forward in the process of modernisation.

But the key question for social policy, and for the efficient and fair functioning of the labour market, remains. It is how to create a system that diminishes the burden on families and which encourages men to take a new responsibility for families and children, one which offers a modern role for men in family life. What can we learn from other industrialised economies on this? What can the US experience, in particular, tell us, as they have been addressing issues of gender for longer, and in more depth, than we have in Europe.

The ageing population

The third important factor driving the need to modernise our social systems is the ageing of our populations. We must face the fact that demographic change is already forcing us to break the mould of our current social structures, and to rethink the ways that we organise work, education, and our very social fabric.

Figure 8

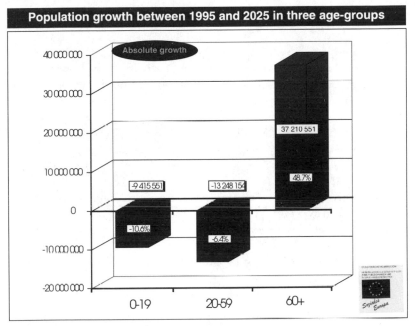

By 2025, the number of people aged over 60 will increase by not less than 37 million, nearly 50 per cent, to more than 110 million pensioners, nearly a third of the population. We are adding years to our lives, and we are adding life to our years. This is to be welcomed. But it also has implications for our social protection systems. Because, during that same period, as we have already seen, those of working age, between 20 and 59, will decrease by 13 million. Fewer people will have to produce the goods and services needed for a growing population. There will be nearly 10 million fewer children and teenagers. That means, for example, that one in ten classrooms will be redundant. It means fewer young people entering the labour market. It means a drop in the injection of skills and energy that society gets from the young.

Europe is ageing and the working age population will soon start to decrease. This profound change in the age structure of the population will place enormous stress on the unwritten contract between generations. If we continue with the passive policies which have brought about low employment rates and high unemployment, a clearly inadequate basis for the pension system, the consequence will be a drastic reduction in benefits, an increase in pension costs, or a combination of both.

There are three types of action we must, therefore, undertake:

- We must develop an active employment policy, to equip more of the potential workforce to contribute to the economy, to bring more people back to work. This is the most important way of making our pension systems sustainable;
- Alongside that shift, we must make the necessary adjustments in the pension system. We must begin this process now; and
- We have to find ways and means to allocate resources to the care of the very old – in twenty–thirty years time.

Should we not, then, ask ourselves how much we can achieve by changing the arithmetic, by improving public health across the generations, rather than just leaving the bill for the workers of tomorrow? Because we can free resources for pension obligations and for the care of the very old, by developing more pro-active policies to improve health and safety at work and public health.

For example, 500,000 people die every year in Europe of smoking related problems. 200,000 people in Europe are, right now, suffering from smoking-related illnesses. In health and safety matters, too, there are things we can do to minimise suffering and costs at the same time. We must be able to improve on a situation where, in Europe, there are still 10 million industrial accidents every year, with 8,000 fatalities.

What, again, can we learn from others? There is the demography issue, which, like many others, is not confined to Europe. For example, some might say it could hit the US harder, as the baby boomers draw their huge stake from the economy. In the US, the anti-smoking movement is much stronger than in Europe, with huge implications for reducing health costs in years to come. We must learn from that success. But is there, perhaps, a down-side in some other areas of social policy, like health and safety at work, and equality, for example, as a result of the more litigation-based and less regulation-based American approach to resolving disputes? What are the implications of this difference, in terms of costs to enterprises and to individuals, in terms of future competitiveness on one hand, and of access to social justice on the other?

All of the issues and questions I have raised here concern the essential need for modernisation of our social model in the European Union. As I hope I have made clear, the reason for undertaking this modernisation process is not that there is anything intrinsically wrong with our hard-won rights and obligations, from education and training to employment support, from safety at work to health and welfare. The reason is this. If our social provision is to continue, in the future, to play the essential role in our economic success which it has patently played in the past, it must be equipped for the new tasks this represents. There is as much danger in trying to preserve our social policy, as a static structure in the face of change, as there is in trying to dismantle our achievements.

Social policy is a productive factor in creating strong economic performance – but only if it is well designed for the problems it is trying to address. Only if it is aligned with the grain of the remarkable pace of change in our technologies, economics and societies.

Will the success of the German Model be its undoing?

Jürgen Hoffmann

In Germany today, registered unemployment has risen to almost five million, with an average rate of 13.5 per cent (January 1997) and up to 30 per cent in some of the 'new' eastern *Länder*; the national debt is increasing and remains above the Maastricht criteria for entry into Economic and Monetary Union; society is split, with over 10 per cent of the population living in poverty and 10 per cent owning over half the country's total private assets; the social security systems are in the throes of crisis. Meanwhile, annual productivity growth has been above 3 per cent; major increases in profits have been accompanied by stagnating investment; 1996 was a record year for foreign trade; and there has been an apparently uninterrupted rise in share prices. All of this taken together would at least appear to indicate that the once lauded 'German model' – in which the interests of capital and the interests of workers (in high levels of profit and investment, job security, high incomes and social security) could be combined on a cooperative basis – has started to disintegrate.

Reasons for mass unemployment

Taking merely the *demand* for labour from the viewpoint of employers, one reason for the current trend in the labour markets in western Germany is still the necessarily high capital intensity of the manufacturing sector – an inevitable factor accompanying high labour productivity – at levels of investment which have fallen off. This is dampening the job-creating effects of investment. On the other hand, the high rates of labour productivity growth in the core sectors of western German industry are not being accompanied by similar increases in production (in 1996 productivity rose by 3.25 per cent, while GDP went up by 1.5 per cent during the same period). This must inevitably result in the loss of jobs and unemployment if other sectors in the national economy with lower productivity growth do not expand. By contrast, the 'employment miracle' in the USA is acknowledged to have been attributable to the fact that the rates of labour productivity increase were lower than those of production, and this was caused not least by the expansion of the human resources-oriented service sector – and within it the employment of women. Further reasons for unemployment in the Federal Republic of Germany are the pressure of ancillary wage costs in labour-intensive small and medium-sized enterprises (SMEs) producing chiefly for the domestic market, and the rationalisation processes which have reached the service sector owing to the use of information and communications technologies. This same sector, both in the area of public administration and in the social and health domains, is currently being massively affected by a policy of cost-cutting measures – faced with the twofold pressure of financing the reunification of Germany and the 'race' to join the single European currency. This economic development is being overshadowed by the dramatic unemployment figures and high costs of reunification: net transfers to the 'new' German *Länder* currently amount to between DM150 and 160 billion. Owing to the position occupied by the Bundesbank in Europe, the high interest rate levels during the first half of the 1990s which were largely caused by this situation also restricted financial policies in the other EU Member States. These, along with the Maastricht criteria, instigated fresh austerity policies which in turn had a negative effect on employment.

The second reason why lasting mass unemployment has persisted throughout the 1990s, accompanied by a restricted demand, is the *supply side* (which is often not even mentioned at all in the debate on unemployment), namely the rapid increase in the number of those seeking work on the supply side of the European labour market since the mid-1970s and 1980s. To some extent this is connected with processes of globalisation, because the streams of migration during the 1960s and 1970s added to the increase in the supply of labour. In addition, besides the entry to the labour market of the so-called 'baby-boomers', changes in the number of working women are another reason for the growing demand for jobs – a (naturally welcome) result of the process of society's modernisation. However, the problem of employment would perhaps be even more dramatic if in Germany – where the employment rate in the 1990s totalled 67.5 per cent (women: 57.7 per cent) – rates of employment could be assumed which corresponded to those in the USA (total: 75.6 per cent, women: 68 per cent). Thus comparison is only valid to a certain extent. For in fact the increased employment of women also brings about a 'commodification', a shift away from household activities to markets ('a working woman needs a wife'), which in turn can bring positive employment effects in its wake – in the USA this has made a substantial contribution to 'wealthless job growth'.[1]

The successful 'German Model' . . .

Although the problems of mass unemployment and funding the social security system have resulted largely from developments issuing from reunification, which tended to be fostered by the naïve/radical market policies of the new *Länder*, I do not wish to focus the spotlight on this so-called 'exogenous' reason for the current economic and social problems. Instead I would like to investigate the preconditions for the development of the 'German Model' which was formerly so successful.

Embedded in the nation-state and a system of fixed exchange rates, this 'model' was based on the Fordist-Taylorist production method, with a highly qualified workforce, and a system of social and political regulation (e.g. for industrial relations) which was compatible with the Fordist production method, as well as the 'co-operative disciplining of capital' (W. Streeck). The cornerstone of this 'model' consisted in the fact that, firstly, the gains in productivity in the highly productive core sectors of the processing industry (electrical engineering, mechanical engineering, motor vehicle manufacture, the chemical and oil industries, optics), which were geared to the world market, not only yielded high levels of profit and investment with positive effects on employment, but also were *re-distributed*, via domestic reproduction links (e.g. supplier relationships), among less productive and labour-intensive SMEs. On top of this, the tax system, a successful, productivity-oriented wage policy, and the nationwide sectoral collective agreement meant that workers and the state all had a share in the successful outcome of productivity. Secondly, a type of social security system was possible which was based on so-called 'standard working relations' (*'Normalarbeitsverhältnis'*, a term coined by Ulrich Mückenberger), which was male-oriented and geared towards full-time gainful employment (and still remains so). Within this system, women were allocated the role of housewives and at most that of 'additional earners' – with the important side effect from our point of view that many human resources-related services remained private and were not exposed to the market sphere (as in the USA) or taken over by the state (as in Sweden). Whilst the subordinate role of women as housewives in the patriarchal family was firmly established in this way in social terms, in economic terms the gainful employment of women was limited, and the development and expansion of the markets for human resources-related services was blocked – which helps to explain the relatively low share of employment in the human resources-related service sector, seen in an international context.

. . . comes up against its limits

The crisis, disintegration and economic restructuring of this successful model[2] can be divided up into several, partly overlapping phases: in the mid-1970s it became clear that the productivity effects of the Fordist-Taylorist production model were tailing off; growth in productivity now had to be paid for with disproportionate capital input – resulting in falling returns on investment and falling rates of investment, structural crises (coal, steel, construction industry) and mass redundancies. At the same time, the modernisation of society meant that the markets turned into buyers' markets which could no longer be supplied solely with standard mass-produced goods: limits were thus imposed on mass production. These problems were overcome by introducing methods of flexible mass production based on new communication and information technologies, and new corporate concepts which culminated in renewed high productivity and profitability effects in the 1980s. However it proved impossible to achieve full employment again. This is because the end of the Bretton Woods monetary system in the 1970s and the world debt crisis during the 1980s enabled the internationalisation of monetary capital, with expected yields from speculative capital becoming a relatively safe bet, and this in turn made alternative forms of investment in monetary capital more attractive. The result was increased investment in financial assets at the expense of productive investment. Parallel to this and almost at the same rate, the supply of workers rose sharply inside the country so that even at times of a strong rise in the level of employment (as between 1987 and 1991) mass unemployment persisted.

At the end of the 1980s and during the 1990s the 'German Model' suffered a loss of quality. This was firstly because, after a brief reunification boom, the economic crisis in the 'new' German *Länder* necessitated enormous transfer payments which placed a great burden on state finances and the social security system, and in the short term proved to be the main reason for the crisis in the social security systems.[3] (It should be noted that these transfers were also used as a pretext by the political elite to justify to public opinion cuts in social spending and redistributions in favour of the owners of capital.) Secondly, the combination of the European Single Market and the internationalisation of capital ('globalisation') brought about new structural conditions in which the functioning of the German model changed. The 'globalisation' of the economy,[4] which – looking at world trade – focused largely on the European internal market, North America and Japan/Southeast Asia (in other words the so-called 'Triad'), brought about two kinds of qualitative change: firstly, internationally, money achieved a relatively independent status as money and thus the speculative profit motive gained ground against the productive investment of capital ('casino capitalism'). This effectively multiplied the investment alternatives for companies, allowing them to opt out of the national production context, or at least threaten to do so ('exit' option).[5] This was accompanied by a change in corporate cultures favouring short-term profit objectives ('shareholder value capitalism'). These processes of internationalisation were preceded by a deregulation of the flows in trade and money, set in motion politically by the nation states, but which led to a loss in the autonomy of national economic policy. Secondly, large companies in particular could now implement a policy involving the cross-border 'external flexibilisation' of production at a new level as part of their strategies of 'lean production' and 'new production concepts', making use of modern information and communication technologies to do so. As a result, the large firms found it possible to mobilise different productivity, qualification and wage cost resources in various countries by relocating factory resources and setting up 'intra-firm' networks.

Although we must beware of over-estimating the globalisation process, the effects of these briefly outlined developments have never-theless resulted in decisive changes in the way in which the 'German Model' functions. On the one hand, under more intense competition, quality production based on the high labour productivity of a skilled workforce and high wages is being put under pressure ever more clearly by products competing internationally on the basis of their price – a development which is also linked to the trend towards stan-dardising the prerequisites for productivity internationally, thanks to the use of modern communication and information technologies (in important sectors, for example, the automotive industry, success on the market depends no longer on competition in terms of quality, based on 'immobile' knowledge of the system, but rather on price-based and therefore cost-based competition). Secondly, looking beyond this, the process of globalisation is, at national level, unhing-ing or even threatening the functional and productive links between sectors as well as between large, highly productive and world-market-oriented companies and SMEs whose production is geared towards the internal market or centred around the role of supplier to these large companies. Thanks to the strategies of 'outsourcing' and 'global sourcing', internationally-oriented companies can now buy in primary products and company-oriented services from the interna-tional market, thereby benefiting from cost benefits (i.e. here too implementing 'exit' options). In this way they escape the redistribu-tion mechanisms on the internal market (via wages and prices). As a consequence of this, the national socio-political standard systems of rules which are tailored to gainful employment are now coming under pressure, because the companies and sectors in question, which were previously indirectly involved in the major companies' success on the world market, often have very labour or wage-intensive production methods, and thus bear the main brunt of ancillary wage costs (through which the social security systems are financed) and of tax revenue (income tax comprising the largest share of tax revenue). At the same time (in the German system) it is these companies which play a leading role in training skilled workers. And this division between large and small or medium-sized companies is being systematically promoted by an economic policy which does not strengthen produc-tive, often regionally linked connections, but is aimed solely at guaranteeing the productivity of large companies. High productivity in the core sectors of the export-oriented economy is now generating extra unemployment, which is being aggravated by the facts that (a) managements are adopting 'shareholder value' attitudes and (b) the German government has embraced a policy of deregulation. Consequently, the development of productivity is no longer part of the solution to the problem (of mass unemployment) – leaving aside the justifiable environmental objections – but is now *part of the problem* itself. All the more so since, coming back to the problem of the gainful employment of women mentioned earlier on, the way in which the social security institutions and labour market are organised in Germany means that the market and/or the state are being deprived of the human resources-related services sector (unlike in Sweden and the USA), which therefore cannot offer additional employment possibilities. Accordingly, the 'German Model' is threatening to self-destruct under the pressure of Europeanisation and 'globalisation', and to perpetuate mass unemployment.

What should be done?

If this diagnosis is correct then there are no simple solutions, because simple solutions would not take account of the complexity of the problem! And here I can only sketch out complex solutions. (1) The institutions governing the European and international regulation of the flows of goods and money must be developed with a view to achieving the social and ecological 're-integration' of the unfettered world and money market. Consequently, the European level (including the plan for Economic and Monetary Union) should be perceived more than ever as an institutionally prescribed opportunity for this type of *political* regulation. (2) The regions, their potential regarding production resources, labour skills and (above all) their capacity for networking should also be bolstered as 'immobile production site factors; as should (3) the area of education, training, continuing training and research – and both these should be fostered with an eye to achieving environmentally compatible production and environmentally friendly consumption. All these policies could be linked to state-run programmes implemented at the sectoral level (within the context of an 'active structural policy'). On the labour markets (4) policies of reducing working time – if possible co-ordinated at the international level! – and (5) of re-distributing work and ensuring equal treatment of the sexes would have to be promoted. Gender equality is particularly important if the number of gainfully employed women is to be increased (for neither the Swedish nor the American model for developing the human resources-related service sector hinders the renewed discrimination against women, who in both cases are now being marginalised in the area of gainful employment). Moreover the social security system (6), combined with the tax system, would in the medium term have to be extended or restructured to turn it into a system of taxation-funded basic security. There are three reasons for this: firstly, to prevent discrimination against those who never had the opportunity, or did not have sufficient opportunity, to achieve gainful employment; secondly, to reduce the ancillary wage costs incurred by the small and medium-sized, labour-intensive producing capitals; and thirdly (perhaps in conjunction with elements of an 'ecological tax reform'?), via financing by taxation to include capital and investment income in funding as a means of social redistribution. The fact that this would in all likelihood hardly be possible without internationally coordinating tax and insurance systems no doubt barely constitutes an argument against this reform in the present era of globalisation. Finally, (7) for social reasons there must be doubts as to whether the target of 'full employment' in the conventional sense (as still featured in the DGB's new political programme) makes sense – in view of the economic conditions and the pluralisation and flexibilisation of individual biographies and life styles in society. To me it seems to make more sense to attempt to regulate flexibility with the trade unions and by political means, so as to protect against the risks of discrimination and to promote the development of opportunities for forms of employment involving different uses of time.

Such a programme would require the trade unions to come up with a policy in which firstly, through resistance (i.e. the protest, 'voice' option) and by demanding systems of regulation at national *and* European levels, companies' perception of the 'exit' options offered by the globalisation process will at least be hindered or diverted in 'socially acceptable' directions (a good example is resistance to reductions in continued wage payments in the event of workers falling ill). Secondly, such a policy would also have to intervene in the economic and social restructuring process to keep open or create future corridors for action geared to a 'social infrastructure policy'. And thirdly, these options for action would have to be combined with nationally and internationally positively discriminating regulations, in the sense of a 'policy of social cohesion'[6], and with a redistribution policy, if this is to result in more than social division, the formation of distinct social groups and new forms of social 'closure' within our own society and *vis-á-vis* other countries and societies. So, in a certain sense this constitutes a political task (not only for the trade unions), the fulfilment of which corresponds to the 'squaring of the circle' so often quoted in this context.

Notes

1. These considerations, which are taken up in further detail below, are based on Gösta Esping-Andersen, 'Equality or employment?', in *Transfer* no. 4/1996 and Hartmut Häusermann/Walter Siebel, *Dienstleistungsgesellschaften*, Frankfurt/Main 1995.

2. The following explanatory model arose *inter alia*, from discussions with Dieter Läpple, cf. also Dieter Läpple, *Que reste-t'-il du 'modèle allemand'?* Inaugural lecture given by the occupant of Chaire Alfred Grosser at the Institutes de Sciences Politiques, Paris 1996/97, 18 February 1997.

3. This aspect is dealt with in detail in the contribution to the conference by Heiner Gansmann; for this reason we do not examine it further here. See also Heiner Gansmann, 'Soziale Sicherheit als Standortproblem', *Prokla-Zeitschrift für kritische Sozialwissenschaft*, No. 106 1/1997.

4. *Cf. inter alia* Jürgen Hoffmann, 'Gewerkschaften in der Globalisierungsfalle?', in *Prokla-Zeitschrift für kritische Sozialwissenschaft* No. 106 (1997) (to be translated) and John Evans' contribution to the conference, which formulates positions similar to those in the contributions cited: John Evans, 'Welfare, Security and Economic Performance – Public Policy Overview' (Draft, IPPC, March 1997) and Jürgen Hoffmann and Reiner Hoffmann, 'Globalisierung – Risiken und Chancen für gewerkschaftliche Politik in Europa', in Rolfs Simons and Klaus Westermann (eds), *Standortdebatte und Globalisierung der Wirtschaft*, Marburg 1997.

5. For the concepts of 'exit' and 'voice' referred to here, see Albert O. Hirschman, *Exit, Voice and Loyalty*, Cambridge/Mass: Harvard University Press, 1970.

6. The terms 'social infrastructure policy' (*soziale Infrastrukturpolitik*) and 'social cohesion policy' (*soziale Kohäsionspolitik*) were taken from a lecture given by Wolfgang Streeck: Wolfgang Streeck, 'Industrielle Beziehungen in einer internationalisierten Wirtschaft' – Gesprächskreis der Friedrich Ebert Stiftung 'Arbeit und Soziales' zum Thema 'Globalisierung der Wirtschaft...' Bonn, 24 June 1996 (unpublished manuscript). However, Streeck uses the two policies in a mutually exclusive form, which in my opinion does not necessarily have to be the case.

The high road to development: Japan and the stakeholder agenda

Sadahiko Inoue and Fujikazu Suzuki

A number of interpretations are possible of the concept of the 'high road' approach as a tool of understanding the process of socio-economic development. One popular, if somewhat simplistic, interpretation would be to take it to mean the growth path of high productivity and high wages.

The concept can be crystallised by contrasting it with the opposite view of development, i.e., the low road approach, which is gaining strength in some quarters as applied to managerial strategy and the conduct of industrial relations. Some corporations in some industrialised countries single-mindedly try to maximise their use of a low-cost and dispensable workforce on a short-term basis, transferring their sites of operation in search of low wages. They do this not just between countries but also within their own country. Theirs is the low road approach. They thus try to reduce trade union strength, or even deny the unions, and limit the arena of public policy. They emphasise stockholders' sovereignty, and take the Return On Equity (ROE) as the sole indicator of management success, with little importance attached to the employment security of their workers or the social consequences of their actions. We might call this low road approach 'competitiveness for the shareholders'.

The high road approach, in contrast, emphasises long-term employment; the adaptability of workers by developing their inherent human capabilities; and the industrial democracy inclusivity of labour-management consultation; as beneficial to management and to technological progress. Their activities are based on the concept of 'competitiveness for the stakeholders', which could also be termed 'competitiveness at high standards of living' or a 'socially acceptable' model of competitiveness, as in John Evans' paper elsewhere in this volume.

The 'solidaristic wage policy' of LO, Sweden, can be understood as one of the approaches to high road development, although it is now facing severe challenges caused by the recent difficulties of the Swedish economy in adapting itself to the European economic integration and a new phase of the world market.

The high road approach – the importance of public policy

In order to secure the sustainability of the high road approach on the micro level it is necessary to enjoy a favorable macro economic performance. In fact, the micro high road approach could well result in better macro performances than the low road approach. Jeff Faux points out that the low road and low wage approach fairly extensively adopted by the United States in the 1980s produced lower per capital productivity gains on average, in comparison with the other nine industrialised countries.[1] When it comes to the sources of economic growth, he notes that most can be attributed to productivity gains in the same nine countries, while the contribution of productivity gains was less than half in the case of the United States.

The high road approach to managerial strategy and industrial relations policy would make one of the main foci of management concerns the enhancement of industrial democracy and worker participation. The human resource management in this approach would make it easier for workers and management to share knowledge and wisdom, on the basis of which technological progress could be envisaged, and staggered investment in plant and equipment could be planned. This is therefore a more appropriate approach to today's highly industrialised and knowledge-based economies. The high road approach would raise labour productivity in a steady manner, help attain a desirable growth rate, and promote more sophisticated industrial and technological structures. In other words, it would work in the direction of the elimination of sectors with low wages and low productivity.

The high road approach, in order to be effective, would require not only efforts by labour and management to achieve stable employment, industrial democracy, and participation, but also strong public policy which would be expected to create the basic conditions for the sustainability of this approach.

First, no expansion of the groups living in poverty should be allowed, and various categories of socially protective policies are essential, including a social security system to guarantee stable living throughout the life of individual citizens.[2].

Secondly, some facilities to allow life-long education, learning and training must be there for every member of the society so that he or she can better adjust himself or herself to the violent changes in society and in technologies.

Thirdly, the social infrastructure in both cities and villages must be improved, and the environment protected, so that there can be sufficient amenities for a pleasant and convenient life. It is also important to maintain social cohesion in a solidarity-based society with freedom and equality. The very basis of the high productivity of the high road approach is better social cohesion, and a high level of communication and social trust. In the high road approach, welfare and security contribute to a better economic performance.

Keynesian macro-economic policy is also important in this approach in order to ameliorate the violent business cycles that are unavoidable in market economies. In this context, it is rather questionable that major economies of the world continue to pursue excessively tight and repressive economic policies in the 1990s, even when the fear of resurgent inflation hardly exists. International policy co-ordination is thus an important task facing the international community.

These are the conceptual features of the high road approach. It is hoped that these will serve as a reference point for more progressive economic policies.

The Japanese economy of the 1990s

Let us try to apply the concept of the high road approach to the Japanese economy in recent decades. Up until the 1980s Japan had achieved exceptionally high growth compared with other industrialised countries. But in the 1990s it stagnated at almost zero growth for three consecutive years: 0.4 per cent in fiscal year 1992, 0.5 per cent in 1993, and 0.7 per cent in 1994. OECD called these years a period of 'strikingly exceptional low growth.' It was only in 1995 that growth recovered to above two per cent. In the context of the prolonged recession there arose internationally a strong neo-market economic view, calling for over-all industrial restructuring. Japan was no exception in this. It was argued that the specifically Japanese type of employment and wage determination system was crumbling down, or it was rashly concluded that it had already died. Such a view was rather popular in the international media. However, we wish to state categorically that such a line of reporting is the result of a thoroughly mistaken perception of the reality, or, at the least, a gross exaggeration.

The Japanese recession in the early 1990s should be characterised as a reaction to the preceding bubble-like boom of the latter half of the 1980s, with the economy growing at four to five per cent per annum, and with the soaring land and stock prices looking very much like those of the pre-1929 United States. The stagnating economy, however, did not register negative growth even in the early 1990s, and this was thanks to the aggressive macro-economic policies applied, including large-scale fiscal measures, involving a total of 75 trillion yen (or 15 per cent of Japan's then GDP; although its net effect is estimated to be around 25 trillion yen, or 5 per cent of GDP), and a major expansionary financial policy, including lower official discount rates and other easy money policies. These policies resulted, however, in Japan's budget deficit swelling to a level above that of many European countries, amounting to seven per cent of GDP.

Here we must note that, in the midst of the three-year stagnation, there were many economists who anticipated a soaring unemployment rate for Japan, due to the dwindling demand for labour, not unlike the German case; many also predicted growing income disparities in the country after a period of relatively equitable income distribution. Many economists of the neo-classical school maintained that it would be impossible for Japan to maintain the Japanese employment system, forecasting an ever worsening labour market situation. Contrary to these views, however, the reality proceeded somewhat differently. On the basis of available data, we can make the following comparison between the year 1991, when the stagnation started, and the year 1996, when it hit the bottom.[3] First, the unemployment rate showed only a slight worsening, of a little above one per cent, from over two per cent to over three per cent. This indicated that there were no major changes being made to the way in which employment had been adjusted to business conditions for the preceding twenty years, i.e., firms tried to maintain long-term employment for their employees as much as possible. Secondly, income distribution did not worsen. In fact, it even improved slightly as far as the wage differentials between industries, firms, and job categories were concerned.

The recent development of Japanese economy and society as seen from the view point of the high road approach

These phenomena would probably be incomprehensible unless one took into account the functioning of the Japanese internal labour market, especially in its flexible adaptability to the economic slump. Our interpretation of the favourable performance of the Japanese economy is as follows. First, macro-economic policies were effective in avoiding the worst outcome, i.e., negative growth. Second, there was a drop in working hours, from about 2,050 hours a year to about 1,900 hours a year. Shorter working hours during this period probably resulted in some form of work-sharing. Third, the specifically Japanese pattern of employment practice, with emphasis on long-term employment, was maintained. This micro factor probably served as the most important factor in the favourable performance of the economy during this period.

Long-term employment and seniority-based wage determination became part of Japanese employment practices on the compound basis of a number of elements, not least through the strenuous struggles against redundancy waged by the trade union movement in the postwar period, the demand by trade unions for wages on the formula of a subsistence wage for the whole family of the workers involved, and the rational organisation of business firms. The internal labour market within individual business firms, or the semi-internal labour market within groups of firms, has been shown out to be as effective as the external labour market in avoiding redundancy or unemployment.[4]

The flexibility of the internal labour market, however, can be secured only when the prevailing conditions give rise to, or further enhance, some specific form of adaptability on the part of both the workers and the firms: while the firms try to avoid worsening working conditions and to guarantee long-term employment, workers try to improve themselves and accept transfers in jobs or work location. Although we ourselves are not completely satisfied with what we have achieved in Japan in the above context, we do feel that the prevailing employment system works more favorably than the external labour market for both management and labour.

There is one institution that has helped Japanese firms maintain their workforce – the employment adjustment subsidy which firms receive, on the basis of the Employment Insurance Act, when they keep redundant workers on their payroll for specific periods of time.

The fourth factor which has helped the Japanese economy is the ongoing changes in the industrial structure of the economy, for dynamic generational shifts in principal product lines, partly supported by the flexible internal labour market. Japan's imports have increased and are increasing rapidly, including manufactured imports from other parts of Asia. This resulted in the loss of over one million jobs in manufacturing at one time. Fortunately, however, there are indications of the situation improving since the latter half of the fiscal year 1996, mainly thanks to a successful shift of the principal product lines to sophisticated capital goods like robots, and, among consumer durables, from colour TV sets and VTRs (more of which were imported) to electronic parts and liquid crystal devices with high technology inputs.

Fifthly, we have a rather unique method of national wage determination, the 'Shunto', or annual spring wage offensive, which makes good use of specific information collection networks. Wage negotiations in Japan take place on an individual enterprise basis, formally highly fragmented. In functional terms, however, they are not at all fragmented or decentralised but quite uniform and national in nature. Let us explain. In spring each year, the national trade union confederation and industrial unions mutually exchange information and formulate a consensus. They present their almost identical demands for wage raises at about the same time. Thereafter national wage guidelines are arrived at, one after another, within roughly a week. The rates of pay increase are not very divergent from industry to industry, and this rate is applied to public employees, and to workers in non-unionised sectors. (Some small-and-medium-sized firms do put a small extra on the national average in order to draw better talents.) Without this form of national wage determination, and its prerequisite, i.e., specific networks of information, the shrinking income differentials among various worker groups in the 1990s would have been impossible.

Thanks are due to these mechanisms, which contributed to Japan's successful avoidance of either the high unemployment of Europe or the growing income discrepancy of the United States.[5]

Social security and the budget reform

By the early 1970s, the social security system in Japan had developed to the level of developed world in the areas of national pensions, medical insurance, unemployment insurance and occupational hazards insurance. The steady institutional improvement stopped during the 1970s due to the two oil crises, but started to pick up again in the early 1990s, despite the prolonged recession, now aiming at reaching the German or Scandinavian standards, from the American standard achieved hitherto.

In July 1995 the prestigious Council on Social Security came up with an epoch-making recommendation, to specifically promote the adoption of the German and Scandinavian type of social security rather than the American one. On the basis of this recommendation, relevant laws will be passed to deal with social care for the aged. The background to this development is a common perception in Japan that Japanese society is very rapidly aging, and will eventually become an even more aged society than in the Scandinavian countries. In terms of the real content of these institutional developments, we come to a somewhat surprising conclusion – that Japan is now becoming the first non-Western welfare state in the world.

At the moment, however, Japan is suffering from a big fiscal deficit, beyond the level of European countries, in terms of the annual level of general account deficit and the accumulated deficits *vis-à-vis* its GNP. This is mainly a result of the large scale fiscal policies mobilised to counter the recession in the first half of the 1990s. Furthermore, there are observers who call for a total review of the welfare system and various public institutions, in order to regain fiscal health in the face of the impending social transformation into an aged society. We feel it to be a task of utmost urgency for us to refute such neo-market ideologues and to pursue a policy of solidly establishing a stable and sustainable welfare system in the country.

Notes

1. Jeff Faux, 'Is the American Economic Model the Answer?', *The American Prospect*, Fall 1994.
2. We probably are justified in applying the high road approach to the case of Japan if we look at its performance in functional terms. But did we purpose-

fully pursue that road of development? The answer is not so straightforward. A major challenge for the Japanese society in these days of globalisation would be the deliberate and intentional adoption of the high road approach in the coming century.

3. See S. Inoue, 'The Change of Employment in Japan,' IIRA Asian Regional Congress, 1996.

4. See R. Dore, K. Tapiola, & J. Cabale, *Japan at Work*, OECD, 1989.

5. In spite of these measures of progress, we are beset with a number of challenges facing Japan's economy and society. Gradual improvements in income distribution still allow substantial discrepancies in wages among firms of different sizes, as well as between men and women. There still are some industrial sectors of low productivity, like agriculture, as the remnant of the once famous dual structure of the Japanese economy.

The political economy of Europe

Paul Ormerod

Discussing the present situation in Western Europe is fraught with difficulties. A great deal of the debate compares the outcomes of the Anglo-Saxon economies – Britain and the United States – with those of the 'Continent' – the rest of Western Europe. This particular disputation raises ideological blood pressures, and is hard to conduct dispassionately. I want to look at Western Europe on its own, by which I mean the countries of the European Union excluding, for these purposes, the UK. Avoiding as far as possible direct comparisons with the Anglo-Saxon world, I am still forced to the conclusion that there is a serious crisis of political economy in Western Europe.

The most striking manifestation of this is unemployment. This now totals 18 million, up from the 1991 figure of 12.5 million, which in itself is a dramatic increase on the 1979 level of 5.5 million. A partial defence, which is often heard in trade union circles, is that unemployment rates amongst prime age males, from 25 to 55, say, are by no means as high as the overall rates. Unemployment falls disproportionately on the young and upon women. It has to be said that this particular distribution of unemployment seems to have less devastating consequences for social cohesion than one under which men are the main sufferers. But it would obviously be much better for all concerned if rates overall were much lower.

In any event, the official figures conceal a great deal. In the Netherlands, for example, the rate of unemployment is low, at 6.5 per cent, but the Dutch have the same number classed as disabled. The problem has simply been redefined. More generally, there are large numbers of jobs in the traded public sector which exist only because of massive state subsidies. Coalminers occupy a special place in the affections of many, so it is easy to sympathise with this group when the withdrawal of financial support threatens their jobs. But airline staff, for example, can hardly be said to command such a prominent position in the mythologies of the labour movement. Yet, throughout Europe, a job with the national airline is to a large extent at the courtesy of the taxpayer, an expensive form of make-work scheme for the lower middle class.

Economic growth has been low for twenty years. But here the conclusions to be drawn are mixed. In the golden years of Western capitalism, from 1950 to 1973, real GDP per capita in Western Europe rose at an average rate of almost 4 per cent a year. Since 1973, there has been a dramatic cut-back in the rate, to just 1.7 per cent a year.[1] This relative lack of growth is responsible for a substantial part of the current set of problems of political economy which face Europe, and I argue below how the growth rate can be raised. But some of the difficulties posed by low growth are caused by expectations of growth being too high. The post-oil shock growth rate has been perfectly respectable by historical standards – higher, indeed, than for any set of years of comparable length in the whole of the 1820 to 1950 period. But electorates seem to expect growth to be even higher.

A partial justification for popular discontent with European growth is the fact that real wages have grown more slowly then the overall economy in recent years, as companies have tried to restore profitability. The concept of the real wage extends considerably beyond the amount in the pay packet at the end of the week, or the sum transferred to the bank at the end of the month. Contributions by employers to pension funds, health care schemes and the like all go to make up the true definition of the real wage. A failure to appreciate this has led many commentators to misunderstand the American experience. The distribution of personal income has widened considerably in the US, but the overall division of national income between profits and wages has been remarkably constant throughout the 1980s and 1990s. The average real wage, properly defined, has not fallen. It has grown at the same rate as the overall US economy.

In contrast, in Europe, the share of wages in national income has fallen over the past ten years or so, typically by 5 or 6 percentage points. From a share of national income of around 64 per cent in the early 1980s, it has fallen to the high 50s as a percentage by the mid-

1990s. Simple arithmetic tells us that real wages have therefore grown by around 8-10 per cent *less* than the economy overall over this period. Given the overall rate of growth, real wages are on average only a few per cent higher than 10 or so years ago. In other words, it is in Europe and not the US that there has been a problem with real wage growth.

Europe's problems are compounded by the serious fiscal problem which many countries face. This is of a structural nature, and exists quite independently of whatever criteria may eventually deemed as being satisfactory in order to meet the Maastricht conditions. Indeed, these latter in many ways veil the problem, and lead people into the false belief that if a country is accepted into monetary union, it necessarily follows that its public finances are sound.

There are two problems which governments in all Western countries face. The first, in the jargon of economics, is caused by the income elasticities of demand for health and education. As countries get richer, the demand for services in general tends to rise faster than the demand for manufactured goods. This is not in any way to dismiss manufacturing as unimportant, but merely to state a fact. The demand for air travel, holidays, financial services and so on have all been amongst the fastest growing sectors of consumer demand. Health and education are no exceptions to this list. The demand for both rises faster than the economy as a whole. In health, for example, many people now survive ailments or injuries which even thirty years ago would have killed them rapidly. The necessary treatments are often very expensive, but once the genie is out of the bottle, it is hard to put it back in. It is very difficult to say to a 75 year old that he or she cannot have treatment which is known to both exist and to prolong life. These two areas comprise a substantial proportion of total public expenditure. And the inexorable rise in demand for these products places long-term pressure on the public finances.

The second general problem also relates to the more rapid growth of services as opposed to manufactures. So far, this switch in the overall composition of output has led to a reduction in the overall base of taxation. Manufactured goods are easy to tax and, with very few exceptions, attract Value Added Tax or excise duty in Europe. Governments have been slow to extend taxes on consumption into the service sector. Meals in restaurants attract VAT. And in Britain, for example, the Conservative government introduced an airport departure tax and a tax on insurance policies, but both these are at very modest rates. Whole swathes of consumer spending either attract hardly any tax whatsoever

– financial services is the prime example – or low rates of tax, such as the use of the car.

In principle, of course, governments could extend the tax base to deal with the emerging problem, but it might be very difficult in practice. The American government, for example, is deeply hostile to the idea of levying tax on activities on the Internet, which are offering more and more scope for legitimate tax avoidance. Unless the Americans change their minds, the European Commission is completely powerless to do anything about it.

There are two further issues of public finance which are more specific to Europe. Firstly, there is the question of ageing populations, on which much has been written. It is sufficient here to note the financial implications. Britain has escaped the problem by the brutal decision in 1979 to link state pension increases to prices and not wages. But this obviously creates serious difficulties for the large numbers who are effectively reliant on the state pension.

My main concern here is with a second issue, which has implications which are both strictly economic in a narrow, technical sense, and more generally, are firmly in the realm of political economy. This is the question of interest payments on the stock of public sector debt.

From the point of view of an individual, the ability to manage a loan depends upon two factors, the size of the loan and the interest rate. A debt of £100,000 is not large if the interest rate is only 1 per cent, but a debt of £50,000 might be punishing for many if the interest rate were, say, 15 per cent. Exactly the same principle applies to governments, though, importantly, the interest rate on outstanding government debt is effectively fixed. With some very minor exceptions, such debt is issued at the then prevailing interest rate, so the rate of interest on debt only changes slowly, as old debt matures and new debt is issued at existing rates of interest. Interest payments are now a source of major problems across Europe.

The German government has a relatively low stock of debt, at just over 60 per cent of GDP. And the average interest rate on this is low. Even so, interest repayments are almost one-fifth of the total tax revenue of the national government. In Italy, with a much higher amount of debt outstanding issued at distinctly higher interest rates, these repayments amount to as much as one half of all the tax receipts of the national government.

For virtually the whole of the 1980s and 1990s, the *real* rate of interest in European countries has exceeded the real rate of growth of the economies. Simple arithmetic tells us that, unless governments raise taxes to start repaying debt, this is not sustainable in the long run. Eventually – and the numbers rise with frightening speed beyond a certain point – debt interest payments absorb the whole of public expenditure.

In the bad old days, a very convenient way of dealing with large amounts of debt issued in nominal terms was to have a burst of inflation. A few years of double-digit inflation did wonders for reducing the stock of debt relative to the level of GDP. Inflation still exists, but at much lower levels, so this method of expropriating the wealth of bond holders to deal with public finance problems is nowhere near as effective as it used to be.

Support for the welfare state and the principle of social solidarity is still very strong in Europe. But, increasingly, taxpayers have been asked to hand over money not to finance the delivery of services now, but to pay the interest on debt incurred for the provision of services in the past. Very few people will actually look at the national accounts and realise explicitly that this is happening. But many will see that their taxes rise but services at best do not improve and may often deteriorate.

The structural fiscal problem varies in severity from country to country. But it is hard to avoid the conclusion that, regardless of the Maastricht criteria, a period of higher taxes on incomes is required if substantial cuts in public expenditure are to be avoided.

Life would be considerably easier if a higher rate of economic growth could be sustained in the medium to longer term. Despite all the difficulties, many European companies are still capable of performing well. Europe is by no means as strongly represented in dynamic areas – computer software, biotechnology, financial services, telecommunications, airlines - as would be desirable. But the economy is hardly on the verge of complete penury, as many Eurosceptics in Britain wish to believe.

The preparations for monetary union have seriously damaged Europe's economic performance. There are two main, and connected reasons, why Europe's growth has been low. First, high real interest rates. Second, high real exchange rates.

Since 1980, real interest rates in Europe have averaged around 5 per cent, the highest which they have been over so long a period in the entire history of capitalism. It is hard to imagine that this has not had a damaging effect on long-term expectations and what Keynes described as the 'animal spirits' of businesspeople. And, although there has been a welcome fall very recently, between 1981 and 1995, the real effective exchange rate of the mark against a basket of other currencies rose by nearly 40 per cent. Not only does this involve a direct loss of potential competitiveness, but as companies respond by holding export prices down, their profit margins are squeezed. And a repercussion of the latter, pointed out above, is that firms then hold real wages down in an effort to maintain profitability.

The overall impact of the pressures on profits can be seen on the chart below. This plots the change in the annual average rate of growth in OECD countries between 1974–94 and 1960–73, against the change in the share of profits in national income. The more that profits fell as a share of total income, the greater was the reduction in the average growth rate.

In order to revive the medium term growth rate in Europe, sharp falls are needed in both real interest rates and the real exchange rate. This shift in macro-economic policy is not a panacea. But it would go a considerable way to easing the crisis of political economy which Europe faces.

Change in average real GDP growth and profit share
OECD economies, 1974-94 on 1960-73

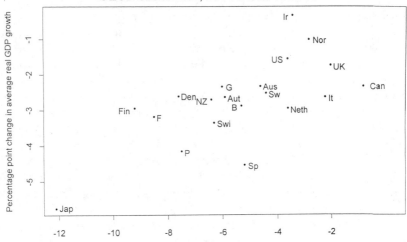

Percentage point change in profit share in national income

The policies adopted in the long drawn out moves towards monetary union represent a folly of the highest order. As a consequence, growth is depressed, unemployment very high, real wage growth very limited, and the public finances placed under severe strain. The future is inherently uncertain, and it is theoretically possible that monetary union will create jobs and prosperity. But such a belief requires a real leap of faith. In the dress rehearsal for monetary union, unemployment has risen to 20 million, and real wage growth has been very low. Maybe it really will be all right on the night, but the best thing to do in the current circumstances is to cancel the performance altogether.

Note

1. The source for figures on growth is Maddison, *Monitoring the World Economy 1820–1992*, OECD, 1995.

Restoring prosperity: Why the US model is not the answer for the US or Europe

Thomas I. Palley*

Over the last two decades, Western European and US unemployment experience has differed dramatically. Whereas the US has been characterised by extensive job creation and comparatively low unemployment rates, Western Europe has been characterised by negligible job creation and comparatively high rates of unemployment. These differences in job performance are shown in Tables 1 and 2.

Table 1 shows how the unemployment rate has inexorably risen in European countries since 1973. As of 1996, the US had a lower rate of unemployment than Europe, though this rate was higher than it had been in 1973. More recent data serves to compound the US's advantage since the US unemployment rate fell to 4.9 per cent in April 1997.

Table 2 provides data on job creation in the period 1979–92, and once again the superior performance of the US economy is evident. Moreover, more recent data again compounds this dimension of superior performance since the US economy has generated a further 8.5 million jobs since 1992.

The severity of the European unemployment problem, combined with the relative success of the US in creating jobs and keeping unemployment rates down, has led many Europeans to believe that they

* This chapter is also published in *The Journal of Post Keynesian Economics*.

Table 1   Comparative unemployment rates, 1973–96

Country	1973	1979	1989	1996
United States	4.8	5.8	5.2	5.4
France	2.7	5.9	9.4	12.3
West Germany	0.8	3.2	5.5	9.0*
Italy	6.2	7.6	10.9	11.9+
United Kingdom	3.0	5.0	7.2	8.2
Europe large country average	3.2	5.4	8.3	10.4
Belgium	2.7	8.2	8.0	9.8
Finland	2.3	5.9	3.4	15.7
Netherlands	2.2	5.4	8.3	6.6
Norway	1.5	2.0	4.9	5.0
Sweden	2.5	2.1	1.4	10.0
Europe 5 small country average	2.2	4.7	5.2	9.4

Source: Bernstein and Mishel (1995) and author's calculations. 1996 data from OECD News release (97) 21
+ = 1995 data: * = all Germany

should adopt the US model. This belief is evident in the 1996 OECD survey of the US economy, in which Chapter III is little short of a panegyric to US labour markets and labour market policy which is described as being 'generally effective in creating a dynamic and flexible economy (p24).'

The OECD's endorsement of the US model is misguided, and can be faulted on a number of levels. First and foremost, the US model is fool's gold in the sense that though it has generated relatively more jobs, these jobs have been produced at great cost in terms of income inequality, stagnating wages, and increased income insecurity. Moreover, this putatively superior employment performance represents a step back when compared with US employment performance in the period 1950–73. In 1973, the US unemployment rate was 4.8 per cent: during the 1960s it averaged 4.8 per cent, and during the 1950s it

Table 2   Jobs created, 1979–92

Country	Total Created (000) 1979-89	New Jobs as Per cent of Employment 1979	Total Created (000) 1979-92	New Jobs as Per cent of Employment 1979
United States	18,518	18.7	18,774	19.0
France	550	2.6	730	3.5
West Germany	1,730	6.8	3,180	12.5
Italy	840	4.2	1,240	6.2
Netherlands	730	13.7	1,130	21.2
Sweden	364	8.7	146	3.5
United Kingdom	1,410	5.7	520	2.1
Europe (6 country average)		7.0		8.2

Source: Bernstein and Mishel (1995) and author's calculations.

averaged 4.5 per cent. These average rates are lower than the current rate of 4.9 per cent, which itself marks the peak of the current business cycle expansion

Second, the diagnosis of the causes of the US's recent superior employment performance relative to Europe is a false one. This diagnosis emphasises microeconomic factors associated with labour market practices and institutions, whereas the real cause of the US's superior performance concerns macroeconomic policy.

Third, the construction of an opposition between the US and European models establishes a false dichotomy in which policy-makers are forced to choose between either high unemployment with moderate social protections, or lower unemployment with low levels of social protection and high income inequality. In fact, both the US and European models are pathological, and both should be rejected.

Economic policy should aim for full employment with a high degree of social protection and relative income equality. These were the conditions that characterised the Golden Age period of 1950–73. Achieving such an outcome demands an alternative economic diagnosis. The current diagnosis implicitly blames workers for unemployment through its focus on labour market rigidities and social protections: an alternative diagnosis de-emphasises labour markets and promotes a strategy that encompasses macroeconomic policy, international economic policy, and appropriate governance of domestic markets, which include labour markets.

Fool's gold: the dark side of the US model

The one clear advantage of the US model over its European counterpart is its employment performance. However, the US model has extensive disadvantages which have been documented by Mishel and Schmitt.[2] At the macroeconomic level, this disadvantage shows up in the rate of productivity growth which is shown in Table 3. Over the period 1960-92, the average annual rate of US productivity growth was consistently below that of the six European economies shown. This sub-par performance holds for all of the sub-sample periods within the overall sample period, and US productivity growth also slowed down in the latter half. However, this is faint praise for Europe, since it too experienced slowed productivity growth. In this connection, it is noteworthy that amongst European countries, the United Kingdom has also experienced very low productivity growth in the most recent period, and it has come closest to adopting the US model.

Table 3 Productivity Growth Rates, 1960–92

	1960-1967 (%)	1967-1973 (%)	1973-1979 (%)	1979-1989 (%)	1989-1992 (%)	1960-1992 (%)
United States	2.7	0.9	−0.1	0.8	0.7	1.1
France	4.3	4.1	2.4	1.9	1.2	2.9
West Germany	3.9	4.3	2.9	1.1	2.1	2.7
Italy	6.1	5.0	2.7	2.0	0.8	3.5
Netherlands	n.a.	n.a.	0.0	0.7	0.1	0.3
Sweden	4.0	2.8	0.5	1.2	1.1	2.0
United Kingdom	2.3	3.4	1.2	1.8	0.4	2.0
Europe	4.1	3.9	1.6	1.5	1.0	2.2

Source: Bernstein and Mishel (1995).

Another downside to the US model has been its tendency to produce wage stagnation. This is captured in Tables 4 and 5. Over the period 1979–92 the US average rate of growth of compensation per employee was 0.23 per cent: in Europe, it was 1.19 per cent. Table 5 reveals that the US performance was even worse in the manufacturing sector, where US hourly compensation growth was negative for production workers: contrastingly, European hourly wages of production workers continued to grow.

Table 4   International compensation growth per business sector employee, 1979–92

	1979–89 (%)	1989–92 (%)	1979–92 (%)
United States	0.12	0.51	0.23
France	0.93	1.28	1.03
Germany	1.11	2.71	1.57
Italy	1.38	1.83	1.51
United Kingdom	1.91	0.51	1.51
Europe (4 country average)	1.03	1.58	1.19

Source: Bernstein and Mishel (1995) and author's calculations.

The US model is also characterised by greater inequality of income distribution. This is captured in tables 6 and 7. Table 6 shows family income of selected percentiles as a percentage of the median income. The last column shows the ratio of the 90th percentile's income to the 10th percentile's income. In the US, this ratio is 5:94: for the six European countries it averages 3.32. Table 6 captures the greater extent of income inequality in the US. Table 7 captures the direction in which it has been changing. This table shows how various groups' incomes changed relative to the median income. In the US, persons at the 10th percentile found that their income declined relative to the median income by 3.4 percentage points: those at the 95th percentile increased their income relative to the median by 25.4 percentage points. The US pattern is one of growing income inequality. In

European countries, it is only the United Kingdom that shows a similar pattern: however, in the UK, those at the bottom have been able to retain their standing relative to the median. In the Netherlands and Sweden, those at the 10th percentile have lost ground relative to the median, but top income groups have not increased their relative standing. In sum, income distribution in Europe has remained relatively stable, while it has become more unequal in the US.[3]

Table 5   Hourly manufacturing compensation growth, 1979–92

	1979–89		1989–92		1979–92	
	All (%)	Production (%)	All (%)	Prod. (%)	All (%)	Prod. (%)
United States	0.2	−0.6	0.8	−0.1	0.4	-0.5
Denmark	0.0	−0.2	1.7	2.0	0.5	0.4
France	1.9	1.9	0.8	0.7	1.6	1.6
West Germany	2.3	1.9	3.0	3.1	2.5	2.2
Italy	1.0	1.5	3.4	0.5	1.7	1.2
Netherlands	0.8	0.5	1.0	1.1	0.9	0.7
Sweden	0.9	0.9	0.1	0.3	0.7	0.7
United Kingdom	3.1	1.7	1.7	2.4	2.7	1.9
Europe (7 country average)	1.4	1.2	1.7	1.4	1.5	1.3

Source: Bernstein and Mishel (1995) and author's calculations.

A final statistic that sheds light on the dark side of the US model is the poverty rate. Table 8 shows comparative international poverty rates. The poverty threshold is defined as 40 per cent of median income adjusted for family size. US poverty rates are an order of magnitude higher than European rates: the percentage of adults in poverty is twice as high in the US, while the percentage of children in poverty is five times as high.

Table 6 Family income distribution: per cent of median income, mid-1980s.

| | Percentiles | | | Distance Ratio |
	10th	90th	95th	90/10
United States (1986)	34.7	206.1	247.3	5.94
France (1984)	55.4	192.8	233.5	3.48
West Germany (1984)	56.9	170.8	201.7	3.00
Italy (1986)	48.9	197.9	233.8	4.05
Netherlands (1987)	61.5	175.0	206.4	2.85
Sweden (1987)	55.6	151.5	170.4	2.72
United Kingdom (1986)	51.1	194.1	232.1	3.80
Europe (6 country average)	54.9	180.4	213.0	3.32

Source: Atkinson, Rainwater and Smeeding (1994), and author's calculations.[4]

Table 7 Change in multiple (percentage points) of median income during the 1980s

| | Change in Distance from median | | | Distance Ratio |
	10th	90th	95th	90/10
United States (1979-86)	−3.4	18.5	25.4	1.0
France (1979-84)	1.8	6.3	1.2	0.0
Netherlands (1983-87)	−3.3	−1.1	−1.7	0.1
Sweden (1981-87)	−5.9	0.6	3.4	0.3
United Kingdom (1979-86)	0.2	14.4	23.2	0.3

Source: Atkinson, Rainwater and Smeeding (1994), and author's calculations.

Table 8 *International poverty rates.*

Country	Poverty rates in the mid-1980s		
	All Persons	All Adults (18-64)	All Children (17 or under)
United States	13.3	10.5	20.4
France	4.5	5.2	4.6
West Germany	2.8	2.6	2.8
Netherlands	3.4	3.9	3.8
Sweden	4.3	6.6	1.6
United Kingdom	5.2	5.3	7.4
Europe (5 country average)	4.0	4.7	4.0
Ratio of US to Europe	3.3	2.2	5.1

Misunderstanding the causes of the lower US unemployment rate

The previous section documented the dark side of the US economy, which offsets its superior job creation performance. The consensus view amongst economists, which is also supported in the OECD survey of the US economy (1996), is that the US has a lower unemployment rate because its labour markets and wage structure are relatively more flexible compared to Europe. Thus, workers in the US have little in the way of job protection, unions are weaker, and unemployment benefit is harder to qualify for, of shorter duration, and marked by a lower wage replacement rate. The argument is that labour markets in both countries have been buffeted by technological shocks and increased foreign competition driven by globalisation, but flexible US labour markets have enabled the US economy to cope better with these shocks.

This explanation is being used to push European countries to abolish labour market regulations and reduce worker protections, yet it significantly misrepresents the true cause of lower US unemployment rates. Throughout the 1960s and 1970s Europe had a lower unemployment rate than the US. However, this situation reversed in 1983, since when the US unemployment rate has trended down, while Europe's unemployment rate has continued trending up. Whereas the consensus view is that this difference is attributable to differential labour market flexibility, an alternative view is that it is attributable to differential macroeconomic policies. Thus, the US has pursued relatively more expansionary macroeconomic policies, and this is the real cause of its lower unemployment rate.

Taking account of macroeconomic factors dramatically changes perceptions of the US model. Europe is trapped in deep recession, while the US is at the peak of a cyclical boom. This raises the question of why Europe has gotten trapped in a slump, while the US has been able to enjoy a cyclical expansion. The answer lies in macroeconomic policy.

During the 1980s, the US pursued a strongly expansionary fiscal policy, and ran budget deficits that averaged 3.6 per cent of GDP. These deficits were caused by the big defence build-up and by extensive tax-cuts for upper income groups, and together they stimulated aggregate demand. European countries have also run deficits, but rather than being the product of expansionary fiscal policy, these deficits have been produced by reduced tax revenues and increased welfare spending caused by recessionary conditions. Thus, the US budget deficit was the result of pro-active expansionary fiscal policy, whereas European deficits were the result of depressed economic conditions.

Just as the US has run relatively more expansionary fiscal policy, so too it has run more expansionary and counter-cyclical monetary policy. The US has pursued an independent monetary policy conditioned upon the state of the domestic economy. Though the underlying stance of monetary policy has not been as expansionary as might have been desired, the Fed has been able to lower interest rates whenever economic conditions have weakened excessively. Thus, in the 1981–82 recession, when unemployment threatened to become excessive, the Fed was able to lower the Federal Funds rate from 16.4 per cent in 1981 to 9.1 per cent in 1983: in the most recent recession, the Fed lowered the funds rate from 5.5 per cent in 1991 to 3 per cent in 1993.

This state of affairs contrasts with that in Europe. First, European monetary policy has been more completely captured by the notion that inflation is an unmitigated bad that is not to be tolerated at any cost: this reflects the more unruly inflation experience of European countries in the 1970s, as well as the domination of the Bundesbank within European financial circles. European monetary authorities have therefore been less inclined to lower interest rates when domestic employment conditions have weakened. 'Inclination' is one reason for Europe's more contractionary monetary policy: 'ability' is another. European economies are much more 'open' than the US economy, as measured by the ratio of imports to total domestic expenditure. This is captured in Table 9 which shows the degree of openness: a measure of 0 is a pure closed economy which has no imports, while a measure of 1 corresponds to a pure open economy in which all domestic spending is on imports. For the US, the degree of openness is .10: for Europe, it is .31. The significance of this heightened openness is that it makes European economies very sensitive to imported price inflation resulting from exchange rate depreciation. Given this, and given their fear about inflation, European countries have been averse to exchange rate weakness. This aversion has locked them into a policy of keeping interest rates high. Worse than that, fearing exchange rate weakness, individual country monetary authorities have had an incentive to push their domestic interest rates fractionally above the average. However, with all countries succumbing to this incentive, average interest rates have been pushed higher.

Table 9   Degree of openness.

	1988
United States	.10
France	.21
Greece	.26
Italy	.18
West Germany	.28
United Kingdom	.27
Denmark	.30
Sweden	.31
Switzerland	.35
Austria	.35
Norway	.37
Netherlands	.51
Europe (11 country average)	.31

Source: Davidson (1994).[5]

During the 1980s, the deflationary impulse in monetary policy was institutionalised through the European exchange rate mechanism (ERM). Countries joining the ERM were forced to keep domestic interest rates high to prevent exchange rate depreciations that would have violated ERM bounds. Ultimately, these attempts to preserve the ERM proved futile, and it collapsed in 1993 after a bout of extreme currency speculation against the British pound.

The big beneficiary from the ERM was Germany, whose currency was kept below the levels that its balance of payments surplus and low inflation rate demanded. France has been a particularly heavy loser, as the French Franc has been tied to the Deutsche Mark through the Bank of France's *franc fort* policy. In order to limit imported inflation, and in an attempt to win lower interest rates through international credibility regarding commitment to low inflation, the French economy has been burdened by much higher interest rates than underlying real economic conditions warranted. In effect, the French monetary authorities have sacrificed the French economy on an altar of the Bundesbank's making.

Exchange rate considerations limit individual countries from pursuing autonomous monetary policy: balance of payments considerations limit them from pursuing full employment fiscal policies. The problem is again one of openness. Since individual European economies are so open, a significant part of any fiscal stimulus leaks abroad in the form of higher import spending. This in turn worsens the balance of payments, thereby putting pressure on the exchange rate. At this stage, expansionary policy must be brought to an end, either by the reversal of the fiscal stimulus or by higher interest rates. In this connection, it is notable that the Mitterrand government in France felt compelled by a sense of crisis to put an end to its expansionary Keynesian policy when the French budget deficit reached a mere 2.6 per cent of GDP in 1983: however, by then the French trade deficit was 2.2 per cent of GDP.[6]

In a sense, European economies are similar to individual state economies within the US or Canada: individual states are unable to purse expansionary fiscal policy because too much of the stimulus leaks outside the state. States that try such policies quickly find that the employment effect is limited while the budgetary impact is huge, and they are forced to reverse course; this is what happened to the Ontario provincial government in Canada in the early 1990s. Fiscal policy in the US only works when implemented at the federal level: a similar logic applies to Europe, where fiscal policy is effective if co-ordinated across countries, and short-lived if tried in isolation.

The problem of excessive leakages, combined with the fear of exchange rate weakness, gives rise to a systemic deflationary bias since every country has a private incentive to adopt contractionary policies. This problem is illustrated in Figure 1. Countries can either choose expansionary or contractionary macroeconomic policies. The top left box yields the optimal outcome, and has both countries expanding. The result is full employment, balanced trade and fiscal balance in both countries: countries import from each other, thereby producing balanced trade, while full employment raises tax revenues and lowers transfers. The bottom right box is the inferior outcome, and has both countries contracting: trade is balanced, but both countries experience unemployment, and may also have cyclical deficits because tax revenues are down and unemployment insurance payments are up.

Figure 1   Taxonomy of macroeconomic policy outcomes

COUNTRY A

	Expand	Contract
COUNTRY B Expand	Co-ordinated Policy	
COUNTRY B Contract		Uncoordinated Policy

Why does the bottom box dominate despite its inferior outcome? With regard to monetary policy, there is a policy incentive to raise interest rates fractionally above the international average, thereby currying favour with the foreign exchange market and reducing the likelihood of capital flight and imported inflation. However, when all countries do this, the result is higher interest rates in all countries. With regard to fiscal policy, there is a policy incentive to cut spending and reduce the budget deficit, in the hope of winning favour with the bond market and generating lower interest rates.

In this structural environment, no country can go it alone. If one country tries to use expansionary monetary policy, it quickly finds itself in danger of an exchange rate crisis, with consequences for imported inflation. This is because lower rates, combined with the prospect of marginally higher inflation, cause capital to flee. Demand also leaks abroad, giving rise to a trade deficit. If a country tries expansionary fiscal policy, there is still the danger of capital flight owing to the prospect of potentially higher inflation, and there is still the problem of demand leaking abroad. The result is it finds itself stuck with both a budget and trade deficit, and is soon forced to reverse policy.

Resolving the adverse incentive structure associated with independent action calls for co-operative policy making. If all agree to expand together, then the demand leakages between countries offset one another. The result is expanded output combined with balanced trade, since all countries are importing from each other. The fiscal deficit is also reduced as a result of the expansion. Finally, the problem of capital flight is minimised as all countries are simultaneously expanding, and finance capital has no country of particular preference to flee to.

The above problems of openness and lack of co-ordination have imparted a restrictionary bias to both monetary and fiscal policy in Europe. This bias in fiscal policy is now being compounded by the Maastricht Treaty's conditions regarding implementation of economic and monetary union (EMU). As part of the transition arrangements for establishing a single European currency, countries are restricted to have government budget deficits that are less than 3 per cent of GDP. However, most countries are running deficits significantly in excess of this owing to current depressed economic conditions which have lowered tax revenues and increased welfare payments. Consequently, many European economies are being pushed to adopt contractionary fiscal policies to reduce their budget deficits at a time when they are already in recession. Given the openness of these economies, whereby contraction (expansion) in one country negatively (positively) affects others, this will aggravate Europe's generalised deflationary climate.

In addition to the relatively contractionary stance of European monetary and fiscal policy, there are other special factors that explain the US's relatively better job performance. One factor, is the US private credit system which is ready to make easy provision of credit. This, combined with America's culture of consumerism, can be a significant expansionary factor. It contributed to the long expansion in the 1980s, when consumer debt to income ratios rose to record heights, and it has contributed to the current recovery during which household consumer debt to income ratios have again risen to record highs. However, it is also true that these debts may become a major burden in the next US recession, just as they were in the recession of 1990–91.

A second special factor behind US job creation was the S&L bailout during the late 1980s. In one sense, the bailout was contractionary since it disrupted the flow of credit from the S&Ls. Yet, balancing this, the rescue brought with it a $125 billion injection of funds into the economy. The initial S&L lending was expansionary, while the contractionary burden of these debts was wiped off the private sector's balance sheet by the Federal government stepping in and paying off depositors.

Beyond the US and European models

The previous sections have highlighted the pathological state of affairs in both the US and Europe. To summarise the argument so far: though the US economy currently has lower unemployment rates than Europe, it has also experienced an upward trend in unemployment rates since the early 1970s; the superior job creation performance of the US model is 'fool's gold' in that it was accompanied by a tendency to generate wage stagnation, and increased income inequality and poverty rates; moreover, the US economy's recent superior job creation performance has been been driven by macroeconomic forces rather than by microeconomic considerations of greater labour market flexibility.

The causes of the differences in performance are shown in Figure 2. This figure contains a two-by-two matrix describing the policies pursued by Europe and the US. These policies are described as 'maintenance of the wage floor' and 'expansionary macroeconomic policy'. Box B corresponds to the US economy, where the wage floor has been undermined, but macroeconomic policy has been relatively expansionary: the result has been increased income inequality, accompanied by job creation. Box C corresponds to Europe, where the wage floor has been maintained but macroeconomic policy has been relatively contractionary: the result has been unchanged income inequality, accompanied by rising unemployment.

Figure 2   *Taxonomy of policy configurations.*

WAGE FLOOR MAINTAINED

		yes	No
EXPANSIONARY MACRO POLICY	yes	A	B US
	No	C Europe	D

The policy that is needed is associated with box A, and its combination of maintained wage floor/expansionary macroeconomic policy. Unfortunately, the current direction of policy is the exact opposite, and is pushing toward box D with its combination of undermined wage floor/contractionary macroeconomic policy. In Europe, the push is to lower the wage floor and reduce worker protections under the guise of creating greater labour market flexibility. This is the policy that the OECD has endorsed in its jobs strategy (OECD, 1997, see Chapter III). Simultaneously, the US is pushing for tighter fiscal policy through a reduced budget deficit, while the Fed is keeping monetary policy tight by linking it to the employment cost index, thereby holding the lid on money wages.

This push toward box D reflects the adverse structure of incentives that exists in today's globalised economic environment. Increased competition in international trade exerts a persistent pressure to improve competitiveness, and this has encouraged countries to implement policies that lower the social wage. At the same time, greater economic integration means that economies are becoming more open, and characterised by greater import demand leakages. This means that domestic macroeconomic policy has become less capable of stimulating domestic employment, since a greater proportion of any domestic demand stimulus now leaks abroad as imports. Consequently, countries that try to expand domestic demand are left burdened with both trade and fiscal deficits. This is the lesson of the failed Mitterand government economic experiment in the early 1980s, and it explains why European governments have been unwilling to adopt sufficiently expansionary policies.

Given this adverse policy setting, there is no single policy that can restore high wage full employment. Instead, a successful programme will have to be multi-dimensional. The outline of such a programme is as follows:

(1) *Structural reform*. Rather than aiming for increased labour market flexibility and lower wages predicated upon reduced worker protections, labour market reform should focus on raising wages by restoring the balance of power between business and labour. This balance has tilted in favour of business owing to technological and organisational innovations. It has also been affected by the decline of unions, and by international trade and international financial policy which have increased the mobility of both physical and financial capital. In the face of these structural changes, policy should aim to rectify this imbalance by strengthening the wage floor through higher minimum wages, improved welfare, and increased unemployment benefits and coverage. Side-by-side, labour laws should be amended to facilitate unionisation, and render employer sponsored deunionisations more difficult.

(2) *Monetary policy*. The doctrine of the natural rate of unemployment, which maintains that monetary policy is handcuffed by a binding employment constraint beyond which inflation accelerates, should be abandoned. In its place, monetary policy should be guided by a more pragmatic stance, that seeks to lower unemployment while experimenting as to where the region where inflation starts to accelerate actually lies. Given the high level of corporate profitability and continued productivity growth in manufacturing, there is room for non-inflationary wage increases. The bond market's implicit domination of monetary policy, which is evidenced by the policy goal of zero inflation, should be replaced by an outlook that balances concerns with employment, wages and inflation.

(3) *Fiscal policy*. The notion of a saving shortage, which has fuelled the push for fiscal austerity, should be rejected. Industrialised economies are awash with savings, as evidenced by the increase in stock prices and other financial asset prices. Saving does not cause investment: rather, investment causes saving. Increasing investment in turn calls for easier monetary and fiscal policy, which in turn will make for more robust market conditions and encourage business to invest. Public investment is important for growth, and should be funded both for growth purposes, and as a means of reflating economies. A more progressive system of taxation, combined with the elimination of

corporate welfare, can help restore income equality while putting money in the pockets of those who spend it.

(4) *International economic policy*. The final dimension of the policy puzzle concerns international economic policy. Here, there is a need to distinguish between international trade and international financial capital markets. International trade is in principle good, conferring the benefits of product diversity, economies of scale, and increased product market competition. However, where trade is exclusively driven by low wages or by the absence of environmental regulations and labour standards, it should be carefully managed: this is the only means of preventing international trade, and accompanying employer threats to transfer production overseas, from undercutting domestic wages. International financial markets also need to be regulated, perhaps through the imposition of capital controls. This is to prevent financial capital from excercising a veto over domestic economic policy. This problem has been particularly severe in Europe, where policy has been held hostage by the threat of speculative attacks against the exchange rate.

Such a programme outlines a consistent economic strategy for restoring high wage full employment. However, European economies are undoubtedly too small to-go-it alone as all suffer from too high a degree of openness. The same increasingly applies to the US, where increased openness means that international trade exerts a stronger effect on wages, while the increased size of demand leakages makes for exploding balance of payments deficits and growing international indebtedness. Economic policy co-ordination has therefore become a necessary condition for acheiving sustained economic prosperity in the new globalised economic environment. By ensuring a concurrent generalised expansion of income across countries, such co-ordination can mitigate the problems of trade deficits and capital flight driven by international differences in inflation and interest rates, and thereby enable countries to stay the expansionary course. In the absence of such co-ordination, the adverse policy incentives that promote the macroeconomics of austerity and lowering of the wage floor, will inevitably assert themselves.

Notes

1. J. Bernstein and L. Mishel, 'A Comparison of Income, Wages & Employment Trends of the Advanced Industrial Economies', in L. Mishel

and J. Schmitt (eds), *Beware the US Model: Jobs and Wages in a Deregulated Economy*, Economic Policy Institute, Washington DC, 1995.

2. Mishel and Schmitt, *op.cit.*

3. Supporters of labour market flexibility side-step the problem of declining real wages for production and non-supervisory workers by referring to 'family income'. This has increased as dual spousal labour force participation has increased in response to the wage squeeze. Similarly, the increase in inequality is side-stepped by focusing on lifetime income mobility. Many young persons from upper-income families begin their working lives with low incomes: this creates the perception of significant income mobility, but those from low-income backgrounds are likely to remain low-income workers all their lives.

4. A.B Atkinson, L. Rainwater and T. Smeeding, 'Income Distribution in OECD countries: The evidence from the Luxembourgh Income Study', OECD, 1994.

5. P. Davidson, *Post Keynesian Macroeconomic Theory: A Foundation for Successful Economic Policies for the Twenty-first Century*, Edward Elgar, Aldershot 1994.

6. The Mitterrand policy experiment is analysed in M. Lombard, 'A Re-examination of the Reasons for the Failure of Keynesian Expansionary Policies in France, 1981-1983', *Cambridge Economic Journal*, 19, 1995.

The 'human development enterprise': pushing beyond stakeholderism

Guy Standing

'A just system must generate its own support.'
Rawls, *A Theory of Justice.*[1]

Those wishing to promote social cohesion and economic dynamism should recognise that, in part because of growing labour market flexibility and the impact of globalisation, old protective mechanisms and policies have been enfeebled. Old forms of statutory protection and welfare and labour market policies seem to suffer from both an incapacity to protect the vulnerable and an incapacity to promote efficiency and flexibility. There is no consensus on what should take their place. We are in an era of experimentation, and although many traditional regulations and institutions still have a role to play, incentives to good practice are more in the spirit of the times, and can be more effective, than sanctions and rigid regulations.

This is the context in which debate on 'stakeholderism' is taking place. In that context, we need to think more about four fundamental questions:

What sort of labour market would we regard as Good?
What sort of regulatory system is feasible and desirable?
What sort of 'firm' should be promoted to be consistent with the answers to the first two questions?
What would be the best way of promoting such firms?

Answers to the first two questions are attempted elsewhere. On the first question, suffice it to note that, because flexible labour markets tend to produce inequality and fragmentation, we should define a Good Labour Market in terms of seven forms of security. On the second question, suffice it to state that improvements in redistributive justice will depend on escaping from the era of market regulation, into one in which statutory regulation establishes standards of decency and in which there are adequate measures to promote and facilitate 'voice regulation'.[2] By the latter is meant that mechanisms should exist to enable *all* groups to bargain and put pressure on the powerful to redistribute the gains of economic growth.

The third question raised above is addressed in this chapter, which is a shortened version of several papers in which the ideas have been developed. One way of putting the issue is to ask: What would be a Good Enterprise for the onset of the twenty-first century? How can substance be given to the stakeholder idea? In trying to answer these questions, one should recognise that the firm is only one social unit, and that not everybody works in firms. Mechanisms to promote exemplary firms must be complemented by policies to spread the benefits to the wider community. Those involved in the stakeholder debates have hinted at possibilities, but so far that aspect has been insufficiently considered.

In contrast to the Chicago school of law and economics, which has dominated economic policy in recent years, the following starts from an ethical position close to what is known as the Rawlsian 'difference principle'.[3] This states that, assuming an institutional framework providing for equality of opportunity and equal liberty, distributive justice improves if and only if a change in a practice or regulation improves the position of the 'worst off' – or most vulnerable – groups. A second ethical principle guiding the following analysis and proposal is: The powerful need protecting from themselves.[4]

Less abstractly, an alternative to the orthodox perspective is one that looks to regulations, institutions and incentive-structures to strengthen human development, while recognising that flexible markets are essential for economic growth. The starting point for constructive rethinking of social and economic strategy is the need to create conditions for thriving competition 'regulated' to ensure that it is based on competition between strong partners who are simultaneously rivals and co-operative. The competition must promote both social equity and dynamic efficiency, and as such it is a fallacy to depict a simple trade-off between 'equity' and 'efficiency'. Dynamic efficiency is derived from having rivals that are strong, and this is a justification for promoting co-operation and consensus as guiding principles of corporate governance.

With respect to enterprises, 'good' conjures up images of socially decent or 'responsible', and this may prompt scepticism from neo-liberals. Accordingly, one must state at the outset that the notion of good enterprise should not be divorced from the pursuit of efficiency and profitability, for without that an enterprise will not be economically viable. Thus, what constitutes a good firm from a labour and employment point of view must be compatible with efficiency.

The objective here is to focus on labour and employment aspects of a good firm, which do not cover all aspects of what advocates of 'socially responsible companies' correctly regard as desirable. This tries to consider a manageable set of issues, with a focus on the development of people through their workplace, relating to the social, political and distributional implications that are at the heart of the 'stakeholder' debate. In no way should this be taken to imply that environmental or consumer issues, for instance, are less important or unimportant; they could and should be taken into account. Because the term seems to capture the sense of desirable development for the principal stakeholders, the term proposed for the exemplary firm is the Human Development Enterprise, or HDE. This chapter attempts to conceptualise and operationalise the HDE, as the type of firm that in the late-1990s has exemplary labour practices and mechanisms to ensure skill reproduction security, social equity, work security, economic equity (income security) and democracy (representation security).

Human development involves all those dimensions. Thus, as individuals we wish to develop and refine skills, which we can achieve only through work. We also want equitable treatment, in which discrimination based on non-changeable human characteristics is a denial of human rights and development. We want a fair distribution of the income generated by the efforts of workers, managers, employers and those working on their own account. And we need to have Voice in the work process, recognising that absence of democracy in the most crucial of places for human development is a denial of democracy in general.

The remainder of this chapter merely identifies indicators of these considerations and, for illustrative purposes, applies the HDE concept to data in two national contexts where the approach has been tested.

Although the indicators are only proxies for what we would ideally like to measure, the longer-term objective is to define an approach, clarify practices that could be regarded as exemplary, and then find ways of measuring them. At the end of this chapter, I argue for an HDE award system. But I also want to put the case for such a scheme in my introductory remarks, to provide a context for the discussion on HDE which follows. If we could identify and agree on the characteristics of HDEs, it should be possible to establish an HDE Award scheme, giving awards to firms with exemplary practices, within specific national (or sectoral or size group) contexts. There are several ways of encouraging firms to be of an exemplary type – regulations, codes, taxes, fiscal incentives, public contract rules, collective bargaining pressures, etc. All have limitations, although some may have a role to play. The attraction of an award scheme, besides its direct function, is that it could also play an information-disseminating function, a confidence-building one, a solidarity-building effect and a demonstration effect on stragglers.

One might also take account of the fact that certain types of firm could not be expected to fulfil the same criteria as others. The same could be said of different economies. For instance, a good firm in Russia or South Africa may be modest by the standards of one in Switzerland, the UK or the USA. So, the criteria for defining exemplary could be made relative to national context, sector or size of firm. However, the principles should be similar in, or adaptable to, all countries, sectors and so on. Allowing differentiation should not be an excuse for allowing basically lower standards.

Although the ethical underpinnings of this concept do not correspond to the neo-liberal model, the proposal is at most an extension of other people's ideas. It was developed and first tested in the late 1980s through a survey of manufacturing firms in Malaysia. In some ways it is comparable to the Malcolm Baldridge National Quality Award scheme in the United States. It also seems to correspond to recent advocacy and analysis in the UK, where debate has tended to focus on principles and the macro-economic framework. If there is anything novel in the following, it is that it tries to create an empirical framework and to integrate the democratic 'voice' elements with those of skill and equity. In an interesting report in the UK issued in 1995 by the Royal Society for the Arts, the authors devoted a great deal of space to their proposed 'inclusive approach' to 'tomorrow's company'.[5] The report cited the 'Balanced Business Scorecard', proposed by several US analysts, and the 'self-assessment models' developed by Baldridge and the European Foundation for Quality Management.[6] However, it did not try to develop measures of what tomorrow's company should be, and it skirted round several crucial issues, such as the positive value of adversarialism in labour transactions. This is recognised in the fundamental contextual principles underlying the following HDE approach. These are:

(a) *The Dynamic Efficiency Principle*: The HDE must be compatible with sustainable dynamic efficiency, which comes from mechanisms that put pressure on managers and workers to raise future efficiency as well as a sustainably high (long-term profit maximising) level of utilisation of resources.

(b) *The Shadow-of-the-Future Principle*: The corporate governance must combine incentives for dynamic efficiency and flexibility with monitoring mechanisms to limit opportunism, 'short-termism' and inequitable practices. Flexibility with security can only be assured through strong Voice Regulation.

(c) *The Efficient Inequality Principle*: Differences in earnings and benefits between members of the firm should be minimised to the point where economic efficiency is not undermined, with the Rawlsian caveat that priority should be given to improving the situation of the 'worst off'.

The main claim about the following outline of HDE indexes is that, albeit crudely, it consciously treats all the elements with these principles in mind. It gives a prominent role to voice regulation, recognising that no amount of good intention today is adequate unless there are monitoring mechanisms to prevent slippages tomorrow.

Constructing HDE indexes

To identify the type of enterprise that could be described as oriented to human development, we need to identify indicators that capture the essence of the practices, principles and outcomes that deserve to be promoted. In most cases, these can be measured by an indirect or proxy variable, which involves some subjectivity and pragmatism, partly because of the absence of data, and the difficulty of obtaining measurable information on some issues.

A few methodological points should be borne in mind. A distinction is made between an index and an indicator. In developing an HDE 'index' with numerical values, we construct sets of 'indicators' of underlying phenomena. In putting indicators together as a composite index for any particular area of concern – such as the firm's orientation to skill formation – there are difficulties in 'weighting' different indicators.[7] There are statistical techniques for dealing with these issues. However, in this exercise there is a virtue in transparency. The more complex the way an index is constructed, the greater the suspicion that the data and reasoning have been 'massaged'. It is better to be able to interpret an index than to have to unravel it to try to make sense of it, even if we have to sacrifice a little in terms of 'scientific' accuracy. This is a justification for the chosen technique of using an ordinal scale for the indexes. In subsequent refinements, that could be modified.

A related point is that inclusion of any indicator is a matter of preference, and does not affect the essence of the approach. Thus, if those who wished to promote the HDE idea did not believe that economic democracy were desirable, the relevant indicators could be excluded. If environmental concerns were deemed desirable, suitable indicators could be included.

In constructing HDE indexes, we need indicators to reflect four considerations:

(1) There should be indicators of *revealed preference*, or *ethical principles*, reflecting the firm's commitment to certain desirable practices and outcomes;
(2) There should be indicators of *institutional mechanisms*, or *processes*, by which desirable outcomes could be translated into actual outcomes;[8]
(3) There should be indicators of *outcomes*, to reflect whether or not preferences and mechanisms are working;
(4) The indicators must be *sustainable*, since they must not be idealistic to the point of jeopardising the enterprise's long term viability, profitability and dynamism.

This set of considerations may seem esoteric, but is not. A firm may say it does not practise discrimination, but the lack of mechanisms to prevent it may reveal a real lack of concern. An outcome, good or bad, may reflect good or bad practice or merely the impact of the external labour market. And it is no use expecting a firm to be operating schemes that could not be replicated or sustained.

In this exploratory exercise, a hierarchy of four HDE indexes is constructed (Diagram 1), built by adding sets of indicators covering the principal spheres of labour practice – skill orientation, social equity, work security, economic equity and economic democracy, in that order.[9] This building block approach could be refined by taking account of other issues, but has been useful in applying the approach experimentally to data collected over the past few years in a series of Enterprise Labour Flexibility Surveys (ELFS).[10] For illustrative purposes, applications of the HDE are presented for South Africa and for Russia. However, the approach is one that should have even greater applicability in the UK, Germany or Belgium.

Diagram 1: Hierarchy of Human Development Enterprise Indexes

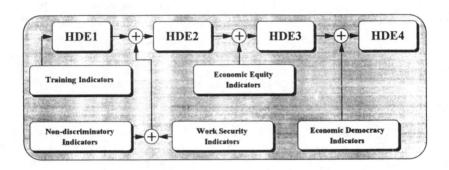

HDE1 = *Training Indicators*
HDE2 = *HDE1 plus Non-discriminatory Indicators plus Work
        Security Indicators*
HDE3 = *HDE1 plus HDE2 plus Economic Equity Indicators*
HDE4 = *HDE1 plus HDE2 plus HDE3 plus Economic Democracy
        Indicators*

HDE1: Enterprise skill formation
It is appropriate to start with what is probably the least controversial dimension. A Good Enterprise should provide opportunities for skill acquisition. Ideally, it should promote a voluntary learning environ-

ment. There is much talk about making firms centres of learning, which may be an exaggeration of their potential. One must also be careful about idealising training. In particular, the notion of lifelong learning, or continuous learning, is not unambiguously good. The thought of having to learn new competences every few months could be unsettling and a source of discordant performance, even deterring workers from trying to become excellent in a particular set of skills. Thus, emphasis must be on opportunities for learning, coupled with reasonable prospects of a personal intrinsic and instrumental 'reward' from the investment in the training. And there must be a voluntary culture of learning, in that those opting not to train or acquire new skills will not be penalised in any punitive fashion. The right to do something must always be matched by a right not to do it.

Taken as indicators of an orientation to skill formation are the three layers of training, namely: (i) entry-level training for newly recruited workers; (ii) retraining to improve job performance or to transfer workers to other jobs with similar skills; and (iii) retraining for upgrading workers or promotion.[11]

In addition, account should be taken of type of training. If a firm only gave informal, on-the-job training, that would deserve less weight than if it involved 'class room' and structured training, including apprenticeship. Accordingly, for each of the three levels, a distinction is made between 'informal' and 'formal' training, with the latter presumed to have greater value, which is not always the case. Given the economic and institutional realities in enterprises, the difference between formal and informal may be exaggerated. Yet concentrated training that involves a quantifiable cost should be preferable to 'on-the-job-pick-it-up-as-you-go' training.

Finally, we include a factor measuring whether or not the firm pays for training, either by funding a training institute or by paying fees to an institute to where it sends workers for training or by giving stipends to workers who go on training courses.

Thus, the first index is constructed by addition of the factors as follows:

HDE1 = (TR + TRF) + (RETR + RETRF) + (UPTR + UPTRF) + TR.INST

TR = 1 if training was usually provided to newly recruited workers, 0 otherwise

TRF = 1 if TR was apprenticeship or off-the-job in classroom or institute, 0 otherwise

RETR = 1 if there was training provided for established workers to improve job performance or transfer between jobs of similar skill, 0 otherwise

RETRF = 1 if that retraining was formal, in class or institute, 0 otherwise

UPTR = 1 if training was provided to upgrade workers, 0 otherwise;

UPTRF = 1 if that retraining for upgrading was in class or institute, 0 otherwise

TR.INST = 1 if the firm paid for trainees at institutes, directly or indirectly, 0 otherwise.

So, the HDE1 index has a value between 0 and 7, with a zero value meaning that the firm gave no training of any sort. What the index implies is that we give each level of training equal importance, and give formal training twice as much significance as informal. Applying this to the fifth round of our Russian Enterprise Labour Flexibility Survey (RLFS5), carried out in mid-1995, and covering 482 industrial enterprises in seven *oblasts* (regions), the mean value of HDE1 was 3.0, with only 2 per cent having a value of 7, and 4.6 per cent having a value of zero.[12] Applying it to data from the South African survey (SALFS1), covering 399 manufacturing enterprises and conducted in October 1995, the mean value was 4.3. In both countries, not surprisingly perhaps, even at the most basic level, few firms scored impressively.

HDE2: Incorporating work security and social equity

The next set of concerns relate to standards of behaviour towards workers and potential workers. One should find little dissent from the view that any good firm should have mechanisms to ensure work security and working conditions that foster safety and health. In the South African survey, the work security index, or set of proxy indicators for this dimension, were as follows:[13]

$$WS = S + A + I$$

S = 1 if the firm has a department or formal worker-employer committee responsible for safety and health at work, 0 otherwise

A = 1 if the number of accidents in the workplace in the past year, expressed as a ratio to total employment, was less than 50 per cent of the sectoral mean, 0 otherwise

I = 1 if the number of work days lost through illness or injury in the past year was less than 50 per cent of the sectoral mean average, 0 otherwise

One could quibble with these, but they are reasonable proxies for good performance, and this is what is needed at this stage.

As for social equity, non-discriminatory labour practices are essential in identifying a good firm. An exemplary enterprise should act in ways that reduce or avoid labour segregation based on personal characteristics such as race, gender or disability. Although measuring discrimination and disadvantage is notoriously difficult, both employer attitude and revealed outcome should be taken into account. Neither alone would be sufficient. For instance, one might have a 'preference' but not put it into effect, or one might have no preference yet discriminate by hiring on the basis of characteristics that had the (perhaps inadvertent) effect of excluding certain groups from various jobs.

Again, complexity in measuring social equity would be the enemy of progress at this stage. In the ELFS, we have measured a social equity index in terms of non-discrimination in recruitment and training. In the eastern European enterprise surveys, the selected indicators of non-discrimination were mainly related to gender. In terms of hiring, if the management reported that there was no preference for either men or women, this was regarded as a positive factor. In terms of training, non-discrimination was taken to involve a commitment to provide training opportunities equally to men and women, although one might argue for greater weight being given to a preference to provide training for women, just as one could for any group near the 'bottom' of the firm's employment structure. Stated preferences in this respect are weak proxies, sometimes being rationalisations of what has happened or a reflection of what the respondent believes should be the social norm. To ignore avowed preferences altogether would be unjustifiable, yet it is important to complement the preference factor with more tangible indicators. The outcome variable for gender discrimination may not be ideal but is a proxy for what is needed. The proxy selected was the percentage of higher-level 'employee' jobs taken by women, with a positive value given if that was greater than 40 per cent. Although this is not ideal, because the outcome could reflect differences in the relative supply of men and women, it does focus on the better type of jobs, and identifies relatively good performance in a key area of discrimination.

One could make the threshold sectorally specific, giving a positive score in the index if a firm had a high percentage of women in training relative to the average for all firms in the sector. Although this has appeal, since the average ratios vary considerably by sector, this is not as easily justifiable as one might suppose. It seems to allow for gender-based industrial segregation of employment.[14] So, presently, a straight-forward average is proposed.

Besides the gender dimension of employment equity, an indicator of discrimination is whether or not the firm employs workers with registered disabilities. Coupled with the gender variables, this results in an index of non-discrimination as follows:

$$ND = Rs + Ts + FWC + D$$

ND is the index of non-discrimination
Rs = 1 if the management has no preference for either men or women in recruiting production workers, 0 otherwise
Ts = 1 if management stated that they had no preference for either men or women in providing training for production workers
FWC = 1 if the female share of employees (managerial, specialist or general service workers) was greater than 40 per cent, 0 otherwise
D = 1 if the firm employed workers with disabilities, 0 otherwise

This would be inadequate in the South African context, and in many others. For South African firms, we defined non-discrimination to give a primary focus to race as follows:

$$ND = Rr + Rs + Tr + Tg + TF + RWC + FWC + D$$

Rr = 1 if the firm is operating an 'affirmative action' recruitment programme in favour of non-white workers, 0 otherwise
Rs = 1 if the firm has no preference for men or for women in recruiting workers, 0 otherwise
Tpr = 1 if the firm has a training programme and has provided production workers with more than 10 per cent of all training course places, 0 otherwise
Tg = 1 if firm has no preference for men in providing training, 0 otherwise
TF = 1 if women's share of those receiving training within the firm was greater than
women's share of total employment in the firm, 0 otherwise
RWC = 1 if over 50 per cent of employees ('white collar') consist of non-whites, 0 otherwise
FWC = 1 if over 50 per cent of employees consist of women, 0 otherwise
D = 1 if over 1 per cent of the firm's employees are workers with disabilities

The value of ND varies from 0 to 8. This and the WS index should be added to make a socially equitable index, HDE2, which for South Africa had a range of 0 to 17.

We now turn to the complex and more contentious issue of economic equity.

HDE 3: Economic equity in enterprises

The literature on economic equity is vast, yet there is little on economic equity within the firm. What is an economically equitable firm? It is surely one in which differences in earnings and benefits between its members are minimised to the point where economic efficiency is not jeopardised. This might be called the 'Principle of Efficient Inequality'. As it is rather utilitarian, one should add a Rawlsian caveat – with priority given to improvement of the 'worst off' workers in the firm.[15]

There are dynamic efficiency reasons to favour economic equity, whatever the bargaining position of various groups. Labour productivity depends on co-operation as well as on individual effort and performance. If there were wide differences between groups in the enterprise, the disadvantaged – or those who feel they are inequitably treated – would tend to withhold 'tacit knowledge' and not commit themselves to the voluntary exchange of knowledge that contributes to dynamic efficiency.[16] There would also be a tendency to sabotage, pilfering and so on. Equity induces loyalty, which usually induces productivity improvement.

To create an Economic Equity Index we took slightly different approaches in our two illustrative country surveys. In Russia, we considered three factors, giving greatest weight to the first, since this relates to treatment of the 'worst off' in the firm. First, one of the worst phenomena to emerge in Russian industry in the mid-1990s was the growth of groups of workers paid much lower wages than anybody else. An economically equitable firm should have few if any workers paid a small fraction of the firm's average. So, we took the minimum wage received by the lowest- paid full-time workers as the initial yard stick. If more than 5 per cent of the workers received this wage the firm was given a low score on economic equity. But as that does not capture any distributional factor, we also gave a positive score if the minimum payment was equal to or greater than 50 per cent of the average wage. These two indicators are only proxies for what we would like to measure, yet with the type of data one can collect in large-scale surveys they are reasonable proxies.

A second consideration is whether the average wage itself is equitable relative to that paid in other firms. We take a sectorally relative measure, to reflect technological and market factors. The proxy is whether the average wage in the firm is greater than the industry's average. If it was, a positive score was given. Finally, equity is improved if the enterprise provides benefits and entitlements that represent security against personal contingencies and that improve the stakeholders' standard of living. Since wages and incomes are only part of the remuneration system, we take as a proxy whether or not the firm provided ordinary workers with more than ten types of fringe, or non-wage, benefit.[17] Thus, the Economic Equity Index is defined as follows:

$$EE = Min/Emp + M + AW/AWM + FB$$

EE is economic equity index

Min/Emp = 1 if the percentage of the total workforce of the firm paid the minimum payment is below 5 per cent, 0 otherwise

M = 1 if the minimum wage paid was greater than 50 per cent of the average paid in the firm, 0 otherwise

AW/AWM = 1 if the average wage in the establishment was above the average wage for the industrial sector, 0 otherwise

FB = 1 if the firm paid more than ten types of identified fringe benefits, 0 otherwise

If we add EE to HDE2 we have what we can call the Socio-Economically Equitable HDE. In the Russian case, this could take a value of between 0 and 18. In 1995, the mean value was 8.5.

The measure of economic equity is slightly different for South Africa, which has one of the most unequal income distributions in the world, including large wage and salary differentials. The following seems to capture the crucial dimensions:

$$EE = Min/EMP + M + AW/Ws + Wnw/W + FB$$

Min/EMP = 1 if less than 5 per cent of the workforce is paid less than half of the average wage in the firm, 0 otherwise

M = 1 the lowest wage in the firm is greater than 50 per cent of the average wage, 0 otherwise

AW/Ws = 1 if the firm's average wage is above the sector's average wage, 0 otherwise

Wnw/W = 1 if the average wage of non-whites is more than 80 per cent of the mean average of all workers, 0 otherwise
FB = 1 if the firm provides workers with more than 8 specified non-wage or 'fringe' benefits, 0 otherwise

Finally, we move into the politically most sensitive sphere of corporate governance.

The economically democratic HDE

'To be governed by appetite alone is slavery, while obedience to a law one prescribes to oneself is freedom'
Rousseau, *The Social Contract*[18]

Something is missing from Rousseau's famous aphorism. To be ruled by laws and regulations alone is not freedom either. What is crucial is that there should be Voice regulation. In the workplace, as anywhere else, the 'stakeholders' who bear the greatest risk and uncertainty should be able to regulate decisions affecting labour and employment. Put differently, what is Human Development without empowerment?

This is the greatest quandary for corporate governance for the twenty-first century. Can the functions of management and productive decision-making be made more democratic and accountable while promoting dynamic efficiency for the benefit of all representative stakeholders, which may include shareholders not working for the enterprise?[19]

Democracy must be more than casting a vote every few years. Democracy requires institutional safeguards, the most effective of which is the capacity of the vulnerable to exercise restraint and direction on those in decision-making positions, giving substance to the Rawlsian 'maximin' principle. Democracy is also about attempts to ensure cooperation in the interest of all representative groups. Successful cooperation requires 'the shadow of the future', that is, mechanisms to ensure that competitive interest groups sitting across the table from one another today will know that they will have to deal with each other and cooperate with each other in the future as well.

In a typical firm, one side (management) has scope for various forms of opportunism through control of information, a limited circle of people and a capacity to take unilateral decisions by fiat.[20] As with other forms of opportunism, to limit managerial opportunism, there must be a process of reciprocal monitoring and a capacity to impose sanctions when abuses are detected.[21] This is particularly important in the context of enterprise restructuring, for if no voice regulation mechanisms existed, the vulnerable would have no capacity to influence the outcome. An atmosphere of dynamic efficiency would also be unlikely if the workers were sullen and became 'excluded insiders'.[22]

So, to complete a Human Development Enterprise we need to construct an Economic Democracy Index. Once again, there are differences in what should be measured in the two illustrative contexts, although the principles are the same. We start with the Russian case, with its historically specific transformation process, defining fledgling economic democracy in terms of six indicators.

First, it is taken as axiomatic that, potentially at least, workers' Voice is strengthened by a high degree of unionisation of the workforce. Having a mechanism to represent workers and employees creates the basis for dynamic efficiency and the proverbial 'sword of justice'. Without a union of some sort, there could not be the 'shadow of the future' to concentrate the minds of managers and workers on developing and maintaining decent, viable and efficient labour practices. This does not mean that there is a presumption that unions will always behave appropriately. However, a strong representative mechanism is a necessary condition for Voice regulation. In the Russian case, this is defined pragmatically as being the case if more than 50 per cent of the workers in a firm belonged to a union, because of the traditionally very high (artificially) level of unionisation. Ideally, it would be appropriate to identify the type of union, but the character of unions would have to change before any refinement would make much sense in the Russian labour market. Elsewhere our indicator would need refinement.

Second, democratic potential is greater if the union is an independent one, which in Russia means that the administration or management should *not* be members of it.[23] In 'Soviet' enterprises management belonged to the union and both managers and union representatives were subordinated to the Communist Party. Thus, as an indicator of growing independence in bargaining, non-membership by management is an indicator of Voice in a country such as Russia. Elsewhere, an alternative indicator of union independence would be more appropriate.

Third, to be meaningful there should be evidence of the existence of an operational mechanism for bargaining. For this, a collective agreement between the union and the employer is taken as a positive sign, even though in the mid-1990s, a collective agreement would in most cases have been more formal than substantive.

Fourth, there is deemed to be greater democracy if workers own a large percentage of the shares of the company, which has been a feature of property form restructuring of Russian industry. The critical level for a positive value is taken to be 30 per cent. Although this aspect of enterprise democracy has long been controversial, empirical studies have suggested that minority employee ownership is conducive to efficiency, economic restructuring and equity.[24] In Russian industry, given the lack of discipline and legacy of the Soviet era, in which workers' effort was low and erratic, and in which monitoring of it was ineffectual, if not distorted, worker ownership and governance should have potential benefits as a means of overcoming the intrinsic incompleteness of labour contracts.[25] Ownership of a flow of income should be distinguished from ownership of property rights. In terms of corporate governance, minority worker share ownership could be interpreted as turning workers into outsider principals – monitoring the performance of the agent (manager), and providing a mechanism for selecting, dismissing and replacing managers. The objection to sole existence of insider principals is that a coalition between managers and workers could result in short-term concerns dominating long-term strategy. However, with share ownership, workers and managers become outsider agents as well, having a direct interest in the long-term flow of income from shares as well as their earnings from work.[26]

Fifth, at least in the Russian context, it is taken as a positive element in enterprise democracy if the top management were elected by the workers, rather than be appointed by a Ministry or by an enterprise board. Elsewhere, this would be controversial, for well-known reasons, although to some extent it is institutionalised in Germany in the system of co-determination. But we introduce it specifically for circumstances of Russian enterprises in the mid-1990s, when other appointment mechanisms were dubious and less accountable. The pragmatic decision recognises the positive value of accountability to stakeholders in the firm, limiting managerial opportunism and encouraging behaviour in favour of sustainable long-term profit maximisation, dynamic efficiency and human development practices. In the 1990s, there has been a diversification in the means by which Russian managements have been appointed and reappointed. Achieving a balance in accountability of managements to workers and the firm is difficult, since sensible commercial decisions might be jettisoned in favour of decisions enjoying the short-term support of the workforce. Appointment by workers could result in managerial conservatism and reluctance to restructure. This is an endemic problem in democracy. However, in so far as workers are both shareholders and wage earners they have become dual stakeholders, which makes behavioural 'short-termism' less likely. This argument is a justification for appointments to be for sufficiently long to encourage managements to take decisions that combine concern both for today's workers and the longer-term future of the firm.

Sixth, economic democracy is taken to be greater if there is a profit-sharing pay system, implying a sharing of risks and rewards. This is a sensitive issue, since many trade unionists have been against profit-sharing pay on the grounds that it introduces income insecurity for workers who are not involved in the decision-making and who rely on their wage. However, if one gives a positive value to democratic decision-making, it is appropriate to balance that by valuing mechanisms that share risks and potential benefits. Moreover, a firm with high income dispersion due to incentive systems should be regarded differently from one in which income dispersion reflects power relations and managerial fiat. Profit-sharing is regarded as a mixed blessing by many trade unionists, since it can be abused to make wages downwardly flexible. However, it is spreading around the world, and can be a means of promoting efficiency and employment, as research has demonstrated.

In sum, taking account of considerations specific to Russian firms, we define an Economic Democracy Index (ED), with a value of between 0 and 6, as follows:

$$ED = TU + IND + COLL + SH + MA + P$$

TU = 1 if more than 50 per cent of the workforce is unionised, 0 otherwise

IND = 1 if the management is not in the trade union, 0 otherwise

COLL = 1 if there is a collective agreement, 0 otherwise

SH = 1 if more than 30 per cent of the firm's shares are owned by workers and employees, 0 otherwise

MA = 1 if the top management is appointed by the workers, 0 otherwise

P = 1 if there is a profit-sharing element in the wage determination system, 0 otherwise

By adding the ED index to HDE3, as shown in Diagram 1, we obtain the full Human Development Enterprise Index, HDE4. For

Russian enterprises, this has a maximum possible value of 24, and if the index is supposed to identify exemplary standards, there should be a tapering in the distribution of firms, with relatively fewer as the scores rise above the median value, and no excessive bunching of values.

For South Africa, economic democracy is measured more simply, as follows:

$$ED = TU + COLL + WF + SH + P$$

TU = 1 if there is a recognised trade union in the firm with more than 50 per cent of the workforce in the union, 0 otherwise

COLL = 1 if there is a collective agreement operating in the firm, covering wages and other labour matters, 0 otherwise

WF = 1 if there is a Work Forum (or the equivalent) in operation, 0 otherwise[27]

SH = 1 if the workers possess more than 10 per cent of the shares of the firm, 0 otherwise

P = 1 if there is a bargained profit sharing payment scheme for workers, 0 otherwise

The share-owning level is subjective, although it does suggest a reasonable level of commitment to broadening capital ownership to those most directly involved in production.

Again, by adding ED to HDE3 we obtain HDE4. Across the spectrum of South African firms, the HDE4 values could range from zero to a maximum of 27. It is most unlikely that any firm would have a maximum value, although a socially responsible firm is likely to have a score of 20 or more.

This summarises the procedure for constructing the HDE indexes. So far it has been tested in several variants with data from hundreds of firms in a variety of countries. The most important point at this stage is not the actual values in the exercise, it is the concept. However, a couple of examples might be of interest.

Identifying the Human Development Enterprise in Russian industry

An attraction of the HDE index is that we can look at a firm to assess its performance in absolute terms, or to assess it relative to others in the country, or even within a sector, region or size category. Thus, in discussing the values of the indexes and patterns, the following is primarily concerned with identification of those enterprises performing relatively well as an HDE in the Russian context.

A first point is that there were 6.8 per cent of establishments with scores above 14 for HDE4, and those should be designated as the leading group in the Russian context, even though there were none with values above 17. At the other end, 35.6 per cent had values of below 11, which should be regarded as unsatisfactory in that context. There are three further points to bear in mind. First, the way the HDE4 index is constructed, heavy weight is given to skill formation. Second, there was a low correlation between the component indexes for non-discrimination, social equity, economic equity and economic democracy, implying that they were measuring distinctive and different phenomena. Third, in considering inter-enterprise patterns, differences in averages for various components may not translate into similar overall differences, since firms that did well on some indicators did poorly on others.

Elsewhere, a statistical analysis is made to try to identify determinants of inter-firm variations in HDE performance. Factors such as sector, property form and size were considered. But even taking account of such structural factors, variations remained. Of course, there is the possibility that correlations between some of the explanatory variables and the HDE indexes mix cause and effect. In some respects, the property form defines the scope for the score on the HDE indexes, but in all cases there was considerable intra-group variation. This is important, for if high scores were simply a reflection of size or one property form, the policy prescription would be a straightforward industrial strategy, with a recommendation to promote a particular enterprise size and property form. That is not the case. There were large firms with low HDE scores and small firms with high scores, and private firms with high and low scores. This implies that if one wished to promote characteristics of an HDE (or variants of them), *incentives* to move in those directions would be advantageous.

Economic performance and the HDE

Beyond the need to refine the approach, three potential criticisms should be addressed. All three are likely to come from an orthodox economist. First, a critic might claim that by being a good enterprise in the HDE sense the firm would undermine its commercial viability. If scoring high on HDE were associated with low dynamic efficiency and poor responsiveness to market forces, the firm's long-term viability would be jeopardised, so weakening the rationale for promoting an HDE. In other words, an orthodox economist might claim that promotion of characteristics of an HDE would result in escalating costs, stronger internal rigidities, plunging economic performance and inadequate responsiveness to market forces, leading to labour hoarding, and so on. This is a legitimate concern.

What is the evidence ? Again we focus on Russian enterprises for illustrative examples. While correlations do not demonstrate causation, it appears that *labour costs* as a share of total production costs were lower in firms with high values of HDE and were lower in firms that scored high on the Economic Democracy Index – which would probably be the most contentious part of the HDE. Labour costs were also inversely related to values of HDE4 (Figure 2).[28] These are encouraging results, suggesting that if a firm does well on its HDE index, and practises economic democracy, it has higher levels of labour productivity.[29] This is *prima facie* evidence against potential sceptics.

Figure 2: Labour Cost Share of Production Costs in 1995, by HDE4 in 1995, Seven Regions, Russian Federation, 1996

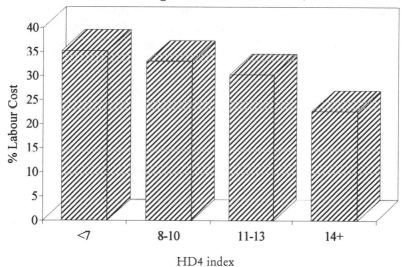

HD4 index

Source: Merged RLFS5 and RLFS6, n = 338

In Russia it has been claimed that enterprises have been unresponsive to market pressures, so high values of HDE might be indicative of resistance to change and a strong protection of 'insiders'. 'Labour hoarding' has been attributed to the persistence of the 'soft budget constraint' and a lack of concern over labour costs. In fact, all forms of enterprise had cut employment by large amounts, and firms with low values of any of the four HDE indexes had cut employment by more than those with higher values (Figure 3). One might interpret this as implying that firms with high HDE values performed better in terms of employment. However, this is neither necessary to support our concept, nor necessarily correct. It merely means that there is a *prima facie* case for believing that being a good firm in the HDE sense was compatible with favourable employment performance. So, high HDE is favourably correlated with both labour costs and employment. It is also positively correlated with what might be called an index of strategic dynamism, where a dynamic firm is one that had made a change in product range, a change in technology in productive equipment and a change in work organisation over the previous year. Firms that had higher values of HDE tended to have higher values for technical change (Figure 4), merely supporting the suggestion that firms which are dynamic in labour terms are more likely than others to be technologically dynamic as well.

A second criticism from an orthodox economist might be that strengthening voice regulation would jeopardise attainment of other aspects of the HDE that managements and owners would value, so that a composite approach would be undermined by internal contradictions. In this respect, one question relates to the effect of trade union presence. For instance, are unions associated with higher values of HDE1 (skill formation practices) and HDE2 (skill formation and non-discriminatory labour practices)? If not, then one would have to raise questions about the effectiveness of unions in two crucial spheres. The evidence suggests a positive association, albeit a fairly weak one. Firms with higher scores of HDE1 had higher average unionisation, and this was also the case with HDE2. Similar positive relationships were found with surveys in Malaysia, the Philippines and South Africa. Strengthening workers' voice in firms may result in internal pressure to achieve greater dynamic efficiency and better HDE performance.

Another question relating to voice regulation sure to arise concerns the association of HDE indexes with wage level. If the value of HDE was

Figure 3: Percentage Employment Change in 1995-96, by HDE4 in 1995, Seven Regions, Russian Federation, 1996

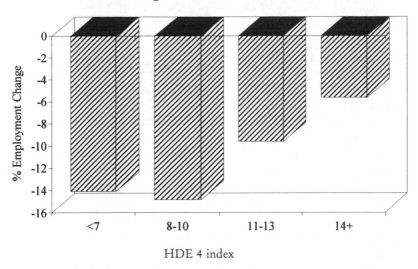

HDE 4 index

Source: Merged RLFS5 and RLFS6, n = 338

Figure 4: Strategic Dynamism Index in 1996, by HDE4 in 1995, Seven Regions, Russian Federation, 1996

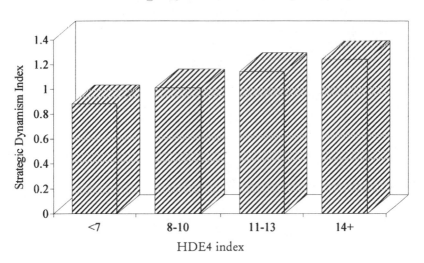

HDE4 index

Source: Merged RLFS5 and RLFS6, n = 338

inversely correlated with wages, the appeal for workers and their representatives would be weakened. In Russian factories, the average wage
was positively correlated with the Economic Equity index, but was not
correlated with either HDE4 or the Economic Democracy index.

This leaves a third potential criticism that a neo-classical economist
might raise. This is the standard argument against market intervention.
If an HDE, however measured, were so desirable and if it were associated positively with economic performance, why intervene? Let the
market work itself out, and if firms with high HDE perform well they
will drive those that do not out of the market or force them to become
better in terms of human development policies.

There has been a protracted debate among economists on these
issues, and one could not do justice to them here. However, to be
compatible with good performance does not necessarily mean that one
causes the other, or that good commercial performance would lead to a
socially desirable outcome of a particular type. And the criticism makes
implicit assumptions about 'externalities', market failures, the dynamics of enterprise restructuring and the reversibility of change. In a
period of economic upheaval, firms taking a low-wage, anti-union,
trainee-poaching approach, discriminating against women or those
workers with disabilities, may undercut firms that pay decent wages,
legitimise genuine trade unions, provide training and so on. This is
more than a matter of externalities, although the bad firm can be a 'free
rider'. It is the nature of a disequilibrium. Once a fragmented labour
market has been created, pressures to generate a virtuous path are
removed. Once a mechanism has been eroded, it is harder to resurrect
it, or create something better, than it would be to create it in the first
place. Once unionisation has declined it is unlikely to rise again, which
does not mean that unions could not play a positive role for workers or
for firms.

Conclusions

Promoting Good Enterprises is a key to the Good Society of the
twenty-first century. This is particularly so in a country such as Russia
where the industrial enterprise has been, for better or for worse, a
crucible for almost every aspect of civil society. It is also true for South
Africa, where apartheid was built on enterprise behaviour. Yet it is true
in every society, and accords with those who have argued in favour of

'mutual gains' enterprise in the United States.[30] It is also apparent that enterprise restructuring is a key to structural or social adjustment.

The idea of a Human Development Enterprise, defined in terms of democratic, equitable practices, is suited to an era in which there is, and should be, increasing emphasis on incentives to good practice rather than sanctions against bad. If 'labour standards' are presented as obligatory and rigid, even those who support them will be inclined to do so with reservation. Some would pay scant attention to the sins of others in case their own sins, real or imaginary, were exposed to scrutiny and condemnation. Rewarding good practices and shining the light on exemplary cases would be in keeping with mature social cultures.

It also corresponds to advanced management thinking, epitomised by top companies in the USA and elsewhere.[31] Enterprises that put the interest of their workers first appear to perform better than others.[32] There are also important externalities. Thus, economically democratic firms – and this is the issue that is most controversial – are likely to promote democratic behaviour *outside* them.[33] One does not have to turn this into an ideological battleground. Rather one should seek ways of refining the approach to secure a broad consensus, and to foster communities of Human Development, bearing in mind the 'network externalities' that come from large numbers of enterprises adopting systems of practices oriented to human development.

In sum, the HDE is a useful heuristic device. Undoubtedly, it could be refined, its components can be challenged and modified to take account of different points of view, and it can be adjusted to meet the conditions of different countries. It is an organising concept, which can be used to grade enterprises by explicit criteria – principles, mechanisms and outcomes – that can be justified as desirable or otherwise.

As one famous economist quipped, the point is not to interpret the world, it is to change it. The objective of identifying HDEs is to change enterprises into something closer to an ideal.

HDE Awards – A proposal

To reiterate the last point, the main objective of identifying HDEs is to encourage enterprises to evolve into something closer to an ideal. As such, a national government or an international agency such as the ILO could achieve much through boldness by promoting HDEs. How?

A few countries could be selected, and an Enterprise Survey carried out to identify HDE performance criteria. Ideally, the survey would be an industrial census. However, it need only be a representative sample survey. An objective should be to have a demonstration effect, legitimising a process to stimulate interest and support from leading companies, trade unions, and government officials.

Once the data had been analysed, a conference of managements, government officials and trade unionists could be convened, and HDE Awards could be presented to, say, the top 5 per cent of firms. The personnel departments of the top ten companies might be presented with financial awards, if a suitable national – or other – funding agency were prepared to sponsor the process, while exemplary enterprises would be awarded with an HDE Certificate and Plaque of approval. The conference at which the awards were presented could be televised, and the public relations given to the firms in question would surely be welcomed by those companies, and would have a beneficial demonstration effect on other firms in the country.

Once the process had been launched, other companies could apply for the Award or the survey could be extended to a new sample each year. Questions of renewal of the Award could then be addressed, much as other such schemes, such as Export Performance Awards, have developed. The concept of an HDE could also be used for framework legislation, and collective bargaining in enterprises could be oriented to pushing firms closer to the desirable model.

Once one thinks about this proposal, one wonders why the ILO has never done something like this. It is consistent with its orientation to standards, and in the 1990s is consistent with the desirability of incentives to Good Practice. Most people relate to the enterprise in which they work for most of their adult lives. Its character and practices shape our achievements, our development, our humanity. Yet there is scarcely a mention of what makes a Good Enterprise in any of the UN system's reports. The United Nations Development Programme publishes an annual Human Development Report, which contains a Human Development Index to rank countries on performance, which conspicuously omits the sort of issues covered in the HDE.

Now is the time to rectify such omissions. More importantly, national HDE award schemes would be a constructive initiative. If there were a will to do something, this would give some enterprising organisation a promotional edge in a vital sphere of human development.

Notes

1. J. Rawls, *A Theory of Justice*, Oxford University Press, Oxford, 1973, p261.
2. For a discussion of points in this paragraph, see G. Standing, 'Globalisation, labour flexibility and insecurity: The era of market regulation', *European Journal of Industrial Relations*, Vol.3, No.1, March 1997, pp7-37.
3. Rawls, 1973, *op.cit.*, p75. It also relates to the less discussed ethical principle of fraternity.
4. It has been stated that power is the facility not to have to learn. Restricting an individual's power induces pressure on that person to keep learning, which is the ultimate source of dynamic efficiency.
5. Royal Society for the Encouragement of Arts, Manufactures and Commerce, *Tomorrow's Company* RSA, London, 1995.
6. See, for example, R.S. Kaplan and D.P. Norton, 'Putting the balanced scorecard to work', *Harvard Business Review*, Sept.-Oct.1993, pp134-47; European Foundation for Quality Management, *Total Quality Management – The European Model for Self-Appraisal* (1992).
7. In constructing any complex index, conceptual and measurement difficulties abound. For the proposed HDE index, the most important concern *scaling* (the justification of any weighting of indicators), *aggregation* (summarising of multi-dimensional information in a single index) and *patterning* (determining that additivity is more appropriate than, say, a multiplicative approach).
8. Here, no attention is paid to an important set of concerns. A good enterprise should have mechanisms to minimise internal *transaction costs*, that is, costs required to ensure internal co-operation. It should also have mechanisms to reduce tendencies towards *bureaucracy*, that is, to avoid a hierarchical control system that exists because of performance ambiguity and goal incongruency (or even goal indifference). On these, see, for instance, W. Ouchi, 'Markets, bureaucracies and clans', *Administrative Science Quarterly*, Vol.25, 1980, pp129-41
9. Not covered in this version is *employment security*, which can be easily accommodated. The basic point is that a firm that employs a large proportion of its workforce as casual, insecure workers is scarcely as good as one that can give its workers reasonable employment security.
10. The approach was developed when the author was acting as an economic adviser in the Prime Minister's Department in Malaysia, in the course of working on the country's human development plan. A survey was

conducted in 3,100 firms; this was followed by one of 1,300 firms in the Philippines. See, for example, G. Standing, 'Towards a Human Resource-oriented Enterprise: A South-East Asian Example', *International Labour Review*, Vol.131, No.3, 1992/3, pp281-96.

11. Possibly, the second and third forms of training deserve greater weight than the first, yet in most labour market analyses only the first is considered.

12. For analysis of the surveys, see G. Standing, *Russian Unemployment and Enterprise Restructuring: Reviving Dead Souls*, Macmillan, Basingstoke, 1996.

13. In South Africa, there exists a scheme for encouraging and rewarding good occupational safety practices, known as the NOSA star system.

14. For instance, would it be appropriate to give a positive score to a firm in the energy sector in which merely 12 per cent of higher-level 'employees' were women just because the industry's average was 10 per cent?

15. Rawls, 1973, *op.cit.*

16. For related points, see G. Hodgson, *Economics and Institutions: A Manifesto for a Modern Institutional Economics* Polity Press, Oxford, 1988, p259. Narrow pay differentials within firms are associated with group cohesion, trust of management and productivity gains. D.Levine, 'Public policy implications of worker participation', *Economic and Industrial Democracy*, Vol.13, 1992, pp183-206. Narrow pay differentials also induce worker commitment to management goals. D.M. Cowherd and D. Levine, 'Product quality and pay equity between lower-level employees and top management: An investigation of distributive justice theory', *Administrative Science Quarterly*, Vol.37, No.2, 1992, pp302-20.

17. This threshold might be lower elsewhere. Yet in Russia, and in other countries of central and eastern Europe, where it was the norm to provide a wide array of benefits coupled with a low money wage, the wage measure of income is misleading.

18. Jean-Jacques Rousseau, *The Social Contract*, book 1, ch.viii.

19. The aphorism that we have reached 'the end of history' with the collapse of 'state socialism' is silly. Now, the challenge is different. Instead of socialisation of property and private management, is there an acceptable way in which privatisation of ownership, through democratic, widespread and accountable share ownership, could be coupled with socially accountable management?

20. There are five types of managerial opportunism, which can be moderated if workers have a monitoring role inside the firm. S. Smith, 'On the economic rationale for codetermination law', *Journal of Economic*

Behaviour and Organisation, Vol.16, 1991, pp261-81.

21. G. Dow, 'The function of authority in transaction cost economics', *Journal of Economic Behaviour and Organisation*, 1987, p22. Dow elsewhere makes the point that unilateral control by management may distort the choice of production technique away from the provision of firm-specific training. G. Dow, 'Why capital hires labour: A bargaining perspective', *American Economic Review*, Vol.83, No.1, pp118-34.

22. One reason for desiring effective Voice mechanisms in enterprises is to limit growth of a 'survivor syndrome'. In firms subject to employment cuts, remaining workers may suffer from a sense of anger and insecurity that reduce labour productivity. If workers are involved in the bargaining process, this 'shadow of the past' can be controlled, to some extent at least.

23. In South-east Asia, the relevant difference is whether the union is an industrial or a company union. This makes a substantial difference to such outcomes as wage levels, wage differentials and training. G. Standing, 'Do unions impede or accelerate structural adjustment? Industrial versus company unions in an industrialising labour market', *Cambridge Journal of Economics*, Vol.16, 1992, pp327-54.

24. See, inter alia, H.A.Henzler, 'The new era of Eurocapitalism', *Harvard Business Review*, July-Aug., 1992, pp57-63; D.I.Levine and L.D'Andrea Tyson, 'Participation, productivity and the firm's environment', in A. Blinder (ed), *Paying for Productivity*, Brookings Institution, Washington, DC, 1990; Z. Acs and F. FitzRoy, 'A constitution for privatising large Eastern enterprises', *Economics of Transition*, Vol.2, No.1, 1994, pp83-94. An argument against worker shareholding is often made by trade unionists who claim it would weaken the workers' desire for improved training.

25. The theoretical point was brought out in a famous article some years ago. A. Alchian and H. Demetz, 'Production, information costs and economic organisation', *American Economic Review*, Vol.62, No.5, December 1972, pp777-95. Worker ownership in the USA is greatest in such 'service' spheres as legal practices, where work monitoring is difficult. It is ironic, however, that in what is often regarded as the bastion of capitalism, the States have *required* law firms to be *worker owned*. This is not highlighted by those who regard worker ownership as incompatible with capitalism.

26. In eastern Europe, there have been efforts to promote institutional *block-holders* – large-scale financial intermediaries holding large blocks of shares – that could control insider managements. See, for example, E.S. Phelps, R. Frydman, A. Rapazynski and A. Shleifer, *Needed mechanisms of corporate governance and finance in eastern Europe*, European Bank for Reconstruction and Development, Working Paper No.1, London, March

1993. Whatever blockholder is created, it should be *active* in corporate governance, and in this respect workers having a block of shares as a group (through the union?) could be beneficial. A danger to be avoided is workers being in substantial control, for this could distort the *management* function. One should be wary about one claim, which is that worker share ownership would lead to short-term investment and profit maximisation, on the grounds that they would be solely interested in the income flow during their work tenure. This is not valid. If the workforce own shares, younger cohorts of workers will be looking to the long-term. By contrast, managements are more likely to take a short-term perspective, since their tenure is likely to be short and they are likely to be closer to retirement age than the average worker. The conventional argument against workers becoming principals and for managers to turn from agents to principals could be reversed.

27. Work Forums are intended to be the South African equivalent of Works Councils.

28. Shown here are the values of HDE for mid-1995 recorded at the time, correlated with the values of labour costs recorded for the year of 1995 from the same firms when interviewed in mid-1996, at the time of the sixth round of the RLFS.

29. For a review of theoretical arguments and evidence from other countries to suggest that economic democracy per se has positive effects on labour productivity, see H. Hansmann, 'When does worker ownership work? ESOPs, Law Firms, Codetermination and Economic Democracy', *The Yale Law Journal*, Vol.99, No.8, June 1990, pp1751-1816.

30. T.A. Kochan and P. Osterman, *The Mutual Gains Enterprise: Forging a Winning Partnership among Labour, Management and Government*, Harvard Business School Press, Boston, Mass., 1994.

31. See, for instance, R. Waterman, *The Frontiers of Excellence: Learning from Companies that Put People First*, Nicholas Brealey Publishing, London, 1994. In the USA, this was published under the title *What America Does Right* Norton, New York, 1994. Waterman, with Tom Peters, was the management guru who promoted the concept of self-managed teams, and recognised a principle of good management: 'Today's leaders understand that you have to give up control to get results.' For an academic view, see T.A. Kochan and P. Osterman, *op.cit.*

32. J. Pfeffer, *Competitive Advantage Through People*, Harvard Business School Press, Cambridge, Mass., 1994. The danger of corporate paternalism is not really recognised in the analyses of Pfeffer or Waterman. Our model is potentially more robust, through emphasising voice regulation.

33. There is evidence that skills learned in participation inside firms improve participation in the wider community. S. Smith, 'Political behaviour as an economic externality: Econometric evidence on the spillover of participation in US firms to participation in community affairs', *Advances in the Economc Analysis of Participatory and Labour-managed Firms*, No.1, 1985, pp123-36.

Welfare, security and economic performance

Peter Cassells

Modernising european economies – the overall context

The European economy is involved, not in some weary recovery from recession to a return to things as they were, but in being transformed by a combination of changes in technologies, values and politics. These forces of change include:

> Changes in people's values and attitudes, including a growing demand for choice, uniqueness and higher standards in the quality of goods and services;
> The pervasiveness of technological change, including the speed of application of information and communication technologies;
> The wider integration of the economies of the globe, in particular the financial markets, which has reduced differences in time and distance to zero.

Commenting on this transition, in the EU White Paper on *Growth, Competitiveness and Employment*, Jacques Delors pointed out:

> This decade is witnessing a forging of a link of unprecedented magnitude and significance between the technological innovation process and economic and social organisation. Countless innovations are combining to bring about a major upheaval in the organisation of activities and relationships within society. Throughout the world, production systems, methods of organising work and consumption patterns are undergoing changes which will have long term effects comparable with the first industrial revolution.

The scale of the transformation required to support the re-positioning of European Society has, however, yet to be grasped. The multiple innovations in technologies, values and structures will bring profound changes in the way we live our lives, just as the earlier industrial revolution changed the world in its time. When we think of the industrial revolution we tend to think of technical inventions and forget that industrialisation radically transformed the whole organisation of society. This included the organisation of work which we now consider typical, the nuclear family, the division of the world into nation states, urban living, and manufacturing industry as the primary source of employment. The industrial revolution also brought many beneficial changes in housing, healthcare, educational standards, diet, leisure, disposable income, travel, and respect for people's rights. These processes did not happen through the guidance of the market place, but required the active involvement and organisation of people in the workplace, in the political arena, and in the development of citizenship generally.

Europe's current difficulties in adjusting to changes, in particular the continuing high levels of unemployment and social exclusion, have led some politicians and employers to blame the European social model of development. In particular, they question the idea that social solidarity operating through the state should care for large numbers of citizens, guarantee individual rights and provide essential services. They also question the social market economy, in which the free market is closely supervised by an administrative state with social partners integrated through institutional participation at all levels. I believe that comparisons with the United States and Southeast Asia, which call for Europe to adopt a more radical new-liberal approach, are distracting and futile. Far more important is deeper research and agreement on how we anticipate, support and underpin the structural changes needed to rapidly modernise our European social model for the twenty-first century.

Forces changing Europe

People are changing – changes in values and lifestyles are important dynamics of change in the economy and society, bringing demands for new types of products and services, and changes in the nature and organisation of work. A significant cause of unemployment has been the failure of organisations and businesses in Europe to identify the new trends in values and lifestyles and create services and products to meet them. Also, many aspects of government, industrial relations and social policy lag far behind these changes in people's values, attitudes and perceived needs.

People Are Better Off: Income per head in Europe is projected to grow by 30 per cent over the next 15 years. This increase in affluence is reducing the lifespan of products and changing the types of services being offered. This in turn will change the world of work, as organisations and businesses respond to these evolving patterns.

People Are More Individualised: The increased range of options available to people in their work and leisure opportunities has resulted in the emergence of a wider concept of personal development, as people take responsibility for defining their own needs and managing their own lives. However, many people find the compulsion to choose in a complexity of options very confusing, isolating and overwhelming, especially at a time when the traditional forms of social cohesion – class, traditional family, trade unions, church, nationality – are weakening. Modernising our European social model means creating new forms of social cohesion, and collective structures that promote and support individual differences and the desire for diversity in ways that do not demand conformity and sameness. This is one of the significant challenges of the twenty-first century.

The Workforce Structure is Changing: The share of the population of working age is steadily declining – the overall average number of workers per elderly person in Europe has declined from about 7.5 per cent in 1960 to about 5.4 per cent today, and is projected to drop to 2.5 per cent by 2040. At the same time, the participation of women in paid employment is growing in all European countries and that of men is declining. In the EU, 30 per cent of new jobs go to men, 70 per cent to women. The ageing of the workforce, the rising participation of women in paid employment and the relative decline in male participation, will be some of the most important formative trends in the world of work of the twenty-first century. Our labour markets and our social protection systems must be modernised to cope with these changes.

Technology and change

The world is undergoing a major technological revolution. A core of new technologies is replacing the technologies which formed the basis of 'industrial' society. This will fundamentally alter the nature of work and the structure of European society in the twenty-first century.

The core technologies of the emerging knowledge based economy are the information and communications technologies. They are major industries in their own right, producing machines (hardware) and programmes (software), but more significantly, they are enabling technologies, and their links with biotechnology, ecotechnologies, energy technology and new materials technologies are giving us a virtual explosion of new knowledge, new products, new ways of organising work and of meeting human needs.

In industrial society, physical labour and natural resources were the primary inputs in economic activity. Information technologies and advances in organisational skills have made possible the development of a system of production based on knowledge and information processing. In Europe in the twenty-first century, the creation, organisation and dissemination of knowledge will be the dominant feature of economies.

The shift to a more knowledge intensive economy can be seen in the products and jobs emerging. Many of the new products and jobs are pure information or relationship in content and have virtually no material content – for example, financial services, the media, entertainment, tourism, sport, education, health, personal services, services to business.

In traditional economic thinking people are a factor of production similar to land and capital – a cost to be reduced. In a knowledge based economy people are a resource not a cost. They are the key resource. Organisations are valued not on the basis of their products or machines but primarily on the knowledge creating capacity of the workforce, the people who work for them, how they work, what work means to them. The rate of innovation and change in products and technologies is so rapid that the competitive advantages of companies and countries will be the capacity of the workforce to create knowledge.

New technologies in themselves do not guarantee increased productivity, economic growth or improvement in living standards – this requires deep attitudinal and organisational change to imbed the technologies within society. The conversion of the potential of technologies into practical improvements in living standards involves a deep and lengthy process of social learning. Crucial to modernising European labour markets is an acceptance that changes in awareness and social innovation are as central as technologies if the vision of improved living standards and quality of life is to be realised.

The new technologies bring great benefits but these benefits do not automatically accrue to everyone. Some individuals and groups are benefiting greatly, others including whole communities are being left behind. Young workers with technological literacy win, older workers lose. With the growth in services many women win; other women, in service jobs protected, to date, from 'information', lose. People with disabilities could be winners; other disadvantaged groups, in particular, the long-term unemployed, lose. Shifting taxes from labour to other areas, as recommended by the Monti Commission, developing effective educational and skill levels for low-skilled workers and the unemployed, and providing substantial personal support for the unemployed to help them return to the labour market, are all essential for a social investment programme to modernise Europe.

Globalisation – A new world emerging

The increasing integration of the economies and cultures of the world, the growing size and power of multinational companies, and the rising economic capacity of the economies of developing countries, will be a central feature of the twenty-first century. This will impact on Europe in a number of ways.

The global flow of information is seen very dramatically in the huge growth in the international financial markets. There is now a 24 hour continuous global flow of financial trading amounting to a thousand billion dollars per day, which is 160 times the size of world trade in goods. Many governments are virtually powerless in the face of these forces as attempts to establish an EU single currency demonstrate. The movement of finance, and a fluctuation in currency, can be more important in determining a company's cost competitiveness than labour costs. A major political issue for Europe is the creation of a system of global economic governance which will give governments more control over these financial markets.

The combination of information and communications technologies with organisational innovations has resulted in the emergence of global companies, which organise their production within a global web of adding value, where different parts of the value adding process are carried out in different countries or continents. In addition, the financial control systems of these companies are now commonly configured in such a way that plants must bid, both for business with the parent company and for further investment, on the basis of indicators of cost and product reliability in competing national locations. The crucial issue for European countries is to place themselves in the part of the 'value adding web' where the high-skilled, high wage, less footloose jobs are located, and not impoverish themselves through bidding against less industrialised countries, or indeed each other, for low adding value, repetitive, low waged, more footloose jobs.

Most of the competition in OECD countries comes, not from low wage countries, but from OECD countries themselves. Trade with non-OECD countries represents less than 5 per cent of GDP in North America and Western Europe. Analysis of trade in goods suggests that there has been a small negative effect on demand for unskilled labour in OECD countries, due to trade with non-OECD countries, but that this has been largely offset by jobs gained through trade in goods produced by skilled labour. The vast bulk of job losses in the 1980s in developed economies came from obsolescence in products and technologies, failure to create new products and services and failure to innovate. The key issue here for European countries is the achievement, from a human rights perspective, of social clauses in the regulation of trade, dealing with child labour, forced labour, trade union membership and the elimination of discrimination.

Radical changes in the world of work

The interaction of new technologies, changes in people's values and lifestyles, and the emergence of global markets and global companies, is bringing about radical changes in the world of work.

The large increase in women workers and the contraction at both ends of the age pyramid have changed the social structure of the workforce. With the decline in manufacturing, two-thirds of the workforce are now working in the services sector. Jobs from heavy industry have been transferred on a massive scale to SMEs. At the same time, the number of professional and managerial posts has virtually doubled in ten years.

Many of the new products and services which are beginning to dominate the emerging economy have little or no material content and are composed of pure information, knowledge or relationships e.g. financial services, computer chips, medicines and films. As a result, there is a shift towards a higher skill and informational content in new jobs, with an across-the-board rise in the threshold of competence required for employment. In manufacturing and services, managerial, professional and technical categories of work are growing fastest. Service jobs in low paid, low skills categories like shop assistants, clerical and waitering are also growing.

Work contracts are also becoming less standardised. The traditional 'standard' work contract of the 40 hour, 40 year package is being accompanied by a growth in part-time work, short-term contract work, self-employment, temporary work, teleworking and home-working.

The impetus for this variety of contracts is coming from a number of motivations. The speed of change of technologies and consumer tastes, and the changing variety and lifespan of services and goods, are resulting in organisations and companies wanting more flexibility in terms of both staff numbers and skills.

This flexibility can be motivated and organised to enhance work and enable the employment of more people in better jobs. However, it can also be motivated and organised to exploit workers, as is the case with a growing number of 'atypical workers', mainly women, members of ethnic minorities, migrant workers and young people. The big challenge for Europe lies in reconciling the two objectives, of promoting more flexible forms of work to enable companies to meet new needs, and of eliminating the negative aspects of such forms of employment by providing greater security and protection for those workers and improving the general quality of their jobs.

Organisations are also changing. A number of trends are reducing the layers of decision-making in organisations, resulting in flatter organisational structures. Information technology does away with the need for layers of supervisors and middle managers, or human information carriers. In the emerging knowledge based, innovative economy, the intelligence and creative commitment of workers is becoming the key resource of organisations. This is leading to more team and project-based working.

In addition, a new system of manufacturing is being created based on highly flexible technologies, integrated with highly skilled workers and organised in small teams. This system of production is called a variety of names – World Class Manufacturing, TQM, Lean Production, etc.

Another big challenge for European companies and unions is how to move *in a positive way* from the traditional Taylorist approach to more flexibility in the organisation of work.

Industrial relations are also changing. Over the past decade, a number of distinct industrial relations models have developed side by side in Europe. These models represent alternative ways of responding to the new competitive order. Flexibility, fluid working practices and a capacity to handle ongoing changes in products and processes are the key concerns. How these principles are realised in practice, however, varies radically and provides the point of contrast between models:

(i) *The Non-Union Human Resource Model* – these companies are mainly in the electronics sector, are US in origin and often grew out of sectors and geographical areas which were effectively union-free;

(ii) *The Partnership/New Industrial Relations Model* – union management dialogue moves beyond collective bargaining alone to embrace business and product plans and strategies, and the design or re-design of production systems, linked to ongoing flexibility in work processes, new payment systems and more investment in training and development;

(iii) *The Deregulation Model* – what defines this model is the search for minimum regulation of managerial action or of labour markets, whether by unions or by statute, with an insistence on managerial prerogative and maximum flexibility in recruiting, deploying, utilising, pricing and dispensing with labour;

(iv) *The Adversarial Model* – management and unions remain wedded to adversarial industrial relations across a wide spectrum of industries in Europe. Sometimes this is obscured by an apparent willingness to embrace new ideas and principles, with mission statements, quality circles, new communications programmes, 'empowerment', adding up to little more than wishful thinking – 'eclectic adversarialism'.

Modernising the European social model will require a renewal of social partnership and recognition that the introduction of work organisation and production methods that depend on training, motivation, flexibility and continuous improvement requires a high trust environment with management, workers and unions acting as partners in the enterprise.

The gap between the haves and have-nots in the world of employment is also growing. Technology both eliminates jobs and creates jobs. It has destroyed low skill, lower productivity jobs, while creating jobs that are more productive, high-skill and better paid. Those workers who lost their jobs and are not able to take up the new higher skill opportunities have remained unemployed for longer and longer periods. The gap between those who benefit from technological change and those who lose from it is becoming socially divisive.

The sectors where employment is increasing are those where educational requirements are highest. And in many areas competition for jobs is pushing up the educational levels beyond those needed to do the job. Again, the long-term unemployed and young early school-leavers are not able to access these jobs. A growing gap is also developing between those with full-time, permanent employment, engaged in the core activity of the enterprise and those who work on the periphery in less secure unprotected jobs.

Tackling social exclusion is, therefore, another key priority for Europe. Modernising European economies will require an integrated programme to promote inclusion, active labour market policies to tackle long-term unemployment and action on incentives to work and poverty traps. Policy should aim to support self-generating social inclusion by disseminating the idea that social investment is crucial for adaptation to change.

Modernising the European model

Modernising the European labour market and the European social model to cope with the profound and rapid economic, social and demographic changes taking place, is the key priority. Our ability to create and manage change, to accept uncertainty, to strike a balance between flexibility and security and to promote social inclusion as essential for adaptation to change will be crucial. All of our key organisations will, therefore, have to adapt their policies, strategies and procedures for these challenges – the pace at which we adapt and the degree of consensus we develop amongst governments and the social partners for these changes will determine the future of the European Union.

These profound changes are occurring at a time when Europe, having created a single market, is seeking, through the Maastricht Treaty, EMU and the Inter-Governmental Conference to introduce political, economic and social controls on that market. The response to-date, however, from the EU has been lack-lustre and lacks focus. In particular, the Social Dialogue between unions (ETUC) and employers (UNICE) has failed to develop a strong social partnership programme to modernise European Labour Markets and European workplaces by striking a balance between flexibility and security and between individualism and partnership.

A strong social partnership programme to modernise the European labour market and workplaces requires us to change some of our attitudes and look afresh at our way of looking at the world and of looking at each other. Changes in attitude are more difficult than altering the terms of a collective agreement or adding a few paragraphs to a joint declaration.

We urgently need a new social partnership in Europe – a social partnership informed and sustained by the following principles:

1. *Acceptance of our Inter-Dependence* In other words, no country, no group – government, employers, workers, the wider community – can achieve its goals without a significant degree of support from others.

2. *Appreciation of the Value of Co-operation* If we accept our interdependence we should be able to appreciate the value of co-operating together to achieve our aims.

3. *Greater Respect for Workers and Entrepreneurs* The contribution of workers and entrepreneurs to our economic and social wellbeing is undervalued by society in general and by each group. This respect should go beyond a recognition of our inter-dependence to a genuine regard for the value of our distinct contributions.

4. *Higher levels of Trust* Greater mutual respect should lead to higher levels of trust, more openness and less suspicion of each other's motives. Workers will accept the need for more profits if they are getting their share. Management will get the changes they require when they show concern for maintaining and improving the quality of jobs.

5. *Commitment to Fair Sharing* All social partners should accept that the fruits of economic growth be shared by all citizens in a manner that reflects Europe's commitment to social solidarity and a better quality of life for *all* our people, and that modernised social protection schemes can contribute significantly to positive economic development in Europe.

Working time and employment

Bettina Agathonos-Mähr

In 1996, Michel Rocard, the former French prime minister, presented his resolution on the reduction and reorganisation of working time to the European Parliament. The resolution was subsequently adopted by a large majority in the European Parliament. The basic idea in the Rocard report is that if unemployment is really a priority concern of the European Union and its member states, then, on labour market policy grounds, there is no alternative to a redistribution of work.

There are different formulae, involving various instruments, for actually redistributing work. They include: the reduction of weekly working time; the abolition of overtime; life-long learning and continuing training leave; sabbaticals and study leave; gradual transition to retirement and early retirement; and the creation of more part-time work. In his report, Michel Rocard squarely places the emphasis on reducing weekly working time. Yet all the other approaches are important instruments in the direction of 'models of life-long working time', and have already been discussed or implemented in various EU member states.

When he first put them forward, Rocard's proposals did not appear to have established a foothold in the discussion on fighting unemployment, and were characterised by many as unrealistic and utopian. This scepticism was unsurprising in the climate of neo-liberal thinking which predominated until recently and which was characterised by proposals for deregulation, increased flexibility, and dismantling of the welfare system. But the wayward and illegal action of closing down the Renault plant in Vilvoorde, Belgium proved to be the last straw which set the forces aiming for a social Europe in motion. Not only were 100,000 demonstrators from all the countries of Europe mobilised at very short notice, but the reduction of working time, and the lowering of ancillary wage costs to create jobs, were placed at the centre of day-to-day politics.

The reduction of weekly working time

Through an irony of fate, while working on this report I gained my own personal experience of the labour battle to reduce working time to 32 hours a week in Belgium. My pre-Easter shopping plan was frustrated by the strike of employees at Belgium's largest supermarket chain, who were calling for a reduction in working time to 32 hours a week. Since then, the workers have received initial responses to their political demands, but these have not been entirely favourable.

France and Belgium were the first countries to conduct feasibility studies on general working time reduction, and to have cost-benefit analyses carried out by finance offices and social insurance associations. France and Belgium are also the countries that have undertaken the first steps toward turning Rocard's proposals into a reality. In France, social insurance contributions for new employees are reduced by 40 per cent in the first year if working time is reduced by 10 per cent. In Belgium, a draft law has been drawn up which contains the following: enterprises with at least 50 employees can reduce weekly working time from the present 38 hours to between 32–36 hours if the workers at the same time forego their pay for the 'lost' time. This can only come about with the consent of the works council. If additional workers are employed as a result, the government exempts part of the associated social security charges. This can represent an annual saving equivalent to as much as 34,000 schillings per new worker, regardless of how much the working time is shortened and how many jobs are created.[1]

Rocard points out that between 1880 and 1970 annual working time in Europe fell from 3,200 to under 1,700 hours annually, and that this development was accompanied by a substantial rise in income. From the time that this reduction in working time reached a standstill, Europe has recorded rising unemployment.

As early as 1991, the European Commission commissioned a comprehensive study on the subject of 'Working Time, Employment and Production Capacities', by D. Taddei, which was published in

Soziales Europa (Social Europe). This study projected a very positive impact on employment if there were a reduction in working time coupled with an extension in factory hours and thus bringing greater flexibility with regard to working times. However, these proposals were not reflected in any of the Commission's main initiatives. Neither the white paper on social policy nor the white paper on growth, competitiveness and employment dealt with reducing working time, although flexibility, the deregulation of labour markets and the promotion of part-time work were recommended. If scientific research and past experience clearly demonstrate the positive effects on employment of a reduction in working time, why has this approach been neglected, despite growing unemployment?

For trade unions and works councils, the problematic nature of pay adjustment has been, and remains, the main barrier to implementing a reduction in working time. Without compensatory pay adjustment, in most cases the proportional reduction in pay is not acceptable. The complete exclusion of any form of pay adjustment would certainly create unacceptable problems for workers on close to the minimum wage, and would result in a disproportionately large drop in purchasing power.[2]

Employers, on the other hand, fear higher charges in the event of a reduction in working time with the retention of full pay, and could react by trimming profit margins (which ultimately jeopardises investments and jobs) or by raising prices, which has an adverse impact on external trade.[3]

One solution to this problem is put forward by D. Taddei, the author of the Commission study. He suggests lowering capital use costs by extending the period of use of investment, as one possible way of making stable unit costs and practically equal pay compatible. The expansion of production capacities could result in stimulating growth and thus lead to the creation of jobs.

Reduction in working time leads to clear productivity gains per hour worked. These result from a more intensive pace of working, a reduction in downtime, less time lost due to absenteeism and sickness, and other related benefits. If higher productivity gains through longer factory hours are added to this effect, then a reduction of working time on full pay would be justifiable, as it would create more jobs without adversely affecting purchasing power.

On top of these external consequences can be added domestic expansionist effects: an appreciation in disposable real income through a fall in prices and a rise in net wages and salaries. According to the HERMES model,[4] this would result in GDP growth amounting to 1.5 per cent (France) to 2.2 per cent (Italy) in the medium to long term.

At the same time, the Taddei study projects a competitive improvement for the countries that undertake a working time reorganisation and reduction relative to those that do not. From the perspective of supply-side policy, the reorganisation and reduction of working time results in an improvement in the efficiency and competitiveness of production, by bringing about an increase in production capacities and, consequently, gains in terms of price competitiveness. These enable gains to be made in market share at the expense of partner countries. In addition, the reorganisation and reduction of working time has clear, more positive, employment effects than other supply-side policies (the employment elasticity to GDP is between 0.35 and 0.70 compared to 0.25 to 0.40 for completion of the Single Market).[5]

The Taddei study sees three further macroeconomic advantages in the reorganisation and reduction of working time:

> 'the expansionist effect has a deflationary impact, since it is caused by a drop in production costs that affects prices. According to the HERMES model, the fall in consumer prices in the present scenario is in the range of −3.0 per cent and −4.9 per cent in the medium to long term, depending on the country involved;
>
> financial surpluses improve since the expansionist effect leads to increased tax revenues; expressed in percentages of GDP, these improvements in the present scenario fall within the range of 0.3 and 0.8 in the medium to long term depending on the country;
>
> balances of goods and services likewise improve, since the reorganisation and reduction of working time boosts external competitiveness; these improvements are in the range of 0.15 to 0.40 points of GDP in the medium to long term, depending on the country involved'.[6]

If a reorganisation and reduction of working time is implemented in several EU countries at the same time, the competitive advantages gained through it will be relativised; however, the simultaneous increase in activity in several member states will lead – via intra-Community trade – to the familiar multiplier effect, which in turn has a further strengthening factor for employment.

If the process of working time reorganisation and reduction is developed in several EU countries at the same time, and is also accompanied by supportive measures implemented by the respective governments (with the state passing on the positive impact on the budget of the reorganisation and reduction of working time by lowering employers' contributions to social security), then the macroeconomic result will be shored up. In addition, the credibility of the reorganisation and reduction of working time will increase, since substantial financial resources can be employed to encourage companies to adopt these structures for their reorganisation. At the same time, the longer-lasting utilisation of plant capacity could serve as a stimulus to investment, especially in cases where the useful life of plant and equipment is limited by rapid obsolescence.

The following five results at microeconomic level have been achieved in numerous studies on and extensive research into the reorganisation and reduction of working time:

> '1. An increase in production capacities and sales: this is obviously the company's prime objective, since in the vast majority of cases studied restructuring was preceded by unsatisfied demand (or an increase in demand was foreseeable); in some cases, unprofitable plants had to be closed down in order to concentrate on the most efficient resources. In some cases, a bankruptcy could be avoided as a result.
>
> 2. Maintenance of or slight reduction in unit costs: the reduction of working time on full pay and with certain added costs related to reorganisation were at least compensated through specifically targeted 'savings of capital'. The result of this was that selling prices could generally be maintained, or at any rate raised to a lesser extent than if no reorganisation of working time had taken place.
>
> 3. Significant improvement in financial results. This is easy to understand, since profit margins per production unit hardly change whereas the volume of sales rises.
>
> 4. Employment increases noticeably, since new workers are brought on. This leads to a capacity effect (more is produced) and a redistribution effect, in the region of 20 per cent to 30 per cent.
>
> 5. Investment activity is greatly stimulated. Of course, an initial analysis reveals that any reorganisation and reduction of working time substitutes for a capital investment that was never made. But two more important and dynamic factors have an opposite effect: on the one hand, the fact that an expensive plant can be used longer can be an absolute precondition for the investment decision, while on the other hand an improvement in the financial situation naturally leads to a willingness to

undertake later investments. Overall, measures associated with the reorganisation and reduction of working time seem to stimulate, rather than discourage investments, even capacity investments'.[7]

Another result of these studies is that, in most cases, the reorganisation and reduction of working time did not result in an increase in night work, Sunday work or holiday work.

In its resolution the European Parliament presented arguments along similar lines. Rocard proposes a reduction in social contributions with a reduction in working time, giving the following justification: the member states allocate almost ECU 350 billion annually, almost 4 per cent of the European Union's GNP, for expenditure related to unemployment. Thus social insurance agencies are the beneficiaries in a reorganisation of production through a lengthening of factory hours with simultaneous reduction in working time. Rocard suggests using the savings to both the state budget and social funds for creating jobs rather than financing unemployment:

'The principle of these mechanisms is extremely simple. Any firm that hires a certain number of recipients of unemployment benefit through an appreciable reduction in working time, and if necessary a simultaneous increase in its machinery's running time, receives a grant from the labour exchange equal to part of the unemployment funds saved, to be determined in negotiations by the social partners.

This grant should prevent or limit wage losses, without which a reduction in working time would not free up the necessary financial resources for hiring new recruits. The extent, duration, and gradual – dependent on productivity increases – reduction in this grant would be negotiated in tripartite talks between the companies, trade unions and government or unemployment insurance agencies, and on a sectoral or company level when firms with over a 1,000 employees are involved.

Subsidies of additional training efforts made by firms for their newly hired workers are also conceivable – always bearing in mind the savings achieved through the large-scale hiring of recipients of unemployment benefit'.[8]

Other work redistributive mechanisms

Rocard also calls on the social partners in each member state to engage in negotiations on the gradual, full or partial abolition of overtime, and its replacement with extra time off, since total overtime in the EU corresponds to some 2.5 per cent of non-self-employed work performed, or put another way, is equivalent to some 3 to 4 million jobs. In the Austrian framework agreement amending the law on working time, the people negotiating collective agreements have a duty to limit overtime, or to compensate it with time off in lieu.

The European Commission stresses the importance of life-long learning in the age of technological change, since it believes that in the next ten years technology will advance very rapidly and only 20 per cent of the technologies currently used will still be employed. 'Consideration should therefore be given to how time devoted to continuous training can be integrated into a concept of life-long working time and, for example, be extended to three years. This would result in a working time reduction of 7 per cent of total life-long working time'.[9]

Sabbatical leave and study leave can also play a role. Study leave is release from work for elective purposes and can be awarded for up to one year. In Denmark, the system operates in such a way that the position involved is filled by an unemployed person. In Denmark, the person who takes sabbatical leave receives 70 per cent of the highest estimated benefit. This model offers a good opportunity for the unemployed person replacing the individual taking sabbatical leave. Study leave is something which is provided very generously in Austria, in comparison to the rest of the EU, through the waiting time rule (*Karenzregelung*). In addition, at EU level, the European social partners have negotiated a minimum regulation for parental leave, Europe-wide, which was adopted by the Council in the form of a directive.

The instrument of early retirement has been used frequently in Germany and Austria in recent years, where certain sectors, especially the steel industry, have been threatened with large-scale layoffs. However, there is a trend towards raising the retirement age in these countries: this is a problem, since early retirement has significantly eased the problems faced by the unemployed aged 50 years and over, and by the long-term unemployed. Other countries are moving in the opposite direction. For example, France, after the conflict with the truck drivers, lowered the retirement age in this sector to 55, and Belgium is seeking an employment pact with an early retirement rule of 58 years. The smooth transition to retirement is of particular psychological importance, since it softens the abrupt break between full employment and full retirement. Michel Rocard's resolution addresses this issue: 'Men or women who can still work only three-quarter time already receive a quarter of their pension, which has already been financed through their contributions. These workers also continue receiving three-quarters of their salary out of which they pay the contributions for the remaining pension they will receive later on'.[10]

Part-time work is clearly a useful means for work redistribution, and it is one of the types of work that is strongly encouraged at EU level; it has correspondingly increased sharply in recent years in all the EU member states. Jacques Delors' white paper, *Growth, Employment and Competitiveness*, stresses the necessity of a 'thorough reform of the labour market: a greater flexibility of work organisation and working time organisation, a reduction in labour costs, etc.' In particular, work organisation should be arranged more flexibly by eliminating barriers to the employment of part-time staff or concluding fixed-term work contracts. The USA is often used as a model for Europe in terms of flexible employment policy. However, it is not always mentioned that every type of employment is counted as the same in the US, regardless of the number of hours worked per week. In other words somebody working only a small amount of hours is counted the same as someone employed on a full-time basis. This means that the volume of employment as such remains the same, but is divided up between several persons through the promotion of part-time employment. In other words, the existing workload is redistributed among several persons through the promotion of part-time work.[11]

Of course, part-time work has its own problems. Those employed part-time in Europe are discriminated against relative to the full-time employed in many ways. For the most part, they: are paid less; have less security; have flexible working hours; have fewer possibilities to participate in continued training measures; have fewer career and promotion opportunities; have fewer trade union rights; lose special privileges gained through works council agreements and bonuses. Further problems with part-time work are encountered with the possibility of returning to full-time work and with voluntary work.

Currently, the European social partners are in the middle of a negotiation process aimed at securing 'more flexible working time and offering workers security', in which part-time work is now the first topic of negotiation. The workers are demanding that there be no discrimination between these kinds of labour relations, the objective being to unshackle them from the image of being 'second-class' situations. The principle of non-discrimination should apply to all necessary types and conditions of work, including equal treatment in labour law, social insurance, social protection, public service and contributions, career advancement, participation in training and labour protection. Moreover, these new types of employment should only be introduced after workers or their representatives have been heard, and only on a voluntary basis.

With the exception of the Netherlands, there are few incentives on offer for part-time work. Depending on the results of the negotiation between the European social partners, the European Union could issue a Directive extensively eliminating discrimination against part-time work and thus providing incentives for its promotion. However, Rocard sees two essential disadvantages in incentive measures with respect to the choice of part-time work:

> 'They increase discrimination between men and women on the labour market and clash with measures aimed at bringing about an overall reduction in average weekly working time. It is important that the individual measures designed to promote the reduction in working time do not cancel each other out, and any government aiming in particular to reduce collective average working time should take care that it does not sabotage its own action via excessively favourable and overly selective incentives for part-time work.'[12]

On the issue of equal opportunity, it can be easily established that part-time work Europe-wide is women's work: over 80 per cent of those in part-time employment are women; in Austria the figure is even 89 per cent. In 1994, 30 per cent of all female employees had a part-time job or were only working a few hours a week.

Most of the rise in part-time work (+9 per cent) occurred between 1990 and 1994, when overall employment fell by 3 per cent. While the 3.5 per cent job loss among men was only compensated by a half percentage point through the increase in part-time work to 3 per cent, the 5 per cent drop in overall employment among women was almost offset by the 10 per cent increase in the number of women employed on a part-time basis (an employment drop of −1/4 per cent).

The increase in part-time employment mainly affected women. While 98 per cent of the newly created employment for men was full-time positions, 30 per cent of the newly created jobs for women were part-time; stated differently, 95 per cent of the newly created part-time employment was taken by women. Consider countries in which special government incentives have been offered for part-time work, such as

Great Britain and the Netherlands. In 1994 45 per cent of all female workers in Great Britain, and 66 per cent, or two thirds, of all female employees in the Netherlands, were part-time employees.

This highlights the clear trend towards a division of the labour market, namely a full-time job market for men and a part-time job market for women, which will continue to lock women into their traditional role in the future. The argument that two thirds of all women employed part-time do not actually want full-time employment owing to family obligations has some justification under today's circumstances; however, the question must be raised as to whether these women ever had the choice of exchanging their part-time job for a partnership sharing of family pleasures, with a general reduction of working time to 32 hours a week for both partners.

The Austrian Framework Agreement on Working Time

In 1997 a breakthrough was made in Austria by the social partners in their negotiation of a framework agreement on working time which should amend the Austrian law on working time. The centrepiece of the framework agreement is that greater flexibility of working time is linked to the conclusion of collective agreements and thus to the consent of trade unions. There is thus a 'trade-off' between greater (sector-specific) possibilities for more flexibility and a compensation for workers – that can be reflected in the form of a reduction in working time, job security, forms of life-long working time, sabbaticals, and training time models.

The calculation of weekly working time (previously over several weeks) can now be allowed by collective agreement over a period of 52 weeks. This paves the way for models of annual working time. And with blocks of time off covering several weeks, the calculation can also be made over a lengthier period of time. Within the calculation period, daily normal working time can be laid down at nine hours, as before. The new feature is that the parties to the collective agreement have the possibility of extending normal working time to up to 10 hours in connection with the introduction of a four-day week or of making longer blocks of time off possible. The normal weekly working times can be extended by collective agreement to up to 50 hours as before, but only if the period over which the calculation is made does not exceed eight weeks. If it does, then only an extension up to 48 hours is possible.

If the parties to the collective agreement do not agree on a flexible working time, then a conciliation procedure is set in motion by the social partners. The ÖGB (Austrian Trade Union Federation) and chamber of commerce appoint two members each for this. If the procedure is not successful, then both parties jointly designate a chairperson with a right to vote. If the proposed solution adopted by this enlarged conciliation committee is not implemented by the parties to the collective agreement, then the ÖGB and chamber of commerce conclude a collective agreement through which the works council agreement in the sector involved – in the event that a works council has not concluded an individual agreement – is empowered to implement the proposed solution at company level.

Additional innovations are that in the new framework agreement overtime can no longer be remunerated via the payment of an overtime bonus but is rather compensated for by time off in lieu via a collective agreement. And great discussion was caused by the paragraph stating that exceptions to time off at weekends and on holidays can now be made not only via a decree, but also via a collective agreement.

The first negotiation result in the framework of the new working time agreement was achieved by the parties to the collective agreement in the metal industry. The weekly working time in this industry can fluctuate between 32 and 45 hours. After 41.5 hours a week, workers receive a credit of 25 per cent for the hours over the normal time of 38.5 hours a week, in other words 15 minutes, which can be used in the form of time off. This has led to a sharp reduction in overtime and a slight reduction in working time.

In the chemicals sector, the collective agreement partners have signed an employment agreement in a paper napkin plant (SCA-Hygiene Austria), which provides for the introduction of a five-shift operation with the use of Sunday work. In exchange, the workers receive a reduction in working time from 38 to 36 hours with no loss of pay and Sunday bonuses. The workers affected thus receive up to 6,000 schillings more per month gross.

Conclusions

Working time is starting to change. In 1997 there was a fight for a 32-hour week going on in Belgium. France is also undertaking certain pilot projects in this direction. In Scandinavia, training, education and sabbatical leave have been realised. A bit of everything was enabled in Austria through the framework agreement on working time. Sabbatical leave for public sector employees will also be realised before long. And in other countries there are also interesting developments.

Technological and social change necessitates adjustments. But these adjustments have nothing to do with the neo-liberal demands for a wilder form of deregulation, greater flexibility and the dismantling of the welfare system. On the contrary, technological progress requires more time – for training, continuing training, and everything which forms part of 'life-long learning', so that workers can adapt to the requirements of the constantly changing world.

Social progress in the direction of 'equal opportunities and partnership' requires more time as well – for the division on a partnership basis of household and family duties and pleasures, if men and women are to obtain genuinely equal opportunities in their professional and family fulfillment.

The 20 million unemployed in Europe have more than enough time!

So why should it not be possible to redistribute existing work more fairly, to everyone's benefit?

Notes

1. Radl Sabine, *Wirtschaftsblatt* (Economic Journal), 26 March 1997
2. Cf. D. Taddei, *Social Europe, Working Time, Employment and Production Capacities, Reorganisation and Reduction of Working Time*, European Commission, Supplement 4/91, p94.
3. *Ibid.*
4. The HERMES model was designed by officials at the Commission and a group of national model design experts.
5. Cf. *Social Europe, Working Time, Employment and Production Capacities, Reorganisation and Reduction of Working Time*, p32.
6. *Social Europe, Working Time, Employment and Production Capacities, Reorganisation and Reduction of Working Time*, p32.
7. *Ibid.*, p121.
8. Michel Rocard, *European Parliament, Resolution on the Reduction of Working Time*, 1996, p9.
9. Reiner Hoffman, *Auf dem Weg zu einem Lebensarbeitszeitkonzept – einige Denkanstösse* (On the Way to a Concept of Life-Long Working Time – Some Food for Thought), paper for the international conference

'New Strategies for Everyday Life, Work, Free Time and Consumption,' University of Tilburg, 12–14 December 1996, p12.

10. Michel Rocard, *Resolution in the European Parliament on Reduction of Working Time*, p10.

11. Michel Rocard, *Resolution in the European Parliament on Reduction of Working Time*, p11.

Social security: Class Struggle from Above

Heiner Gansmann

German uncertainties

In Germany, as everywhere else, there are some people whose actions and decisions have binding and far-reaching consequences for a majority of others within a particular social, national or territorial group. For brevity's sake, let us call them elites, using the term not in a cultural or academic sense, but rather to refer to elites in the fields of politics and economics. In an interview in *Die Zeit* in 1996, about Franco–German relations, former French minister Chevènement recalled that on numerous occasions in the past German elites have failed to resolve problems relating to the processes involved in modernising society. In the Weimar Republic, for example: 'The German elites, caught up in a frenzy of irrationality and in their ideology of a conservative revolution, in most cases ended up betraying the nation out of their panic at the prospect of democracy, a panic which was rooted deep in the nineteenth century'. What is interesting about this description by an outsider is that the action of German elites, at a time which we generally perceive to have been one of excessive nationalism, is described by Chevènement as a betrayal of the nation. In contemporary Germany he sees the following risk: 'Today, Germany is in a position – and does not even seem to be on its guard against this – to impose its model in Europe, particularly in France: the market economy; competitiveness considered as the highest level of human society; the desperate urge for consensus; a form of politics that has been reduced to the technical administration of problems; and a hierarchical ordering of states based on their respective wealth' (*Die Zeit*, 2 August 1996, p40).

In what follows, I focus on the discernible costs *within* Germany of this 'model', and ask whether the actions taken by German elites regarding the present political and economic problems give more cause for optimism than is suggested by those experiences from the past evoked by Chevènement from outside – regardless of whether or not one wishes to use such strong words as 'betrayal' and 'nation'.

Present economic and socio-political discussion in Germany has all the signs of a misdirected attempt by society to put itself on the alert. Political jitteriness stands in stark contrast to the almost oppressive stability of the major trends in this society's development. Of course, some 'fundamentals' are slowly changing – not least because of unification – but nothing is happening which might justify the hysteria characterising the 'production site debate' currently taking place; or the nervous attitude towards a 'tax reform' which will be unworthy of the name; or the shrill discussions about the 'health reform', the 'security' of pensions, abuses of social security and so on and so forth. There are, in fact, at least two stable, and negative, trends which merit, but are not resulting in, well-informed, ongoing public debate and counter-measures – namely the inexorable rise in mass unemployment and the state's increasingly dubious financial conduct – amounting to a mixture of effectively deflationary cuts and a rapid rise of the national debt. By 1991, unemployment in western Germany had slowly dropped from its 1985 peak (an annual average of 2.3 million unemployed) to a figure of 1.7 million. Aggravated by the contribution of the new *Länder* (federal states) it has since been rising inexorably, reaching new record levels. The federal economics minister expects an annual average of 4.2 million unemployed in 1997. The national debt is also growing, and is likely to hit a record high. 'At the end of 1995, the government budgets contained a deficit of just under DM 2 billion. The level of debt has now virtually doubled since 1990, the year of German unification. This trend went hand in hand with a tremendous growth in interest burden. In 1990, the federal, *Länder* and local governments spent DM65 billion (including special assets) on servicing their interest payments, which had risen to DM128 billion in 1995. Currently, one in every six deutschmarks raised from tax revenue is spent on paying interest charges.[1]

However, as issues for public debate, these two negative trends tend to be misused rather than subjected to proper analysis. Unemployment is used to justify political decisions (the so-called Growth and

Employment Promotion Act, for example) which are designed to reduce the costs of labour and unemployment, but in fact bring more unemployment in their wake. And the rapid rise in the national debt is repeatedly wheeled out to legitimise the government's policy of reacting to a drop in income by cutting expenditure, but these cuts are continually failing to keep up with the drop in income, which is caused mainly by unemployment. The problem which needs to be solved is getting worse; meanwhile, the debts and the related interest burden on public finances, are continuing to rise.

What can we learn from this? Apparently nothing. An unshakeable unwillingness to learn, which remains impervious to both accumulated experience and rational argument, and which means that the same old recipes keep being offered everywhere, by all the political parties, is the really surprising element in the Federal Republic's economic and social policy debate.

What lies behind this stubbornness? There are two possibilities. Either the issue is beyond the intellectual capacities of those figures in political life, the media and academia who are discussing it. Or it is beyond their moral capacities, blinded as they are by their own interests, which force them to ignore blithely all those experiences or arguments which could end up curbing the advantages from which they stand to benefit. Both these possibilities are equally chilling. It is normal for us to be able to expect actions guided by no more than self-interest on the part of Germany's political and economic leaders; indeed this is desirable as it increases the predictability of their behaviour. But such self-interested conduct at an increasingly sub-rational level does pose a problem. For example, when businesspeople, their associations and their political and media representatives take up the chant of 'intolerable tax burden', it matters little whether (in the light of a per capita tax burden for the economy as a whole which has remained stable for decades[2]) they are motivated by ignorance or whether they are simply lying. What is beyond doubt is the role played by self-interest. Anyone seeking to maximise profits will moan about costs, whether in the form of taxes or wages. What is significant is that no member of the political and economic elite (which now includes opposition leaders, as well as those in the media, trade unions, etc.) is now able to point out clearly and audibly to the public that the (average) tax burden on business has been steadily falling since 1982,[3] and that by international standards (comparing not the nominal top tax rates, but the effective tax burden) the figure is rather low.[4] Even more importantly, in this self-imposed ignorance, political decisions are being made in reaction to phantom problems. The elites, caught up in their collective self-serving frenzy, are obviously increasingly losing all contact with reality. And in view of Germany's previous experiences with failures by the elite, it may well be justified to categorise such processes as somewhat risky. Once the money dries up, and when they see the failure of the economic and socio-political policy currently being conducted, with its labels of production site problems, globalisation, competitiveness, deregulation, and its concomitant view of personal responsibility as amounting to a merciless form of bottom-up redistribution, how likely are these elites to react soberly and rationally? The option of reverting to the old style of German nationalistic megalomania is probably no longer available – the interdependence of imports and exports will see to that. Otherwise, though, between the poles of, on the one hand, a bashful farewell to the half-hearted adaptation of western democratic traditions, and on the other, the compulsive aping of American capitalist Yuppiedom, anything is possible.

My intention in what follows is to define more precisely the current problems associated with Germany's economic and social policy, and to describe how the major political and economic actors are responding to the related challenges. Companies and their interest groups on the one hand, and the overwhelming majority of the so-called 'political class' on the other hand, are in the process of destroying the institutional system – comprising interplay between the state and companies – which has been very successful in the Federal Republic of Germany's past. I should particularly like to show that the costs of unification or regeneration of the new *Länder*, and the excessive unemployment arising from Germany's monetary and fiscal policies, constitute the major economic problems; though they naturally have to be seen against the backdrop of demographic change, i.e. the trend towards an ageing population, structural change in the economy tending towards a post-industrial society, globalisation and attempts at European integration.

Capitalism and the welfare state: a little theory

A capitalist economy can be regarded as a sort of parlour game, essentially involving two kinds of players: owners of capital, entrepreneurs and managers on the one hand, and wage-earners on the other.[5] In one way, the game is cooperative – it is about utilising production factors in a coordinated manner and achieving market success with the productivity achieved, success being automatically measured in terms of sales and profits. But, in another way, the game is non-cooperative: the distribution of the net production results (minus the rate of input effort) is the subject of a permanent conflict, revolving essentially around the relative shares of wages and profits; and the outcome of this conflict simultaneously determines, from a dynamic viewpoint, what growth potential is available to the capitalist economy via the growth of its components, firms.[6] Here, though, once again there are reasons for cooperation: provided profits are invested, rather than consumed or exported, in the later stages of the game they can benefit everyone, even wage-earners, or any other participants in the outcome of the game, through growth. Thus there is a trade-off between present consumption and higher consumption in the future – and this involves an assessment of the risk of being outmanoeuvred in the meantime, which is associated with the delay in hand-outs.

What has all this got to do with the welfare state? The game of capitalism does not involve the whole of society, but takes place in a social context which can initially be considered in the following, simplified way. Not everyone can/may/must take part in this game: Germany's present employment rate is around 47 per cent; in other words a majority of the population are not starting the game. On top of the present total of just under 35 million gainfully employed people, there are at present an average of 4.2 million unemployed, who would like to play, but whose efforts are – at least temporarily – not in demand. There is also a range of other groups who, for different reasons, are not in employment. However, those not playing must/should/can also be economically provided for from the profits from the game, as outside the game of capitalism there are only very limited and inadequate means of gaining access to economic resources (for example, in the form of domestic subsistence economies in the 'black' economy). The welfare state is one way of organising access to economic resources for 'non-players'. In this respect, the modern German welfare state has something to do with democracy, even though the story of its origins under Bismarck would hardly lead one to expect as much. In a democracy, non-players can mobilise political resources (their votes, loyalty, lawful entitlement) relatively easily, to enable them to use politics to intervene in the game of capitalism. The opportunities for intervening are numerous, ranging from regulations about who may/must play, to the removal of resources through taxation and transfer systems. The game's dependence on its social context can be simply characterised as follows: players must purchase from non-players their agreement for the game to continue. The game requires this agreement, because it has negative external effects in the form of a variety of burdens on the economy's natural and social environment. What is important here is the demarcation between players and non-players, through the definition of conditions, and the temporal structure, of employment, i.e. when it starts, participation, when it ends, in the form of unemployment, bankruptcy or retirement, and so forth. Then it is all about the forms, conditions and scale of access to resources. What kind of personal and material resources are made available for the game of capitalism, how are they transformed, and who participates in the results of the game? Non-players are not merely restricted to the spill-over or trickle-down effects. Rather, the greater the (politically underpinned) power of veto that non-players have (or can credibly claim to have), the better their share in the resources arising from the game. However, for non-players as much as for players, it is important not to kill the goose that lays the golden eggs. In other words there is also a (dynamic) problem of optimisation in determining the share of the resources non-players hope to attain. If they sap the game of too many resources now, then it will generate fewer in the future.[7] For the players themselves, on the other hand, the important thing is to obtain permission to take part in the game as cheaply as possible. Complications arise from the fact that the members of the numerically dominant class of present players, namely the wage-earners, are highly likely (depending on their own individual plans for the future) to become future clients of the welfare state, mainly as pensioners, though also as unemployed or sick individuals or even invalids. For wage-earners, therefore, payments made to non-players have the character not only of 'rewards for keeping quiet', but also of 'insurance premiums' against the risk of loss of income in the event of their potential labour not being sold.[8] Companies, on the other hand, have few reasons for adopting such an ambivalent attitude, with payments made to non-players being regarded as costs that need to be reduced as much as possible.[9]

What has all this to do with Germany, and its present economic and political problems? Firstly, in this general characterisation of the welfare state, I wish to make it clear that, within the system characterised by capitalism and democracy, it is a major component of most modern societies[10]. There is a functional complementarity between capitalist economics and the welfare state. But the latter derives no stability from it. The extent to which there is a need to ease the burden on the state via a politically organised transfer of resources is a matter of ongoing debate, not only because the corresponding assessment depends on incompatible vested interests, but also because of the variation in factors which are crucial for determining this extent, such as the level of prosperity, and both cyclical and supracyclical growth rates. And although previous decisions are continuing to have their effect in the form of institutional fixtures, which restrict the path along which the welfare state can develop, once a welfare state has been established it creates new angles of interest and resources, which prevent the dismantlement of institutions of the welfare state from being regarded as a mirror image of its establishment.[11] Dismantling the welfare state must of necessity be a more complex process than creating it, as the relationship between losers and winners when social security systems are introduced is differently structured, in terms of quantity and transparency, than when it is being dismantled: but in Germany a particular structuring of opportunities has arisen for its dismantlement, which has always been on the agenda for certain major players in the game of capitalism. The opportunity has arisen as a result of the relatively sudden problem of politically organising the former German Democratic Republic's transformation process, to bring about a convergence with the economic and political institutions and situations characterising the old Federal Republic of Germany.

The unification process in retrospect

Among the different prescriptions on offer after 1989 for transforming the true socialist economies into capitalist ones, so-called shock therapy was the most prominent. The first stages of this therapy involved lifting price controls, accompanied by the opening-up of foreign trade and the introduction of a convertible currency. This was to be followed by a more rigid monetary and fiscal stabilisation policy, intended to stem the inflationary pressure caused by lifting price controls. The monetary policy was intended to depress domestic demand, and public expenditure was supposed to be kept low, which in turn was bound to lead to unemployment and the loss of income for many social groups. The accompanying privatisation was intended to impose strict budgetary restrictions on the former state-owned firms, thereby forcing them to restructure production. The newly created enterprises would thus gradually become competitive on the world market, enabling an endogenous, self-supporting growth process, intended finally to reduce unemployment and boost incomes. It is questionable whether the complete shock therapy was ever actually applied in any one of the countries concerned – but in any case, it was not effective. Capitalism did not arrive in 500 days, as promised by the advocates of the shock therapy; but they can argue, in the light of their failures, that the therapy was not applied strictly and rapidly, and hence not consistently enough. This argument will always be possible, as it cannot in principle be disproved.

There was, nevertheless, at least one economy, that of the former GDR, which was exposed to a harsh, sudden shock – with devastating effect. Only some of the recommended components of shock therapy were applied, however. At a stroke, monetary union brought about convertibility, opened the economy up to the global market and created freedom in setting prices. However, contrary to the prescription, the national debt – now covering the whole of Germany – was substantially driven up. Subsidies were removed, if at all, in trust agency style (*Treuhand*), i.e. with many subsidies woven into the privatisation process. Wages were not kept in check, but instead gradually adjusted to western German levels (until the adjustment process got bogged down). Wage adjustments, together with the 1:1 currency parity, meant that the vast majority of existing firms were unable to transform themselves into capitalist enterprises, or not at least without drastic reductions in their levels of employment and production, without going into the red for a lengthy period, and thus without subsidies.

This kind of selective application of shock therapy, amounting to the shock without the therapy, had one clear result: barring support from outside, it was not possible to transform former state-owned concerns successfully into capitalist enterprises; but without subsidies there was insufficient incentive to attract foreign companies: 'There is no precedent, either in other transformed societies or in the history of the capitalist states, for such a politically induced handicap to economic concerns.'[12]

What were the intentions behind this selective shock, ordered from outside, by the government of the old Federal Republic? With the currency change, which had the effect of a massive revaluation of the GDR mark, the government ignored the opinions of economic experts,

but enriched the former GDR population with respect to their experience of their role as consumers. Thus there are grounds to suspect –
with elections looming in the foreseeable future – a populist calculation
combined with economic naivety, as amply demonstrated by the chan-
cellor with his glib talk of 'blooming landscapes'. Alternatively, or in
addition, it could be assumed, with a slight pinch of conspiracy theory
in the Stamokap vein, that the object was to ruin the GDR's economy
even more then the GDR regime had already done on its own, thus
leaving it ripe for takeover by capital from western Germany.
However, as such ruin meant that, apart from real estate, there was little
scope left for wealth creation, a different interpretation of these events
is more plausible. The government in Bonn was fully aware 'that introduction of the western German currency would mean that GDR
companies would at a stroke no longer be competitive', as Schäuble,
one of the main protagonists, commented in retrospect.[13] 'We could
also imagine just how dramatically visible this intervention would
become.' It was political motives, rather than economic ones, which
made Bonn opt for the shock.

The rapid transition to the institutional system of western Germany,
opted for along with economic, monetary and social union on 1 July
1990, was intended to protect this very institutional system – in
exchange for promising the inhabitants of the GDR prosperity –
against the pressure for change arising from the unification process.
'The political logic of shock therapy consists of committing oneself to
necessary, interdependent, but simultaneously unpopular measures, the
benefits of which will only be discernible some time in the future.'[14]
This commitment 'allowed the political elite to guarantee an important
self-imposed subsidiary condition, namely the preservation of the
federal German institutional system from any impulses for change
which might occur as a consequence of unification.'[15] In face of the
threat posed to the integrity and continuity of the west German institutional system by the unification process, the economic risk resulting
from the shock was deemed to be of secondary importance. The
economic transformation by way of destruction could be accompanied
at the political- administrative level by the transfer of the institutional
model of the old Federal Republic to the new *Länder*. Of course, the
institutions also had to be operated by western German personnel, at
least at the management level. 'If importing the west German institutional system was the price for a materially comfortable path to transformation, then the monopolisation imposed by an imperial gesture of

the new sphere of action by western Germany's corporate players was the inevitable corollary of the institutional transfer.'[16]

Although the institutional transfer resulted in technical success under these conditions, the result was a deficit in the skills required to operate these institutions, which were new to GDR citizens. And the necessary learning processes were rendered more difficult by the paternalistic attitude adopted by the players from western Germany. All this was bound to give rise to an ambivalent situation. On the one hand, there was the promise of prosperity, as long as those sectors of the population who were sentenced to economic passivity (the unemployed, those who had taken early retirement) could also be made to swallow it; but on the other hand, owing to the former GDR population's lack of opportunity to handle their new institutions in an independent manner, the transfer of institutions and management personnel has led to deficits in articulating their interests, and hence to the frequently-noted experience of 'colonialisation'.

Thus the shock process initially succeeded, to the extent that the old Federal Republic's politico-administrative and judicial institutions were transferred virtually unaltered in their existing form, and the problems of adjustment were 'absorbed' by generous assistance in the wake of the so-called 'rich uncle solution' to the transformation problem. This solution will come under pressure if the hoped-for economic upturn is delayed too long and the institutions in the 'acceding area' fail to be effective. The costs of unification will then be increased as a result of the repercussions that will inevitably follow for the West. Western German institutions, which were supposed to be kept stable as a result of the shock transition process, are now to some extent being overtaxed. This raises the question of how stable the institutional system of the old Federal Republic will remain following its transfer to the new *Länder*, and when the problems associated with unification have reached their peak.

State of the transformation

The transformation process in the former GDR can be considered from various points of view – economic, political or cultural. I shall confine myself in what follows to the economic dimension. How great is the economic distance between the eastern and western part of the country approximately five years (for the time being, most relevant data only cover the period up to 1995) after unification? The transformation of the former GDR is neither completed, nor is it yet successful, in the sense of constituting a form of convergence with the situation in the old Federal Republic. The simplest indicator of the continuing 'adjustment gap' is economic strength. Labour productivity (measured as real GDP per completed hour of work) is around 40 per cent of the western German figure.[17] From 1991 to 1995, the 'acceding area's share of industrial employment in Germany as a whole (gainfully employed persons in manufacturing industry) fell from 20.7 per cent to 17.9 per cent,[18] while the share of the gross value added product in manufacturing industry rose from 7 per cent to 11.3 per cent.

Similar values result for the overall economy. With an 18.5 per cent share of the gainfully employed, the new *Länder* contributed 10.9 per cent to the GDP of Germany as a whole in 1995.[19] Unemployment remained substantially higher in the east than it did in the west, with the official rate of unemployment in the east being 15.9 per cent (as opposed to 9.6 per cent in the west) in December 1996. If market economy criteria are used as the basis for determining what is to be regarded as a normal working relationship (whereby persons in job creation schemes, continuing training, short-time work and early retirement count as hidden unemployed), then the figure comes out at 25 per cent. Almost one in every two jobs (for dependent employees) has been lost since the end of 1989.[20]

Table 1   Manufacturing Industry – Share of the New Länder

Year	Gainfully Employed	Gross Value Added
1991	20.7	7
1992	16.8	8
1993	16.7	9.5
1994	17.4	10.7
1995	17.9	11.3

Source: Federal Statistical Office, *Collected Tables on the Economic and Social Situation in the new Länder*, 3/96, p15, 201.

Despite these problems, the (available) income of private households in the eastern part of the country rose rapidly from 40 per cent

147

of the western German level in 1990 to 68 per cent by the middle of 1995. The fact that average incomes and the average standard of living rose so markedly, and so much more rapidly than economic productivity, is due mainly to the transfer of purchasing power from the west to the east (see below).

Though, overall, it can be said that the rate of development of economic strength in the new *Länder* is improving considerably, the distance between west and east remains substantial. This is no wonder, as developing an economy which will be able to compete in the global market costs a great deal of time, not least because the necessary capital stock is expensive, and cannot be suddenly created out of nothing. According to the Council of Experts, 'the equipment owned per inhabitant ... at the start of 1991 [attained] only 26 per cent of the west German level, though this ratio rose to 43 per cent by the start of 1995.'[21] In its latest assessment, the Council of Experts estimates that 'the capital stock in the business sector of the new federal *Länder* ... calculated per inhabitant only reached just over 60 per cent of the west German level in 1995.[22] Moreover, private investment (per inhabitant) in the new *Länder* rose only with considerable delay to a level above that of the old *Länder* (and only from 1994 in the case of equipment). In view of these figures (five years after unification!), and owing to the weak growth rate which also dogged the new *Länder* last year and during the current year, it is easy to work out that the east's convergence in terms of economic productivity, as aimed for (and promised) by the politicians, will take some years yet – if it is ever achieved at all. This fact has now been conceded by the government. Bonn's professionally optimistic special envoy to the east, Ludewig, is assuming a catching-up period of fifteen years (*Tagesspiegel*, 20 September 1996). If, as we sporadically hear in particular from FDP (Free Democratic Party) circles, state support for development in the east were to be withdrawn, then the goal of convergence will in any case be abandoned. To boost productivity to the extent necessary for the convergence of economic productivity, investments need to be made in the form of independent investments by companies in eastern Germany, which has not happened for the sole reason that these companies lack sufficient profits. This is no wonder, given the average wage unit costs, which amount to over 160 per cent of the wage unit costs of the western federal *Länder*.[23] In large areas of processing industry (including mining), until 1994 production costs still significantly exceeded GDP.[24] Capitalism cannot work like this.

Financial burdens of unification

West-East transfers and their financing

In 1995, state cash payments to the new *Länder* (including East Berlin) amounted to around DM160 billion (SVR 1996/6, p. 151) net (i.e. after deduction of revenue from the new *Länder*).[25] This is equivalent to over DM5,600 per year per gainfully employed person in the west (or over DM2,500 per inhabitant), thus representing substantial proportions of income.

Table 2 West-East Transfers, Public Sector Payments in Billions of DM

Year	GDP (New Länder)	Net Transfers	as % of GDP (New Länder)
1991	206	105.7	51.3
1992	262.6	131	49.9
1993	308.6	135.9	44
1994	346.9	130.9	37.7
1995	376.1	161	42.8

Source: SVR 1995/96, p151

However, taxpayers do not at present incur the full burden of these transfer payments; what they incur is for the most part the interest burden for the growing national debt. Although, in view of the tiresome moaning about the so-called Solidarity Surcharge (*Solidarzuschlag*) it seems unbelievable, the overall tax burden in the Federal Republic of Germany has not gone up in proportion to the increase in the national debt caused by unification.

Table 3 Taxes and Social Security Contributions (as % of GDP)

Year	Direct Tax	Indirect Tax	Overall Tax	Social security contributions
1991	11.6	12.6	24.2	18
1992	11.9	12.7	24.5	18.3
1993	11.5	13	24.5	18.9
1994	11.1	13.4	24.4	19.3
1995	11.3	12.9	24.2	19.4

Source: DIW 35/96, p578

The tax burden remains stable for the economy as a whole (as in the overall history of the Federal Republic of Germany), despite the substantial additional costs arising from unification. There are shifts between direct and indirect taxes (with the latter gaining in emphasis) and there continues to be an ongoing progressive reduction in tax revenue from business activity and assets (*cf.* footnote 2) at the expense of payers of income tax. How can financial policy specialists keep the overall tax burden constant and still finance the considerable additional costs of unification since 1989/90?

The inevitable conclusion suggested by the parallel development of the new *Länder* transfer capacity and rising national debt is that 'the tremendous rise in national debt is primarily a reflection of the high transfer payments which have flowed from western Germany's public sector budgets to eastern Germany . . . Overall, between 1991 and 1995 over DM700 billion flowed from west to east in the form of transfers from regional authorities. Including social security and the *Treuhandanstalt*, the figure works out at DM970 billion, or an annual average of almost DM200 billion.[26]

As most of the financial resources gained from national borrowing are channelled to east German households in the form of welfare benefits and are used for consumption, this borrowing means that those particular (saved) parts of people's income which have been allocated by western German economic players as being not for current consumption, but for the creation of capital, are not being used for their specific designated purpose and are again being used by the state to satisfy its current needs. As a result, the creation of capital intended by the state's creditors, and funded through their savings, is not taking place. However, along with their government bonds they acquire a claim on a proportion of current tax receipts – and obviously for many companies this seems more worthwhile than making investments.

What does it actually mean when the state is using an ever-growing proportion of its tax receipts to make interest payments and repay its debts? Interest payments are only a simulation investment income when the state – as is now the case in the Federal Republic of Germany – uses the loans it has received for the purposes of consumption. Its assets are used up. This can work well, because, despite the continuing demands on the state, it still retains the capacity to appropriate for itself a part of the current social revenue in the form of taxes and use it for interest payments.[27] The interest payments thus amount to a transfer of income from taxpayers to the holders of government bonds. In this way, the – normally economically active – taxpayers are deprived of part of the return on their productivity in favour of profitable income. And if there are any complaints about the lack of productivity incentives in the Federal Republic of Germany's economy, then this would be the right place to make them.

Burden from social security
In contrast to the substantial constancy of the tax burden, an unbroken growth trend in social security contributions can be detected (see Table 3). However, for the social groups burdened with these contributions, this trend is not offset by any additional welfare benefits, with the exception of the newly introduced care insurance: in most cases the growth is going hand in hand with a decline in benefits.

The uses to which the growing social security contributions are put can be roughly gleaned from the directional trend of the so-called social expenditure ratio (volumes of the welfare budget presented as a percentage of GDP), if western and eastern Germany are considered separately (to the extent that this is possible).

The social expenditure ratio hardly varies for western Germany (its 1990 figure of 29.5 per cent was the lowest since 1973), whereas in eastern Germany it has doubled. It can only have reached this size in the east as a result of having been fed by transfers from the west. For example, in March 1996 the adjusted total of contributions paid to the Federal Labour Office (*Bundesantstalt für Arbeit*) amounted to DM 964.8 million, while its outgoings totalled DM3.19 billion, plus DM 547 million in unemployment benefit financed by the federal government.[28]

Table 4   Social Expenditure Ratio

Year	West	East
1991	29	60.9
1992	29.4	67.9
1993	30.3	64.6
1994	30.2	60

Source: Tegtmeier 1996, p5

The fact that there is now universal grumbling (even in the trade unions' monthly journals[29]) about excessive welfare benefits (or excessive wage-level costs, which amount to the same thing within the context of the existing social security system), and complaints about exorbitant public expenditure, can only be explained in terms of people suppressing their awareness of the problems created by unification. Excluding the effects of the burdens imposed by unification, and those of mass unemployment, which has not been restricted to east Germany, the increase in welfare benefits has been quite undramatic.

Firstly, the fact is that the deficits in the social security systems – with the exception of compulsory health insurance – and the resumption of an increase in public expenditure were caused primarily by unification. This becomes clear when the debit and credit balances of the social security systems are compared.

Table 5   Debt and Credit Balances of Social Security Systems (in billions of DM

	1991	1992	1993	1994	1995
Pension Schemes					
West	11.2	10.8	0.5	8.5	9.0
East	0.7	−1.4	−7.9	−12.3	−15.4
total	11.9	9.4	−7.4	−3.8	−6.4
Health Insurance					
West	−5.2	−9.1	9.1	2.3	−6.0
East	2.6	−0.2	1.3	−0.2	−2.0
total	−2.6	−9.3	10.4	2.1	−8.0
Unemployment Insurance					
West	20.2	21.7	15.1	19.3	17.0
East	−20.8	−35.5	−39.5	−29.6	−23.0
total	−0.6	−13.8	−24.4	−10.3	−6.0

Source: Meinhardt 1995, p695

Secondly, again with the exception of health insurance, there is no apparent evidence that welfare benefits, measured as proportions of GDP, are now still exorbitantly high.

Table 6   Social expenditure ratios (by welfare budget as per cent of GDP)

Year	Overall	Age	Health	Family
1982	33.4	13.2	10.4	4.5
1989	30.7	12.4	10.1	4.0
1990	29.5	11.9	10.1	3.6
1991	31.5	12.1	10.7	4.1
1992	32.7	12.4	11.2	4.2
1993	33.6	12.9	11.2	4.2
1994	33.3	13.1	11.2	4.0

Source: BMAS 1996, 7.2, till 1989 former federal territory, from 2nd half of 1990 Germany as a whole.

In Table 6, the social expenditure ratio of approximately 33 per cent, which was typical during the social-liberal coalition government period starting in the mid-1970s, is given for 1982, the first year of the Kohl era, as a comparative figure. By 1989, the Kohl/Waigel government had managed to reduce this ratio (and also its separate components) significantly. The resumption of its rise in the 1990s was caused by unification and unemployment, but is not exceeding what used to be the normal level.

The same also applies to pensions (see the 'age' column). This may be surprising, in view of the present debate about pensions. But this debate, with its emphasis on the 'demographic threat' posed by the foreseeable ageing of German society, has, all in all, more the character of a scenario painted by the insurance company lobby than any objective core of truth. The fact that health insurance contributions are going up in the 1990s is unrelated to the fact that German society as a whole is spending a relatively larger share of its wealth on providing for those who are no longer gainfully employed (between 1975 and 1983 the ratios were on average higher than in recent years[30]). It is, however, related to the fact that this share is deducted from the income of those individuals covered by social security, with this income having shrunk in relative terms as a result of unemployment and the reduction in the wage ratio.

The present scaremongering about the possibility of an inability to honour the generation contract, and the belief that either the system needs to be changed in favour of one which covers capital, or the compulsory pension scheme needs to be limited to a basic provision, is so astonishingly transparent that one can only shake one's head in disbelief at just how seriously such proposals are being taken. If the issue really revolved around demographic factors, then the debate would need to proceed in an entirely different manner. Firstly, demographic changes take effect only very slowly, and in tiny stages. Furthermore, the truth of Mackenroth's old saw, dating from the discussion of pensions reform in the 1950s still applies: whatever a society uses to provide for its old people has to be set aside from its current national product, regardless of whether the aged have acquired their claims in the form of contributions paid to the compulsory pension scheme or to private insurance schemes or in some other way, e.g. via their status as citizens. For current consumption, claims are balanced against nothing other than actual [sic] current production. There is no escaping the rising 'age burden quotient' (unless via claims directed abroad), even if representatives of the insurance industry would like to see things differently. Therefore, some form of generation contract will always be necessary – and though the young generation now entering its earning phase can rescind it in its present form, such a move follows a self-fulfilling prophecy: anyone who regards provision for the aged as uncertain is merely saying that, theoretically, it is not possible to know what the next generation will do. To conclude from this that the generation contract cannot work, and to cancel it, only means provoking the next generation into treading a similar path. Instead of adding fuel to such uncertainties, it could be explained that pensions are (always only) as secure as the social consensus on what provisions to make for the aged and the means with which to do so.

Thirdly, thought should be given to the consequences of the cuts in welfare benefits which are repeatedly being called for, or of a reduction in the government's rate of expenditure. For economists trained in cyclical thinking, the result is obvious: 'The trend in the government's rate of expenditure and taxation is the clear outcome of the particular nature of German unification, and the transfer problem thus created. If a causal therapy is considered appropriate, and the aim is to bring down the government's rate of expenditure, then transfers to eastern Germany must be reduced. If the eastern German market for western German business is to be maintained, then industry and the banks must step in in place of the state, and close the gap between eastern Germany's exports and imports.'[31]

However, this gives rise to a new problem. The government's

attempts to make demands on companies to step in, via the obligations incumbent on their associations (for example, via the so-called 'Banking Initiative' or the 'Buying Offensive for the New *Länder*') have largely failed, in contrast to previous actions undertaken in the Federal Republic of Germany's early history. The associations in the eastern part of the country have lost their organisational capacities, with the result that individual commitments negotiated on a corporatist basis by the associations' leaders can no longer be honoured at grass roots level.[32]

However, if companies do not – voluntarily and coordinated via their associations – step into the breach which is bound to be created by the state's withdrawal, then they will inevitably suffer considerable losses, because demand in eastern Germany will vanish to a large extent:

> Evidently, the general limitation of welfare state benefits in Germany as a whole is regarded as a variation, avoiding such knock-on effects, without taking any special account of transfers from west to east . . . Yet this path is also misleading. Wherever and whenever the state makes savings to compensate for the increase in expenditure arising from the transfers to eastern Germany, and thus to reduce the rate of taxation without enlarging public deficits, negative repercussions for the business sector will be inevitable . . . The only thing that can be achieved is a redistribution of the primary burden resulting from German unification. When for example the state introduces welfare cuts, those who pay for the additional burden resulting from unification – a burden from which many people in both the western and eastern parts of Germany are benefiting in some way or other – are overwhelmingly those dependent on welfare state benefits. There is no justification whatsoever for this.'[33]

Supply-side policy

Here, though, even the economist trained in cyclical thinking is mistaken. There *is* certainly some justification for this policy, albeit one which might no longer be regarded as particularly legitimate in public discussion. And economists arguing in favour of supply-side policy refer to this justification constantly, saying that the climate for investment in Germany as a production site has to be improved. To this end, the taxes levied on companies need to be reduced even further, as do wage costs, particularly ancillary wage costs. In other words, social security contributions must be reduced.

This is a familiar recipe, but it does not work. Social security is already extremely heavily burdened by the fact that a relevant proportion of the costs of unification were passed on to it, while at the same time mass unemployment caused a considerable drop in tax receipts as well as greater expenditure. Furthermore, the shift in income distribution in favour of profits which has been taking place since 1982 has, by reducing the share of wages in the national income, diminished the base variable on which social security contributions are calculated. The extent of the shift in distribution in the Kohl/Waigel/Lambsdorf era is clear from the trend in the composition of the available income of private households.

Table 7   Composition of Available Income of Private Households (in %, without non-deducted profits)

Year	Net Wages & Salaries	Profit & Investment Income	Transfers Received	Transfers Made
1982	51.4	26.3	27	-4.7
1991a	46.7	33.2	24.1	-3.9
1991b	48.2	30.2	25.3	-3.7
1992	47.4	30.5	26.1	-4.0
1993	46.7	30.3	27.2	-4.2
1994	45.0	31.8	27.5	-4.3
1995	43.7	33.0	28.0	-4.7

Source: BMAS 1996, 1.17 (till 1991a old Federal Republic, thereafter Germany as a whole)

For 1995, the share of net wages and profits in private households' available income reached its lowest level in the history of the Federal Republic of Germany, whilst the previous high for incomes from business activity and assets (of 1991a) was almost reached again. The level of transfers received, which was driven up following unification (from 1991b) may also have been a record (the term 'transfer' refers essentially to transfers of welfare payments).

The role played by the state in contributing to this trend is reflected quite clearly by a comparison of both the net ratios of wages and salaries, and of profits and investment income. These net ratios indicate what proportion, on average, of the respective gross income is left after the deduction of direct taxes and – in the case of wage earners – social security contributions; in other words, after the state's intervention.

Table 8 Net Ratios

Year	Profits and Investment Income	Wages and Salaries
1982	79.1	70.6
1991a	85.3	67.5
1991b	84.5	68.5
1995	89	64.3

Source: BMAS (1996, 1.10 & 1.14)

As is obviously considered to be correct in terms of supply-side policy, the state is encroaching less and less on profits and investment income, but in contrast is encroaching more and more on the incomes of wage earners, probably because they are not major contributors. However, the clearly detectable, state-aided, improvement in companies' opportunities for generating profits is not producing the results expected by supply-side policy advocates. Evidently higher profits are not – or are no longer – being translated into higher investments, and hence into more employment. In Keynesian terms, the following applies: if the effectively anticyclical 'built-in stabilisers' of incomes fed out of welfare transfers are reduced on the demand side, as caused by various programmes of austerity measures, this cannot fail to have repercussions for companies' expectations in terms of sales, and hence of profits. Their capacities will remain under-utilised. So why invest, other than in the form of programmes of replacement and rationalisation investments?

This question highlights a fundamental failing of so-called supply-side policy: it can be granted that it takes account of the experience of the state's failure. But what is the justification for the permanent faith placed in businesses and businesspeople, when for them it is nothing short of logical to continually push up the price of their cooperation?[34] In any case, the Federal Republic of Germany's experiences of what has now been over fifteen years of supply side-oriented economic policy no longer justify this faith. Although the profit-yield relationship has constantly improved since 1982[35] – apart from the slump in 1992–93 – the investment ratio is on the decrease. The investment ratio (which in this context means the ratio of investment in equipment and investments in economic infrastructure to GDP) fell during the 1974 crisis by approximately 11 per cent, then recovered again to fluctuate around 12 per cent; rose in the late 1980s and in the wake of the unification boom to just under 14 per cent (a figure which was finally exceeded in the golden age phase); but now – in the 1990s – it is significantly below the figures applying in the days before the supply-side policy era. It is becoming clear that the Kohl-Waigel-Lambsdorf project is ailing: however high profits may be, they do not automatically bring investments in their wake. Instead, such a policy opens up the possibility of blackmail. If investment is not forthcoming, that is merely a reason to call for higher profits, and to make policy concessions accordingly. Why should businesses seeking to maximise their profits stray from this strategy? The 'production site conditions' can still be improved further, even if the argument that companies are handicapped by excessive taxation and wage levels – including excessive social security contributions – is wrong. Where taxes are concerned, though nominal maximum tax rates are in part considerably lower in comparable industrialised countries, the rate of return from corporation taxes is higher. In 1994, Germany's trade tax, corporation tax and corporate wealth tax yielded 2.2 per cent of GDP, at a marginal cost of 62.3 per cent. In the USA, with a marginal cost of withheld profits of 45.3 per cent, tax receipts yielded 2.6 per cent of GDP; in the UK, with a marginal cost of 33 per cent, the figure was 2.7 per cent. The notion that lower tax rates generate more income for the state is not due to some mystical property of a Laffer curve; it is simply attributable to the fact that the Federal Republic of Germany's legislation offers ample scope for tax avoidance, and ample use is made of this.

As for wages and ancillary wage costs, the international comparison of wages by the media's usual method of converting everything into dollars is misleading. The crucial factor for determining international competitiveness is relative wage unit costs, which depend on labour productivity and exchange rates.[36] However, if the observable wage trend in Germany in an international comparison brings a revaluation of the German mark in its wake, then competitiveness in export markets can hardly improve. During the first half of the 1990s, such a revaluation of the German mark did take place. A comparison of the G5 countries leads to the following result: 'The notion of Germany as a high-wage country could not be substantiated: high hourly wage levels appear justified if labour productivity and working-hour productivity are taken into account. At the level of the economy as a whole, real wage unit costs are neither high, nor have they risen at a rate greatly above the average in recent years. In relation to nominal wage unit costs in other countries, converted into German marks, Germany's nominal wage unit costs have in contrast significantly increased. However, this is not a labour cost problem, but the inevitable consequence of the revaluation of the German mark.'[37] The associations representing business interests reacted to the publication of this finding in the same hysterical manner as they did to that of a similar finding by the DIW (German Institute for Economic Research) in 1995, where the answer to the question of whether western Germany had a production site problem was 'no'.[38] The whole grand, profit-oriented topicalisation of the production site issue had been called into question by economists who had no right to do so.

Self-paralysis of the economy

A more plausible explanation for what is at the root of Germany's economic problems, apart from the burden of unification, could make use of a somewhat unorthodox version of the NAIRU (non-accelerating inflation rate of unemployment) concept. Advocates of the NAIRU concept postulate a connection between the levels of unemployment and inflation, which unlike the old Philips curve has the refinement that a certain level of unemployment is necessary to keep the inflation rate stable. Empirical NAIRU estimates for the Federal Republic of Germany (Langmantel 1996, p.11) conclude that it rises in stages, i.e. ever more unemployment is required to stem wage demands accelerated by inflation.[39] Interestingly, profits do not figure among the key parameters of NAIRU (or only do so indirectly, via Companies' utilisation of their capacities). When there is an observable reduction in the wage ratio and a shift in income tax distribution in favour of profits which depresses wages, with attempts to increase wages stifled in accordance with monetary policy to damp down inflation, then higher unemployment appears as an unintentional side-effect of the interaction between government-supported attempts to maximise profits and measures induced by the Bundesbank to control inflation. If the share of profits in the national income is to be constantly increased in real terms, then unemployment also has to increase, in order to reduce the rise in wage-earners' latent readiness for conflict, resulting from pressure exerted on wages. The fact that the economy as a whole is stagnating, since profits are not being translated into domestic invest-ment, does not seem to concern those enjoying income derived from profits, provided they can blame this stagnation on the existing institu-tions of the welfare state. However it is wrong to impute such blame. It is the problems of unification which are putting a strain on the German welfare state, notwithstanding the fact that some of its compo-nents are – and will remain – in need of reform. The refusal to recog-nise the problems of unification as such can probably only be explained by the fact that such recognition would also imply a certain commit-ment to take on some of these burdens. Finally, this is not a question of a 'national' problem, or of the game of capitalism's usual conflict over distribution. If one is not averse to such strong language, then Germany's economic and political elites could again be accused of 'betraying the nation'.

Class struggle from above?

In the debate over economic policy, the observable symptoms of the crisis, particularly the fiscal crisis and the permanently excessive level of unemployment, are portrayed as if they can be traced to an inade-quate adjustment to the present overall constellation of world markets. It is claimed that inherited, excessive claims lead to forms of rigidity, that excessive regulation prevents rapid and flexible reactions to new challenges and that labour costs are too high, conditioned by the welfare state. The effect of such arguments is to attribute to the welfare state various burdens that are caused mainly by unification, using them as a lever to reconstruct and dismantle the welfare state. The conse-quences at the level of distribution (of functional income) are clear: following the American and British models, a furious state-supported redistribution in favour of profits and investment income is taking place. The costs of this strategy are not that clear: to enforce these distributional changes, the economic and political elites are willing to accept not only excessive unemployment and a serious fiscal crisis, but are also using these to forcibly bring about far-reaching changes in the familiar rules of conflict and cooperation. This is not only changing the players' attitudes towards each other, but also increasing the bitterness of conflicts and the ways in which they are carried out. A lesson of the global economic crisis and the Nazi era which moulded the history of the Federal Republic of Germany was that social policy had to lead society 'beyond the class struggle'.[40] Today there are many indications that things are going backwards again, and that the class struggle is being restarted from above.

Notes

1. D. Teichmann and D. Vesper, *Offentliche Haushalte 1996/97: Finanzpolitik weiterhin auf schmalem Grat*, D/W-Wochenbericht 35/96.
2. Since the 1960s, tax revenue as a percentage of GNP has fluctuated around 23 per cent, ranging from 22.4 per cent (the minimum figure in 1990, prior to German unification) to 25 per cent (the maximum figure in 1977). The figure for 1996 is 22.7 per cent. The income tax burden has risen constantly during this period (for the Kohl era, the figure ranges from 7.8 per cent of GNP in 1982 to 8.2 per cent in 1995), and the tax burden from assessed income tax and corporation tax has constantly fallen (from 3.3 per cent in 1982 to 0.9 per cent in 1995) (BMAS Statistical Handbook 1996, Table 1.23: Tax rates).
3. C. Schäfer, 'Mit falschen Verteilungs-'Götzen' zu echten Standort-problemen, in *WSl-Mitteilungen* 10/96.
4. See R. Köddermann, 'Sind Löhne und Steuern zu hoch?' in *Ifo Schnelldienst*, 20/96; and T. Sarrazin, 'Mit Mut ist eine gute Steuerreform möglich', *FAZ* 110.8.96.
5. For simplicity's sake, I am assuming a partnership between players representing capital owners and entrepreneurs. This is not always appropriate, as the entrepreneurs' opportunities for action and income may be restricted by property owners' opportunities for action and prospective income (and vice versa).
6. A. Przeworski and M. Wallerstein, 'The Structure of Class Conflict in Democratic Capitalist Societies', in *American Political Science Review*, vol. 76, 1982; and Przeworski and Wallerstein, 'Structural Dependence of the State on capital', in *American Political Science Review*, vol. 82, 1988.
7. Differing time scales, depending on individual life prospects, play a role here. For example, an age bias in distribution could be explained by the fact

that rational pensioners tend towards so-called 'bang bang' solutions, throwing their weight behind the radical, short-term realisation of their interests, as they are indifferent to the pension situation of the next or next-but-one generation.

8. Since one still relevant (albeit limited) alternative to having a welfare state take care of non-players is to have them looked after by their family, there is a further difference between the interests of companies and wage-earners where non-players are concerned: Companies do not have sick grandmothers or unemployed sons, so they have no need to fear another form of direct taxation in the event that the social security organised by the state disappears.

9. This is true regardless of the fact that 'social policy has an economic value' (cf. Vobruba, *Der wirtschaftliche Werte der Sozialpolitik*, Berlin 1989) insofar as state-run social security systems can result in greater efficiency and gains in productivity for companies for many reasons (conduct at work, forms of pay, frequency of conflict and settling of any disputes).

10. Particular exceptions, measured in terms of the extent of the provision of the welfare state, are the USA, Japan and Switzerland. The historical peculiarities (migration, late comers, etc.) which account for these exceptions could be identified if need be.

11. P. Pierson, 'The new politics of the welfare state', *ZeS-Arbeitspapier* 3/95, Zentrum für Sozialpolitik, Bremen.

12. H. Wiesenthal, 'Die Transformation der DDR: ökonomische, politische und kognitive Koordinaten', in H. Sahner, (ed) *Transforrnationsprozesse in Deutschland*, Opladen, 1995, p85.

13. Cited in J. Steffen, 'Rentenfinanzen unter dem Einfluss des Arbeitsmarktes', in *WSI-Mitteilungen* 4/96, p222.

14. Wiesenthal, *op.cit.*, p86.

15. *Ibid*, p87.

16. *Ibid*, p93.

17. In its most recent report, the Council of Experts [*Sachverständigenrat*, or SVR] estimates productivity (measured GDP in respective prices per gainfully employed individual) for 1995 at 55.2 per cent, and for 1996 at 56 per cent of the level in western Germany. See SVR 1995/96 und 1996/97, Sachverständigenrat zur Begutachtung der gesamtwirtschaftlichen Entwicklung, Jahresgutachten, Stuttgart, 1975. See also K.D. Bedau, 'Löhne und Gehälter in Ost- und Westdeutschland gleichen sich an, Lohnstückkosten jedoch nicht', *D/W-Wochenbericht* 8/96, p140.

18. In this context, it is interesting that the total number of people employed in industry in Germany as a whole in 1995 was, at 8.35 million, exactly the

same as it had been in the old Federal Republic prior to unification in 1989 (SVR 1996/97, p. 351).

19. Federal Statistical Office, Collected Tables on the Economic and Social Situation in the new *Länder*, 3/96, p13, 203).

20. K.F. Zimmermann, 'Labour Responses to Taxes and Benefits in Germany', in A.B. Atkinson and G.V. Mogensen, (eds), *Welfare and Work Incentives*, Oxford 1993, p20.

21. SVR 1995/6, *op.cit.*, p55.

22. SVR 1996/7, p71.

23. Bedun, *op.cit.*, p140. For a different calculation, see SVR 1996/7, p106.

24. SVR 1996/7, p79.

25. *Ibid*, p15.

26. Teichmann and Vesper, *op.cit.*, p577ff.

27. The state can of course also appropriate the assets of private individuals, e.g. by levying inheritance tax. Although the usual problem of negative productivity incentives does not arise in connection with inheritance taxes (since it is the productivity of the deceased which is being taxed), they are somehow unpopular.

28. W. Tegtmeier, 'Umbau des Sozialsystems für eine wettbewerbsfähige Wirtschaft', in *Ifo Schnelldienst* 24/96.

29. *Cf.* S. Papcke, 'Solidarität oder Sankt-Florians-Prinzip?' in *Gewerkschaftliche Monaishefte*, 11-12/96, pp751, 753.

30. The argument that such generous welfare is no longer 'affordable' means nothing more than that there is no *will* to afford it.

31. H. Flassbeck, 'Die deutsche Vereinigung – ein Transferproblem', in *DIW Vierteljahreshefte zur Wirfschaftsforschung*, Vol.3, 1995, p411.

32. G. Lehmbruch, 'Die Rolle der Spitzenverbände im Transformationsprozess: Eine neoinstitutionalistische Perspektive', in R. Kollmorgen, et al. (eds), *Sozialer Wandel und Akteure in Ostdeutschland*, Opladen, 1996.

33. Flassbeck, *op.cit*, p411.

34. In this respect, the disappearance of the competition between different systems may be significant; at any rate, the competition between countries for investment is certainly so.

35. SVR 1996/7, p302.

36. K. Hübner and A. Bley, *Lohnstückkosten und internationale Wettbewerbsfähigkeit*, Marburg 1996.

37. Köddermann, *op.cit.*, p7ff.

38. DIW 'Hat Westdeutschland ein Standortproblem?' *DIW-Wochenbericht*, 95/38.

39. E. Langmantel, 'Halbierung der Arbeitslosenquote bis 2000?' in *Ifo Schnelldienst* 17-18/96, p11.
40. A. Rüstow, 'Sozialpolitik diesseits und jenseits des Klassenkampfs', in B. Külp and W. Schreiber, (eds), *Soziale Sicherheit*, Köln, 1971.

Japan as the first non-western welfare state

Sadahiko Inoue

The social security system in Japan has shown new developments in the 1990s, and is due to be upgraded, beyond the American standard, to reach the German and Scandinavian one. The prestigious Council on the Social Security System issued a recommendation of signal importance in July 1995, the third such recommendation since World War II, where the goal was explicitly stated to the effect that Japan's social security system be not of the American type but of the German and Scandinavian type.

A specific law addressing the need for high quality care of the aged, financed through public funding, is due to be passed by Japan's parliament on the basis of this recommendation. Adequate long-term care of the aged requires the installation of networks of welfare service provision at the local government level throughout the nation, and this has not been instituted so far. Such a network will be completed, and will start functioning in the whole of Japan in the year 2001, following a few years preparations.

Looking at the contents of these institutional developments, we find ourselves a bit surprised: Japan is becoming the first welfare state in the non-Western world, although Japan's conservative and business elements continue to deny it. I remember reporting to the ETUC/ETUI conference in Dublin in 1993 that Japan was on the threshold of becoming a welfare state. And during the ensuing three years Japan has been coming along this path of providing greater welfare to its citizens, at a time of 'strikingly exceptional low growth' as the OECD Ministerial Conference calls it.

By the beginning of the 1970s Japan had already developed one of the better social security systems in the world in such areas as national pension, medical insurance, unemployment insurance, and occupational hazards insurance. During the 1970s, however, with two oil crises, institutional development faltered temporarily, under pressure from those who claimed a review was in order. Universalism of welfare provision was rejected, and greater responsibility for families emphasised.

Fortunately, in the 1990s, there emerged a societal trend to look back with some remorse at the hitherto excessive emphasis on the industrial development of the country. Unification of the trade union movement by RENGO, as well as the coalition government's assuming power with the participation of the Opposition, also helped this trend to take off. Public opinion, too, was gradually approaching a consensus in demanding a welfare state of Western European standards, particularly with the social care of the aged as an essential ingredient. The 1995 Recommendation of the Council on the Social Security System specifically called for a new stage of social security development, from the stage of poor relief and poverty prevention to that of 'the social institution to guarantee everyone a healthy and secure life throughout his or her life.' Universalism of welfare provision, thus, is upheld. The Recommendation also emphasises that the independence of individuals can be better supported by social security as a means of social cohesion.

Improved social security at a time of economic stagnation

There is also another plan being implemented by local government, the 'Ten-Year Plan for the Improved Welfare for the Aged', started in 1989 and expanded in December 1994. Its initial stage is due for completion by 2001.

It is indeed a big step forward for the social security system to shift its emphasis, from being a means of income redistribution and income guarantee, to the stage of having individual local communities provide the aged with all sorts of social services, like daily meals and a hot bath, in their own ways. (I mention a hot bath, because taking a hot bath is one of the most important basic needs of the Japanese people.) A network of social service provision is being formed now in various parts of the country, through which both the aged and the handicapped are guaranteed access to these services both at home and at specific institutions designed for the purpose, to suit individual preferences and needs. The objective is to enable them to lead as normal a life as possible. These services will be on a similar basis to the compulsory primary education in every community.

Such a trend is never simply an automatic result of a higher stage of economic development. Rather, it is more of a result of various social factors, such as the changing social and family structure, and people's consciousness. Let me be more specific. First, the public is now better aware of the rapid transformation of Japanese society, with fewer children and more older people. An international comparison of the speed at which various societies age tells us the following: it took Sweden 85 years for its proportion of people 65 years of age and above to increase from 10 per cent to 20 per cent of the total population. It took Germany 56 years to do the same. It took Japan merely 32 years to do that. Simple extrapolation of the trend will take Japan to the level of the most aged society in the world by 2010, overtaking Scandinavia. The second social factor is the structural change brought about by an improvement of the status of women and their greater independence, smaller families, and more and more people remaining unmarried. It is because of these factors that Japan is trying to improve its social security in the 1990s despite the prolonged economic stagnation.

However, we must also note that this economic stagnation of the 1990s, and the resulting budgetary constraints, compels the Government to review its fiscal expenditures, including the traditional methods of providing medical care and national pensions, while establishing and consolidating the new welfare services such as those I have just mentioned.

Up until now, both the general tax level and social security contributions and expenditures have remained at about the same level as the United States, because of the relatively slow development of the pension system and the younger demographical composition of the country. As the population ages very rapidly in the coming years, both the general tax level and the social security-related burdens will quickly reach the Western European level.

Conservatives, as well as some in the business community, anticipate a problematic course of events for Japan, with rising taxes and social security burdens leading to lower savings ratios, and then on to lower growth and lower plant and equipment investment, ultimately resulting in the loss of international competitive power. At a time when Japan is only at the threshold of a solid welfare state, there are already critics who claim that public welfare payments should not be universal but limited to certain poor and other socially vulnerable groups. We, on our side, stand on the universalistic principle and maintain that welfare should be a life-support system for everyone. What is needed is not to regress but to come up with a system which can survive economic fluctuations and social changes so that stable benefits can be provided. Regular reviews and reforms of the system after a time will be unavoidable or even necessary, but not from the standpoint of the neo-market approach of leaving the whole of welfare provision to private insurance principles. This is where we stand on this issue. (Here I must also note certain deficiencies in Japan's social security system. In particular, we only have inadequate institutions for child care, as social responsibility for the rearing of children is not part of the social consensus in Japan. This might be the next area of societal reform, as women become more active in the economy and society).

Supplement: social relations in Asia

We all know that Korea is now going through the greatest period of labour unrest that it has experienced in the post-war era. The issue is the revision of labour law, through which a modern industrial relations system is to be established as Korea becomes a member of the OECD. Recent developments in Korea include the following: in the spring of 1996 a tripartite Labour Reform Committee was formed on the basis of a Presidential decree in order to arrive at a consensus on the content of the labour law revision. The management representatives, however, refused to accept plural unions in an enterprise, and the principle of non-intervention by a third party, which was tantamount to the denial of the freedom of association. Furthermore, they adamantly insisted on greater management discretion on issues of redundancy, and greater flexibility in working hours.

At the end of December 1996, they even refused to accept the compromise formulae proposed by members representing public interests, and went on to force a bill through parliament while the Opposition members were absent. The bill was sponsored by the party in power, but incorporated many of the points advocated by employers' representatives. Ever since this irregularity in parliament there have been waves of orderly strikes and demonstrations throughout the country, through close cooperation between the two trade union national centres.

Trade unions in Korea are highly critical of the revised labour law, on account of its dubious stand on plural unions, which has serious implications for the freedom of association. The law also gives greater discretion to management in making workers redundant, in the American style of management, allegedly to better meet economic and technological needs, whereas Korean industrial relations have generally striven to achieve long-term employment. Korean workers are indignant also at the blatant infringement of the tripartite principle between management, labour and the Government. The revised bill was forced to a vote at a year-end night session of the parliament, when no Opposition members were present.

We would also like the rest of the world to be better aware of the more recent Korean situation: there has been a recent trend for democratisation, with the trade union movement taking the lead, dismantling various oppressive measures, and growing ever stronger to be able to organise a long-term campaign nation-wide on labour and political issues in a very difficult overall situation.

It is not only in Korea but in various other Asian nations that social development and democracy are taking notable strides forward, propelled partly by the economic growth since the 1980s. Conspicuous social and institutional progress is occurring in various fields, such as education, medical and health services, social security, and environmental protection.

A World Bank report, *The East Asian Miracle of 1993*, speaks of rapid economic development concurrently accompanied by greater socio-economic equality. This achievement is not unrelated to the progress made in social development and improved legal institutions in these countries. One must note, however, that there is one area of change where the Governments are quite cautious, and therefore progress is slow, and oppression remains, i.e. that of social rights and social movement, in particular industrial relations and the labour movement.

But the general picture that has emerged from various JTUC-RIALS surveys of Asia is one of modern industrial relations spreading gradually, albeit intermingled with some setbacks: industrial democracy, in the broad sense of the word, in the form of collective bargaining and labour-management consultation, is becoming a little more prevalent and is taking root in Asia, except for Continental China. Asia, one might say, is trying to achieve within a short span of ten to thirty years what took the European trade union movement one hundred or even two hundred years to achieve. The ICFTU Asia-Pacific Regional Office (APRO) adopted the Asian Social Charter in 1993, and is in other ways following the suggestions of the ILO Asian Office and APEC Summit meetings, in promoting social aspects of development in various parts of Asia. It is also expected that a greater network of inter-governmental contacts will be established among Asian countries on the issues of social security and environmental protection.

Social development in Asia is altogether on a different level from that in the European Union, with substantial distortions and delays here and there. It should by no means be overlooked, however, that Asia is making steady progress in the social aspects of its development.

Tax and public finance: Some issues from a UK left perspective

Dan Corry

This chapter raises a number of questions that need to be addressed for the formulation of new, and equitable, approaches to public finance.

Public finance

Spending and progressive policies

UK debate has quite often revolved around the issue of how high the ratio of government spending to GDP should be. The Conservatives made a lot of the aim of reducing it, but they actually failed in this. However they have kept it relatively constant at a time when most EU countries saw rising trends (Monck in *PE*).[1] In fact, the idea that there is some sort of glass ceiling on the spending/GDP ratio on economic grounds is hard to assess, at least at the sort of levels that the UK is at the time of writing – around 40 per cent (Cooper in *PE*).

On the other hand, there has been a tendency on the left to assume that the more spent by the public sector, the more progressive the government. This may turn out to be fairly accurate at some stages of history, but work by Tanzi and Schuknecht illustrates what we all suspected: after a certain level of the spending/GDP ratio, further increases do not seem to lead to more progressive outcomes.[2] A more particular version of this is preached by the UK Labour government at present. The leadership now state that they want to spend less on welfare by the end of their first period in office, since spending on welfare is a sign of failure not success.

Off balance sheet financing issues and regulation

All countries engage in off-balance-sheet-funding of what is essentially public infrastructure. By this I mean projects where there is some sort of public-private partnership but control and/or risk (largely) remains with the public sector, and/or the funding in fact comes via tax revenues. Strictly speaking, since there is a public sector liability (contingent or firmer), then the expenditure should be accounted for in the public accounts. But often only elements of it are accounted for – if at all. Interestingly, the process of deciding who has met the Maastricht convergence criteria for EMU has led to an increased focus on such funding arrangements, and it is clear that something counted as public sector in one country is often not so counted in another.

In the UK some of these things have been taken to extremes, in what is known as the Private Finance Initiative (PFI). Here the initial funding is put up by the private sector, which also operates the service (eg, a prison, or a hospital) in exchange for a contractual guarantee of a stream of payments over time (often up to sixty years). There has been much criticism of the PFI.[3] The cost of raising money in the private sector is more expensive than in the public and I have doubts that any extra efficiencies from having the private sector put up the money are outweighing this; the PFI, essentially, simply 'posts bills to the future', making this year's accounts look good, but pre-spending part of the budget for the next thirty years or more; and it tends to privatise decision making, since only projects the private sector are interested in are likely to go ahead. And these drawbacks are all in addition to the usual problems with contractual relationships (various principal-agent problems).

The reality is, however, that with massive constraints on government ability to borrow (formally), it may be that PFI, and its cousins, are the only way of delivering the public infrastructure – and, increasingly, services – that we want. This problem is exacerbated in the UK by Labour's great reluctance to categorise public corporations as being outside government spending totals, partly for good principled reasons, and partly for fear that financial markets will smell a rat.

Rather than taking a position against such wheezes, then, we perhaps need to focus on the end product delivered and try to ensure that the more grotesque misuses of such approaches are minimised.

This probably implies tightening the rules for proving value for money – which might kill some projects. It also means moves to better systems of accounting (as in New Zealand – see Pallot and Ball in *PE*), which might stop manipulation of the figures from being an incentive to act in these ways. Steps to resource accounting are taking place in the UK but there are doubts as to what they will achieve. Certainly they would not totally reveal the net worth position of the UK, which has deteriorated badly as a result of privatisations, and other policies of the last government (Corry and Gray in *PE*).

There are also other ways of trying to leave the financing of public services off the public sector accounts. One is to use regulation to impose duties on private firms to carry out certain social functions, possibly in return for some sort of carrot, like a tax relief. While attractive in some ways, there are dangers with this approach. One is that the whole process becomes increasingly opaque. In reality, duties imposed by regulation raise costs and ultimately use resources so that the citizen pays – either as employee, shareholder or consumer. But transparency is lost (Corry in *PE*). Another danger is that one can be tempted to 'over' regulate in order to entice firms to break out of the regulation by doing something you want. For instance local authorities might be tempted to impose ridiculous development plans so that firms wanting to develop land have to pay a great deal in 'planning gain' to get round them. Similarly, and controversially, Labour has recently tempted BT to be involved in making the information super-highway real in return for ending certain restrictions on its ability to compete against cable companies.

An additional problem is that flexibility is often lost. UK utilities would clearly prefer to present their own plans for helping the long-term unemployed in their area, rather than to pay a windfall tax to central governmment to do the job with that revenue. But letting them do this would have severe drawbacks. Monitoring that the firm actually did what was required would be a nightmare, and creative accountants and PR people would have a field day. The allocation of monies fairly across spatial areas would become more difficult since the private sector would essentially be in the lead. In addition, it is not clear that business likes this general approach much more than it does direct taxes. For instance, in the UK, the Labour Party's old policy of imposing a training levy on firms, with exemptions for those investing a certain proportion of payroll in training, did not make it popular!

A last way of avoiding public accounts is to delegate more and more to community, intermediate and self-help groups, under the rhetoric of decentralisation and giving power to the people. The problem here is the usual one of equity and of those in most need being least able to help themselves.

EMU and the growth and stability pact (GSP)

As is well known, to join EMU countries have to reduce their deficit to 3 per cent of GDP. Further, the GSP is to govern certain aspects of fiscal policy for countries inside EMU. In practice it will probably become the standard for all EU countries, in or out. Some on the left see this as inherently anti-progressive and especially anti-Keynesian. And there is certainly a danger that it does act in a deflationary way.

However, so far, the details leave room for common sense. We know that the 3 per cent is not a binding entrance fee (although the politics of letting in some who miss it and not others are horrendous – especially in Germany). In addition, the GSP is not quite as hard as it looks. If the deficit as a percentage of GDP is greater than 3 per cent then this is allowed if GDP has fallen by 2 per cent. And if GDP has fallen between 2 and 0.75 per cent then this may be allowed. But in fact, since the 0.75 per cent figure is in a resolution not a regulation, ECOFIN (voting on QMV) could decide not to punish even if GDP growth is above –0.75 per cent. If the deficit is considered excessive then countries are given four months to take action to reduce the deficit. If no adequate steps are taken, sanctions can be imposed within ten months of the time the figure came out. These can be postponed if the country does start taking steps. Indeed there is still great ambiguity on all this.

The sanctions are non-interest bearing deposits with the EU of 0.2 per cent GDP plus 0.1 per cent for every 1 per cent of GDP deficit over 3 per cent – up to a maximum of total deposit of 0.5 per cent. If the deficit is still 'excessive' after two years, these deposits become a fine.[4]

The basic point the left has to come to terms with, however, is that it is not necessarily progressive to run big deficits for prolonged periods. A commitment to make sure that – on average – the deficit is not overly large should not be regarded as the property of the right. First, a budget deficit tells you the difference between spending and revenue, and puts no restriction on how big either of these two are. Second, there is an error in thinking that tough deficit ceilings mean one can no longer use Keynesian policies. As recent work by Barry Eichengreen shows, if deficits averaged zero, then the swings in the deficit in recessionary times that most EU countries have historically had would almost always have come in under the 3 per cent ceiling.[5] It is therefore no surprise that average deficits *below* this level are implied by new Labour's commitment to the 'golden rule' of public finance (borrow only for investment), and to keep a stable debt/GDP ratio.

The problems are, of course, the speed at which countries are having to hit such targets, the fact that having the same targets on deficits for countries, irrespective of their starting debt/GDP positions is mad, and the nonsense of making the timetable irrespective of cyclical conditions. The optimists (me) see these kinds of issues as being taken on board in practice if not totally in the letter: the pessimists see them as leading to doom and gloom.

Efficiency of spending money

For various well-known (if exaggerated) reasons, public sector provision of services has some tendencies to inefficiency, lack of innovation and producer capture. There is debate on the pros and cons of moves away from public sector provision (see Jackson in *PE* for a hostile view: most other authors in *PE* are more sympathetic). Overall, it seems that the question of who should provide services should be an open one, with decisions on what should be done depending on issues such as the nature of the usual principal-agent problems, as well as more long term strategic issues. Getting regulation right in these areas is crucial and too often neglected.

However, one advantage of shifting provision to the private sector is that the concept of state action no longer becomes confused with inefficient service delivery. In some ways the new 'contract state' emerging in the UK may rescue the idea of state action from its associations with failure and incompetence (Corry in *PE*).

Raising money

How optimistic should we be?

The left has tended to get itself depressed by believing that tax resistance among the population is enormous, and that, therefore, any ambitions that we have that depend on raising money first have to be scaled down.

In the first place we should not be overawed by the task. We need to recognise that in the UK tax burdens have *not* reduced: they have increased. There has been a switch to indirect taxes. On the whole these are, of course, less progressive, but if it is the case that revenue can be raised only through them, then progressive packages can be assembled.[6] Second, some believe that people are now ready to pay more taxes even in the form of income taxes. Kellner, in *PE*, argues that the trend is very much for more taxes. He explains the fact that Labour has lost several elections not on the tax issue, but because, unfortunately, the party that is associated in people's minds with tax increases has also been associated in their minds with economic incompetence. Others doubt that the evidence is that strong (see, eg, Cooper and Corry, intro, in *PE*).

Public views in expenditure vary by sector

The problem of raising money may be less if money is spent where people want it. Work in *PE*, by Hall *et al*, shows big variances over subject and by things such as income level. Such disaggregation is needed if policies are to be better targeted.

Perhaps not surprisingly, higher income groups do not favour spending on unemployment benefit and other measures to aid those without work. Keeping higher income groups tied into this system is a vital mission for the left and much of the welfare reform vogue can be seen as an attempt to convince the non-poor that their taxes that go on benefits are well spent.

It is astonishing, too, how money within public services is often spent with little regard to what the user actually values. It is small wonder we cannot therefore maximise support for public services. Yet techniques are now available to elicit whether people want marginal funds to go, for instance, on cleaner trains, or more trains (Cave in *PE*).

One thing which is clearly emerging is that demands from public services are changing. As wealth increases, many – particularly the middle classes – are demanding higher quality and more choice in their services, including public services. They are – it seems – willing to pay for these things for themselves, but, crucially, do not appear to be prepared to pay for these things for everyone else, particularly the poor. This means that one must face the issue of how to provide services to the standards required by the middle classes, or face mass opt-out by the middle classes into, for example, private health cover. These problems are not insurmountable but do raise difficult issues for the left. For instance, we may be happy for people to top up for 'hotel' services in hospitals (eg, a TV or private room) but what about certain non-essential operations (Cooper and Corry, intro, in *PE*)?

Hypothecation and asking citizens more

One view of how to crack the tax resistance problem is to go for hypothecated taxes. The case against this approach is strong on efficiency, fairness, transparency and other grounds. However, elements of such approaches may well be needed to gain support and to rebuild trust between citizens and government. They may also be necessary if we are to see a switch towards green taxes.

What we can certainly try to do is to engage the public more in the debates about spending allocation across areas. For instance, citizens' juries can open up debate and help enfranchise the public on allocation issues at all levels.[7]

Green taxes

The future is undoubtedly green. Environmental taxes have both economic justification and (potential) popular support. They probably have fewer macroeconomic dis-benefits than other ways of raising money and – carefully handled – need not be regressive. There are also arguments for double dividends if revenues are used, for example, to cut labour taxes.[8]

However, popular support will depend on these taxes genuinely helping the environment, and not simply being seen as easy revenue raisers. Finance Ministries will have to actually be green and not just pretend to be!

Radical moves to fund public services: private sector and Community Funds

If the problem of funding arises partly because, in areas like health and education, expenditure demands rise faster than growth – due to labour intensity, ageing populations, etc (so that a static share of taxes in GDP is not enough) – then in the long term radical lateral thinking and new solutions will be needed.

The right agenda is a simple one of privatisation. The left, too, will not be able to completely ignore the role of private finance in keeping such services going, whether this is via private provision with public funding, compulsory savings schemes, user charges (outside core areas) or other means. The task will be to make sure that such changes are brought in in ways which avoid them leading to the development of social inequity.

Another way of approaching the issues is to note that share prices have vastly outstripped GDP in recent years. If the state had taken a stake in a proportion of firms listed on the stock exchange they would have had a very good return which could have been used to fund state services. Thus the core mission of a left government, which is to make sure that public and merit goods are provided, would have been more easily secured.[9] Such ideas find echoes in thoughts of, for instance, allowing government to invest pensions fund money in the markets, as an alternative to full privatisation. Such a stake would carry no voting rights (thus is nothing to do with old left ideas of directing the activities of the private sector) and might even be managed at arm's length, fully commercially, with the trustees simply handing over the money made to the Government at intervals.

This agenda of course demands some way of starting up the fund. Various ideas have been floated by its promoter, Gerry Holtham. One is to use a windfall tax, of the type currently proposed for the utilities in the UK by Labour. Another would be to use money from a wealth tax (in the UK the inheritance tax) to achieve this. There is also an assumption in this idea that future returns in the markets will be as good as they have been over the last twenty years, rather than the twenty years before that.

Notes

1. This chapter draws on various pieces of work which have been done at IPPR recently. In particular it draws on Dan Corry (ed), *Public Expenditure: Effective Management and Control*, Dryden Press\IPPR 1997. This book is referred to as *PE* throughout the chapter.
2. V. Tanzi and L. Schuknecht, *The growth of the state and the reform of government in industrialised countries*, IMF working paper, 1995.
3. See D. Corry, 'Public and private partnerships', *Renewal*, April 1995.
4. See D. Corry and G. Holtham, 'EMU issues for a new government', paper presented to IPPR/Friedrich Ebert Conference in London, January 1997.
5. See B. Eichengreen, 'Saving Europe's Automatic Stabilisers', *National Institute Economic Review*, January 1997.
6. See D. Corry, 'Indirect taxes are not as bad as you think', Annex, in S. Tindale and G. Holtham (eds), *Green Tax Reform*, IPPR 1996.
7. Citizens' juries have been pioneered in the UK by IPPR. See IPPR, 'Citizens' Juries: towards best practice: a working paper', IPPR 1996.
8. Tindale and Holtham , *op.cit.*
9. G. Holtham, 'It's not all over yet', *Observer*, 24 September 1995.

Recent tax reforms in Norway: What have we learned?

Eystein Gjelsvik

Perhaps the first question to address in this chapter is 'why do we have a tax system?' The Green Tax Commission[1] offers the following reasons: taxes provide real economic room for government consumption, investment and transfers; they can improve equity; and they exist for efficiency reasons, to reduce distortions and possibly correct externalities. The first reason cited is concerned with macroeconomic stability: unless private sector purchasing power is adjusted properly, there would not be productive capacity at the disposal of government services, and market forces would create inflation. This issue is therefore related to the overall tax level. The level has developed from around 30 per cent of GDP in 1965 to around 45 per cent in the mid 1980s. After 1990 the level decreased somewhat, to 41 per cent as of 1995. This compares well with the EU average. Note that while the EU and OECD levels have increased steadily, the level in Norway seems to have peaked.

The second reason for taxation, equity, is a major concern, especially for trade unions. Norway had a strictly progressive system from early 1970s aimed at taxing high income groups. However, after some years of high wage inflation, the LO chairman had to admit in the early 1980s, 'The progressive levels were never meant to harm our people'. The distribution effects and increasing distortions were major concerns behind the tax reform (see below). The new system is flatter, thus less redistributing between different wage levels (up to 50 per cent at the margin). However, capital taxation is lower, flat at 28 per cent for all capital income, including capital gains. The equity effects are discussed below.

The third reason for taxation – its capability as an instrument to reduce distortions and correct externalities – is a complex matter, because of the many types of taxation, and the segmented labour markets both with respect to sectors and qualification. The Green Tax Commission arrived at the following general recommendation:

> First, use efficiency improving taxes so as to improve the market outcome (carefully implemented green taxes) as much as possible
>
> Second, use neutral taxes
>
> Third, use distorting taxes, but only to the extent of satisfying fiscal constraints or equity requirements
>
> Fourth, implement distorting taxes such that the total tax system yields minimum deadweight loss for a warranted (income) distribution.

A broad presentation of the Norwegian tax system in an international context

There are several different forms of taxation which can be looked at in different ways. Income taxes for persons and firms are the most important source of income in OECD countries. Income taxes' share of total receipts was 26 per cent in 1965 and 32 per cent in 1980, decreasing to just below 30 per cent in 1993. At that time income taxes on firms were 7 per cent. Social security and pension taxes amounted to 25 per cent, and indirect taxes were 30 per cent, down from 38 per cent in 1965. Property taxes share has been decreasing and was 5 per cent in 1993.

For the purpose of efficiency, it is more important to distinguish between input factors, such as labour, capital, energy and other natural resources and the environment. There is a lack of information on this. Estimates done for the Commission indicate that taxes on labour (including most income taxes, and social security taxes paid by both employers and employees) increased rapidly from around 40 per cent of total taxes in 1965 to around 50 per cent in 1985–93. Capital Taxes (including a proportion of personal and total firm income tax and property taxes) amount to around 15 per cent, down from 20 per cent in 1965.

Environmental and energy taxes are closely related. First, it is important to note that it is end user prices that determine the actions of firms and consumers. Thus, whether you call them petrol taxes or carbon taxes, they amount to the same effect. Norway applies both, as do other countries. The Commission concluded that the level of green taxes is high in Norway. Only five countries, the Nordic countries and the Netherlands, have introduced carbon taxes, but taxes on fuels are commonly applied. A major problem is that those taxes are not carbon based; thus, they are not optimal and not cost efficient. The worst problem is that, often, coal is subsidised, while oil products and even natural gas are taxed. There is a lot to gain for the environment from harmonising these taxes, internally and externally. There is limited information about environment/energy tax rates, but they seem to be below 10 per cent.

As a broad measure of the distortionary effects of taxation, tax 'wedges' are used. The OECD has estimated total marginal wedges for persons with average manufacturing income. The wedges are high in all countries, higher in Europe than in other OECD countries. The Norwegian wedge has come down below the European level as a result of the tax reforms implemented after 1985. The reforms were completed in 1992.

In 1985 one dollar paid by the employer (labour cost) yielded 27 cents to the worker in after-tax income. The Commission concluded that high wedges might have distortionary effects on employment. Neither theory nor empirical evidence is clear on the importance of such wedges for wage formation and employment, but the Commission found enough evidence to believe that lower wedges improve conditions for employment, and it believes that indirect taxes on labour are most harmful.

Major tax reforms

One of the most important reasons for tax reform in Norway, as well as in many other OECD countries, was to reduce discrimination between different types of capital income. For example, capital income taxes on firms were 50 per cent, but, thanks to a plethora of exemptions, tax free funds and favourable depreciation schemes, average tax income from firms was less than 10 per cent. Bank deposits hardly yielded real returns due to inflation and administrative interest rates, and, after-tax returns, were negative for years both for firms and even more for high income persons with high marginal income tax rates. While at the outset income taxes for most workers were low, average and high income groups faced marginal tax rates of 65–75 per cent. Thus, a high or even average income earner could receive huge government subsidies by investing in property financed by bank loans.

It follows that the major elements in the tax reform were to cut high marginal tax rates. Gross rather than net revenues (after deduction of costs, mainly interest payments) were established as the tax base. The tax on all personal net income was reduced to 28 per cent, which also applies to firms. Double taxation on dividends was abolished, such that taxes on dividends paid for by firms are fully deductible for individuals.

This more neutral tax system has made a sounder base for investments, and the tax system was approved by an almost unanimous parliament after negotiations that took years. However, some problems remain. Some argue that it is unreasonable that capital income is taxed at 28 per cent, while wage earnings are taxed at 50 per cent for incomes somewhat above average earnings (and about 38 per cent for below average earnings). Certainly, this creates incentives for high income groups to seek rents by converting labour incomes to capital incomes. Therefore, there is a complicated model aiming to separate the two sources of income for self-employed persons and owners of small firms. Thus, small entrepreneurs feel discriminated against, compared to stockowners and big firms, and there are a lot of complaints.

Conflicting aims: What is a good system?

The gap between capital and labour taxes, and the lack of consistency in carbon and energy taxes in Norway (and elsewhere), are sub-optimal. But the Commission concluded that this did not matter, at least not in the long term. According to equilibrium theory, it is the tax wedge that matters most for employment, which is the major concern. This theory suggests that the mandate of the commission, namely to shift taxes from labour to environment, will not create more employment if the workers carry the burden of environmental taxes. Both forms of tax enter the wedge formula symmetrically. One response would be to shift the burden to non employed groups or to foreigners. The first is socially unacceptable; the latter may cause international tension, but can be done. Carbon taxes on exported electricity are one example, which could be done if it did not render exports unprofitable. But, if carbon taxes are not internationally implemented, that is precisely what happens. Unfortunately, even the Nordic neighbours have trouble agreeing on this, and the current taxes are distorting the market, which now is opened up. If these problems are not solved, total carbon emissions from the Nordic countries will be much higher than needed, and there will be less substitution of gas and other cleaner fuels for coal. The Swedish decision to phase out nuclear power sharpens the dilemma. It would be a shame if these opportunities were lost because of lack of international cooperation.

In the shorter term, with high levels of unemployment, and in 'out of equilibrium' economies, the tax shift from labour to environment is more likely to create employment. International experience suggest that direct taxes on labour, and especially payroll taxes, are most harmful for employment in the short to medium term.

Since deadweight losses from tax wedges are non-linear, it makes sense to have smaller taxes on broader tax bases. However, taxes on less qualified labour seem more harmful than on more qualified, suggesting that progressive taxes make sense also from the efficiency point of view. This is an important observation that should be exploited by the labour movement.

Another point here is that tax wedges seem particularly harmful for household services. Danish research suggests that efficiency and employment gains can be achieved by subsidising household services. The word subsidise may even be misplaced. The principle of Ramsay taxation for the second best in case of a fiscal constraint says that taxes should not be neutral, but vary by the elasticities of demand in each segment. Where deadweight losses are high, the optimal tax is low.

Finally, simulations on the econometric macroeconomic model 'MODAG', suggest that a minor employment gain could be achieved by the substitution of payroll taxes for a harmonised carbon tax. However, such a shift would render important export industries less competitive, and threaten employment in key firms located around the coast of Norway. The global result of such a unilateral carbon tax is uncertain and may even be negative, due to relocation of such industries. Even though the Commission majority favoured the strategy, the more powerful minority (Government, LO (trade unions) and employers) warned against unilateral carbon taxes.

The Commission hardly analysed the question of equity, and that is why it failed to reach consensus. It might not have reached consensus in any event, but when suggesting reforms, equity should be in the forefront of consideration.The tax reform has reduced progressive elements of taxation for reasons of efficiency, as outlined above. But this does not mean that it is worse than before. High income groups were favoured by the previous plethora of deductions. Even though capital taxation is lower, it brings in more money in the end, somewhat above 15 per cent, about double the level before the reform.

It has been suggested that one should go further in this direction, by omitting all deductions, and having a common flat rate of 30–35 per cent on all types of income combined with a tax free income of about 25 per cent of average income. While still progressive, this would be a rather flat regime, and probably hard for trade unions to accept. A serious analysis of the income distribution effects has not been offered by the (noisy) proponents of this concept. Until this happens, I am sceptical.

One problem with the tax shift from labour to environment and energy taxes is that they tend to redistribute from poorer to richer people. That is valid if the indirect tax on consumption is higher than the marginal tax on income. Thus, the outcome of this shift in terms of equity depends on the income elasticity of demand and the marginal tax rate.

Suggestions for future reforms

- It makes sense to introduce harmonised green taxes in common markets. While it may cause problems for some industries in the short term, it makes the economy more sustainable, and more efficient. If it makes room for reducing taxes on labour, it will probably reduce unemployment in the medium term.
- Unilateral carbon taxes do more harm than good. The equity effects are unacceptable.
- A certain level of taxes is a precondition for the welfare state. Anyone who defends it, cannot be in favour of lowering tax levels, given the deficits in most countries.
- The obsession with neutrality across segments in the labour markets should be questioned.
- Widening the tax base combined with lower tax rates improves efficiency, but I believe that equity considerations put a limit on efforts in that direction.

Notes

1. NOU 1996 *Grønne skatter – en politikk for bedre miljø og høy sysselsetting* (Green Taxes – a policy for improved environment and high employment), The Department of Finance, Oslo 1996, White paper, p9.

Should Europe import US supply-side economics?

Max B. Sawicky

Europe nurses profound concerns about its economic performance and future prospects. Topping the list of worries is unemployment, but close behind are problems anticipated from the aging of the population and world-wide economic liberalisation. It is natural under such circumstances to feel a need to review how all of the major tools of economic policy are being employed, including tax systems.

The US has undergone nearly two decades of tax reform.[1] This US reform is of interest to Europe, firstly because it provides a major case study of tax policy in a federalist framework, and secondly because the US is Europe's most important competitor. To an overwhelming extent, this question of tax reform, in the US and Europe, has come to be viewed through the prism of so-called 'supply-side economics' – which means the economic slogans, nostrums and ideas popularised during the presidency of Ronald Reagan (1980–1988).

This conservative cast of tax reform is not inevitable, however, nor is it reflected in expert opinion. But, because the US economy is perceived as a success story, US tax reform invites emulation. From the European standpoint, US unemployment rates are enviable. In the international arena, there is evidence that US competitiveness has improved in recent years. Even US debt and deficit positions compare well to the norm in Europe. The question arises of whether the US deserves the envy it is accorded in Europe. More importantly, should US tax policy and tax reform get a large share of the credit? Is the wisdom of 'supply-side economics' at the root of the alleged American success story? This chapter offers a 'consumer report' to European policy-makers who are attracted by the promise of a US-style tax reform.

Our basic theses are: that US economic performance since 1980 is an unworthy goal for the advanced economies of Western Europe; that US tax changes, especially those of a 'supply-side' nature, deserve little credit for US economic progress; and that supply-side economics is driven by an ideological bias against the public sector, it takes a cavalier attitude towards the conduct of fiscal policy, and it threatens basic sources of economic security in the advanced industrial nations of the world. At the same time, constructive directions in tax reform can be identified in the US and applied to the European context.

The US economy and the economics of tax reform

Was the whirlwind of tax reform in the US since 1980 associated with US economic success? If progress from 1980 to 1990, roughly speaking, was no better than in prior decades with no tax reform, one could question the logical basis for crediting US tax reform with any important accomplishment.

Economic trends, now and then
The basic indicators of economic performance discussed here are real output, as embodied in GDP, employment, investment, and saving. We want to compare long periods of time in these terms, roughly the post-1980 to pre-1980 period.

A chronic error in popular debate is the failure to separate political regimes' economic policies from unrelated economic trends. Political decisions take some time for their effects, if any, to be visible. Such effects can easily be overshadowed by business cycle movements of GDP. Particularly inappropriate is the characterisation of a political period by reference solely to either the 'upside' or 'downside' of a business cycle. One may contrast the beginning and end of cycles with presidential terms. The key economic dates for our story are 1973, 1979, and 1989, all peaks in the US business cycle. The salient political dates are 1981, Ronald Reagan's first year in office, and 1982-88, the period over which an assortment of tax changes were phased in.

US conservatives like to showcase economic performance between

1983 and 1989 to support their case for supply-side economics. This period conveniently excludes the major recession period of 1980–1982.[2] Less remarked is the fact that after 1981, in an effort to replace lost revenue and prevent ballooning deficits, significant tax increases were passed with the approval of Presidents Reagan and George Bush. These included the Tax Equity and Fiscal Responsibility Act (TEFRA) of 1982, the Social Security Amendments of 1983, and the Deficit Reduction Act (DEFRA) of 1984. Now if tax cuts boost the economy, tax increases should have an offsetting effect. While the specific nature of a tax cut or increase matters, any tax change which raises revenue is likely to affect incentives in one way or another.

What can be said for economic performance if one separates the business cycle effect and compares pre- and post-1980? To compare we should average over the lows as well as the highs of a cycle. If the average for one cycle exceeds that of another, there is at least the possibility that some policy could be responsible. A second consideration is that it makes sense to compare percentage increases, not simple quantitative ones, and where dollar magnitudes are involved, to remove the effect of inflation.

The business cycle which brackets the period of supply-side tax policy began in the peak year of 1979 and ended in the peak year of 1989. During this period, GDP grew at a real annual rate of 2.74 per cent; employment rose by 1.85 per cent per year; investment grew by 2.43 per cent; and gross private saving grew by about 1.2 per cent. By contrast, from 1973 to 1979, GDP growth was 2.87 per cent, employment 2.65, investment 4.66, and saving grew by about 1.8 per cent. (Personal savings *rates*, savings relative to disposable income, fluctuated between 6.6 and 9.3 per cent from 1973 to 1979, while they fell to 4.8 per cent by 1989.) Thus, during the 1970s business cycle, a time when the real tax burden on capital rose,[3] when inflation was volatile, when social movements could have shaken investor confidence, economic performance was above that of the later period of conservative ascendancy in the US.[4]

Partisans of Reaganomics may object that basing any summary on a period which includes the economic decline from 1980–82, after Jimmy Carter had been president for three years is unfair. But the deeper any cyclical economic decline, the easier it is for an economy to improve, relative to its low cyclical ebb. Earlier cycles also began at peaks from which declines unfolded, and those declines are reflected in the comparable figures above for GDP, employment, and the like. Separating the effects of cycles should reveal the underlying, long-run supply capacity of an economy.

Supply side economics focuses on the unleashing of productive forces, which means it looks forward to increases in labour supply, personal saving, and investment. To know if *policy* is effective in this context, it must be possible to show that productive capacity has been raised to levels over and above what could have been expected given underlying trends. By our basic indicators, it is clear that the 1980s fail to provide a record of accomplishment, relative to earlier periods. This does not prove that supply side policies were without value, but it does mean there is no simple achievement upon which to base broad, positive evaluations of the Reagan era policies.

In the heat of Robert Dole's presidential campaign in 1996, 500 leading economists in the US emphasised their opposition to further experiments in supply-side tax cuts. A petition opposing Senator Dole's plan for tax cuts asserted: 'The plan's assumption that a substantial part of the revenue lost by reducing taxes will be offset by new revenues from additional economic growth are not credible. The so-called 'supply-side' tax cuts of the early 1980s were based on the same claim, but what subsequently occurred between 1982 and 1990 was demand-side growth – a recovery from the deepest recession since the 1930s. No sustainable increase in growth of supply took place. The presumed sources of such an increase (more work effort and a higher savings rate) never materialised.'

Tax reform, American style

For the purposes of this paper, we distinguish between two basic views of tax reform. One has long been held by the mainstream of the economics profession. The second enjoyed a take-off in popularity after 1980 and is characterised as the supply-side view. Both views influenced the actual course of reform in the US over the past two decades.

One of the most fundamental choices in tax policy is whether or not capital income – rent, interest, dividends, and capital gains – should be subject to tax. The supply-side view in the US holds that, for the sake of economic growth, capital ought not to be taxed. The centrist view, held by the vast majority of economists,[5] is that capital, including capital gains and estates, are appropriate objects of taxation.

In the most basic sense, putting aside some secondary qualifications, a tax that exempts capital from taxation amounts to a tax on labour compensation or on consumption. The distinction between taxes on labour and on capital is obvious enough; from the standpoint of income, exempting capital essentially leaves only labour for taxation.

The point about consumption will not be as clear without some explanation. Anyone using capital income (interest, dividends, or profits) to finance consumption would seem to bear a tax on consumption, but this neglects the beginning of the process – the act of saving or investing. From the standpoint of a comprehensive tax on all income, the treatment of saving or investment under a consumption tax is a tax preference (known in the vernacular as a loophole or, more neutrally, a tax expenditure). Under a consumption tax, personal income used for saving is not taxed. For business firms, money spent for investment is deductible from taxable income. At the point where income from the returns to saving and investment is used for consumption, broadly speaking the time value of the tax savings is equivalent to the tax liability under a consumption tax. Consequently, economists view consumption taxes as lifting the burden of tax on capital altogether, even though income from capital is used to finance consumption and associated taxes. Individuals bear no *lifetime* tax burden from the standpoint of income taxation.

In contrast, the worker who pays tax on total wages, who saves part of his wages, and who then pays tax on savings and accumulated interest income used for consumption, is taxed twice from a lifetime standpoint. A wage-plus-consumption tax system is double-taxation.

A second basic distinction in tax policy is the choice of flat versus progressive tax structures. The centrist view is amenable to some degree of graduated tax rates, while the supply-side view puts more emphasis on flatter, though not absolutely flat, rate structures. Thus, even if labour compensation were the sole source of taxation, the supply-side view would favour relatively flat rate structures. Consumption taxes collected from business entities necessarily tend towards flat rates, which is one source of their appeal to the supply-side view.

The third basic theme in supply-side tax policy is the special emphasis accorded to income from capital gains. Taxation of capital gains in the US is relatively high, compared to European countries. In the supply-side view, capital gains are uniquely associated with entrepre-

190

neurial effort and the proliferation of venture capital, unlike the more mundane sorts of capital income.

Surveys indicate that the overwhelming majority of US economists, including those who specialise in taxation, favour the taxation of capital on an equal footing with labour.[6] Even the centrepiece of supply-side tax policy, the flat tax (a single-rate tax whose base is consumption) has been rated an unlikely prospect for improving economic efficiency and growth.[7] The notion that a supply-side revolution has swept economic thinking in the US is utterly unfounded.

What actually happened in the 1980s

The key supply-side tax bill was the Economic Recovery Tax Act of 1981 (ERTA), which reduced marginal income tax rates for households and corporations, indexed tax brackets, exemptions, and the standard deduction, and instituted the Accelerated Cost Recovery System (ACRS), among other measures. The revenue loss from ERTA when fully phased has been estimated at 6 per cent of GDP and 28 per cent of revenue by 1990.[8]

Hard upon the passage of ERTA, looming deficits caused the Congress to scramble to recover lost revenue. The leader of this effort was Senator Robert Dole, who for his trouble earned the title 'Tax collector for the welfare state' from Newt Gingrich. So began a series of tax increases over the next five years, as noted above. The first major one was the Tax Equity and Fiscal Responsibility Act of 1982 (TEFRA), which recovered five of the 28 per cent of lost revenue.[9]

In 1983 changes in Social Security, including payroll tax increases, recouped another nine per cent of the tax base as revenue. The following year, the Deficit Reduction Act of 1984 recovered three more per cent. There were eight other increases of a billion or more in this period. Every tax increase enacted by Congress was signed by President Reagan. Obvious design flaws in ERTA, and lingering problems in the tax code, resulted in the most significant comprehensive reform of income taxes, the Tax Reform Act of 1986. This bill lost two per cent of the tax base in revenue.

By the early 1990s, the failure of supply-side tax policies had become obvious. Even the centrist variety of tax reform, while lauded as positive, was acknowledged by its advocates to have shown little in the way of significant effects.[10] Given the hue and cry for deficit reduction, the stage was set for increases in taxes at the very top of the income scale for those who had done extremely well since 1980.

Accordingly, marginal tax rates on high-income persons and corporations were raised in 1992.

Evidence and its lack

Since the effects of saving and investment take time to show up in GDP, the *only* short-term boost to growth that is possible in the supply-side context must be from growth in employment and hours of work. Even in the long run, investment does not guarantee future growth unless the investment projects undertaken prove to have positive rates of return in the future. As noted elsewhere in this chapter, lack of care in formulating investment incentives can promote investments that reduce tax revenues but have little or no economic value.

In the field of labour force supply, one must separate the effect of taxes from pre-existing secular trends in population and labour force participation by women. Burtless and Bosworth[11] could detect no more than a very small effect of this type, while Baker[12] suggests that with some corrections in methodology any such effect vanishes.

After 1980, a number of factors were expected to boost personal saving. These included financial deregulation (which broadened choices available to savers), reduced marginal tax rates, and new tax-based savings incentives. Moreover, the real rate of interest in the US went from negative at the end of the 1970s to historically high levels.[13] Notwithstanding this favourable shift in incentives, personal savings rates in the US fell in the 1980s after being relatively stable for many years. Evidence exists for a *negative* relationship between the rate of return and savings levels.[14] This is plausible in a model of 'target saving' where individuals only save enough to fulfill goals defined in terms of amounts rather than rates, so that increases in the rate of return reduce the need to save as much.

Despite the axiomatic association of saving with growth, the intention to reward saving with tax policy by increasing the after-tax return to saving is not promising. This means that efforts to broaden the scope of exemptions for savings threaten to deplete the public treasury and thereby exert downward pressure on *national* savings, due to the potential for higher fiscal deficits. An added danger of savings incentives in the personal income taxation is that savings deductions can have the effect of reducing the tax burden on labour income, especially for higher-paid workers.

For example, if the taxpayer faces a lower tax rate during retirement than during his or her working life, then the taxes foregone by virtue of an exemption of the amount saved from current income exceed the tax ultimately paid on funds cashed out for retirement. The effect is to levy a negative tax on capital or, to exempt part of the high-wage worker's income from tax. Thus savings incentives have the dual disadvantage of increasing fiscal deficits and worsening the distribution of income, while failing to encouraging savings.

The behaviour of gross investment in the US is not much of a boost to the cause of supply-side tax policy. Doctrine held that a liberalisation of depreciation rules for business firms, typified by the ACRS enacted in 1981, ought to raise investment, and conversely that the withdrawal of such a regime or the repeal of the investment tax credit (ITC) should have adverse effects on investment.[15] But this did not occur after the ACRS and the ITC were repealed in 1986.[16]

Research on business firm behaviour begins with the standard concept of the cost of capital as a key determinant of investment volume. Empirical studies have been very inconsistent in documenting such an effect. Fazzari, among others, has found that the cost of capital (which includes the effect of interest rates and marginal tax rates, among other things) is not very important in determining business investment.[17] There is a US literature which locates investment behavior in macro-economic behaviour. In the Keynesian framework, investment and savings are effects rather than causes of income generation, and the latter chiefly depends on fiscal and monetary policy.

Past practice with investment incentives provides a cautionary tale for growth-oriented reformers. The ACRS reforms in ERTA created serious distortions in investment incentives. Some types of investment effectively escaped tax altogether, and others actually enjoyed negative rates of tax, thus encouraging investments with zero or negative rates of return.[18] This is the very opposite of what is required for growth. Given the exceptionally loose coverage of capital income under the personal income tax, weakening the corporate income tax through the implementation of investment incentives endangers the government's ability to tax capital income at all.

Dogs that didn't bark in the US tax debate

Some themes relevant to the European debate that one might expect to arise in the US failed to do so.

The US political system is more decentralised than all European countries with the exception of Switzerland. US states have substantial responsibilities and powers in the field of taxation, public expenditure, and regulation. Political decentralisation has stifled discussions of tax harmonisation at the national level of US government. In the US, some states do not have income taxes, others lack sales taxes, and others corporate income taxes. Definitions of the tax base vary substantially across states. Any harmonisation would entail tax increases somewhere. Combined with the general disfavour in which government finds itself, tax harmonisation entailing tax increases has been a political non-starter in US politics.

Europe is different because most European countries use the same set of core tax instruments: the value-added tax and corporate and personal income taxes. Setting general minimum rates is less of an issue. Definitions of the tax base remain a difficult matter. For the same reason that taxes in Europe are more uniform, formal harmonisation has somewhat less significance. There is also a real question as to the practical impact of tax differentials. To the extent that differentials are meaningful, there really is an added constraint on European governments' fiscal policies.

The US experience provides some comfort. Despite the considerable diversity among US states' tax systems, evidence of significant effects on the location of business firms is lacking.[19] In light of the relative ease of mobility between US states, in comparison to present or prospective barriers among European countries, this should mitigate concerns about tax competition. In the same vein, globalisation of the economy notwithstanding, there has been no melt-down of state and local revenue levels in the US over the past twenty years, as some observers had feared. US state and local own-source revenues were about 11 per cent of GDP in 1975 and 13 per cent in 1993.

Harmonisation should be understood as the most basic type of tax reform in a federal context. By coordinating definitions of the tax base, the aggregate tax base is broadened, creating the flexibility to either reduce rates across the board, to limit the use of less desirable taxes, or to meet public expenditure priorities. Another important dimension of harmonisation is sharing information about taxable assets and transactions. This can also be seen as a form of base broadening. To the extent that tax authorities can enforce accurate reporting of taxable activities, the tax base is larger and the same boost to flexibility noted above is enjoyed.

In the US, the basic source of information is the Federal tax code, upon which many states 'piggy-back'. This has no analogue in Europe, which will be obliged to develop a federation-wide information system to prevent both legal and illegal tax avoidance activity. This system will require information which to some extent is now protected by bank secrecy laws, another disadvantage relative to the US from the standpoint of tax enforcement.

The US tax system is at odds with those of its major trading partners in the sense that US income taxes apply to income accruing to US business firms, regardless of the country of origin. (There are credits for taxes paid to foreign governments.) In contrast, under the value-added tax, taxes are 'border-adjusted' so that taxes on exports are rebated and imports are fully taxed. It has long been thought that harmonisation of US and European business taxes could benefit US manufacturing, although that position is controversial. The general point is that the public does not relate tax reform much to exports.

For Europeans, tax-based export promotion ought to be more relevant for several reasons. First, the labour movement holds more sway in politics. Secondly, Europe relies more on trade than the US. For these reasons, border adjustment of taxes ought to be more salient in Europe than in the US.

Environmental concerns have never played an important role in US tax reform. By this I mean that discussion of the basic design of existing or prospective taxes has never given allowance for the fundamental environmental premise that market prices of goods and services diverge from their actual social cost or benefit.

This leads to the suspicion that an in-depth revamping of European tax systems could utterly ignore environmental considerations. There are simply too many other issues with which to deal, many of which are much closer to everyday concerns than are many environmental hazards. This is not at all to say that environmentally-motivated taxes (EMTs) lack a firm rationale. It does suggest comprehensive tax reform is not a congenial setting for advocates of EMTs to promote their concerns.

In the EMT context, tax rates would properly reflect the divergence of price from social value. This could mean, for instance, that goods whose manufacture generated pollution would face higher rates of consumption tax than those with lower costs of this type. It could entail excises on the use of energy, or on assorted fuels which adversely affect global climate or the ozone layer. In the US, such initiatives face general scepticism about government and distrust of complexity in the tax code. This scepticism is fed by an obvious thirst for public revenue in the US, whether for purposes of deficit reduction, new public expenditure, or selective tax cuts. The public is justified in fearing that the desire for revenue could easily outweigh legitimate issues in the effective design of an EMT.

A second problem in the US context is that, for all the conservative drift in all areas of public policy, the electorate remains very resistant to changes in the tax code which have the effect of rendering less progressive the distribution of the tax burden. EMTs which are not offset by parallel changes in other taxes or in public spending are as likely to run foul of this concern as any sort of business tax incentive.

A third problem is that EMTs cut across the more customary political alliances – labour on one side and business on the other. For political support, EMTs must find allies among both labour and business, which means that such taxes face the daunting task of disrupting long-standing political relationships.

All of these difficulties played out in the most recent EMT initiative in the US: the Clinton Administration's effort to institute a BTU tax. Business and labour on the whole were lukewarm for the tax, business more than labour because the tax was part of a package of revenue increases.

In the European context, government and its efforts in the EMT area are likely to be held in higher repute, at least at the outset. Such credibility will tend to be undermined to the extent that revenue concerns outstrip environmental ones, and to the extent the distributional effects of EMTs are neglected. The political difficulties faced by EMTs in Europe are daunting, although social-democratic forces would seem more congenial to their goals.

A shift from taxes on labour or consumption to EMT sources has political appeal, but it also has some underlying problems. EMTs must fall on selected portions of either labour, capital, or consumers. The benefits of EMTs may well outstrip their costs, but the distribution of these benefits is unlikely to closely match the distribution of costs.

Distributional motives for US tax reform

It should not be surprising that some players in the tax reform debate have not focused their energies on improving the quality of the tax system or the performance of the economy. For the foreign observer of US politics, however, not all such motives may be obvious. This section discusses political dimensions of the US tax policy debate. In contrast to economists, the popular appetite for tax reform focuses on the magnitude of statutory tax rates, on the level of revenue (and implicitly, on the size of government), on the complexity of income taxation, and on the 'fairness' of taxes. Among elite, business-oriented sectors, there are also concerns about the effect of taxes on personal saving and private investment.

Conservatives have successfully conditioned the public to equate high marginal rates of tax on income with high revenue levels, complex tax rules, and anaemic economic growth. The liberal response has been to concede much of the argument over growth, but to successfully defend the idea that growth-oriented reforms should be rejected because they worsen the distribution of the tax burden. On the whole, this is not a fruitful debate since both sides are mistaken and there is little ground for compromise. In this section we discuss popular concerns in the tax reform debate.

Our favourite tax
The conservative political movement's impact has led to the odd situation that the tax reform most favoured by the public is also a political impossibility. We speak of the so-called flat tax developed by Hall and Rabushka[20] and promoted by such conservative personalities as Jack Kemp and Malcolm 'Steve' Forbes, Jr. The flat tax embodies the public's hopes for tax reform. It is relatively simple to comply with, its rules can be summarised in a very brief space, and it appears to eliminate opportunities for upper-income taxpayers to avoid taxes with complicated financial schemes. When people learn more details of the flat tax, such as the elimination of popular deductions, many recoil.

The politics of the flat tax was tested in the Democratic presidential primary of 1992 and the Republican primaries of 1996. In both cases the proposal rapidly achieved a high threshold of popularity while simultaneously provoking an even higher level of opposition. Advocates of the flat tax failed in their bids for the Presidential nomination. The Republican candidates eventually sought to capture popular support for the flat tax without literally embracing it, hence the call for a tax that was 'flatter, fairer, and simpler'. Here again the contradiction of tax reform in the US becomes more obvious: the public wants to 'square the circle' of tax reform.

The flat tax is promoted as a triumph of simplicity by virtue of its single rate. Of course, all of the work in figuring taxes lies in the determination of taxable income. Once this is done, finding one's tax is no more complicated than reading a number off a table. To most tax-payers, complexity lies in the proliferation of deductions under the personal income tax. To economists, the real complexity of income taxation lies the difficulty of formulating and complying with rules for calculating the net income of business firms. In both cases the flat tax provides relief, but on the personal side the relief is greeted with mixed feelings. Taxpayers welcome the general elimination of deductions but are reluctant to part with the preferences that benefit them the most. Popular views in this context border on the schizophrenic, with the effect of paralysing those in political authority. American views on the flat tax point up the inherently contradictory mixture of concerns, desires, and realities which embody the public's aspirations for tax reform. Our favourite tax cannot be inaugurated, and if it were we would forsake it.

The question of high marginal rates

The overriding concern of supply-side economics is the magnitude of marginal tax rates. Rates affect the prices of goods and services, includ-ing the price of labour, and the impacts of prices on the incentives to work, save, and invest are held to be the prime movers for economic growth. The simple cure for this simple diagnosis is lower rates, more generous rules for depreciation, and tax credits for specified categories of investment. All of these are purported to increase the rate of return to investment and saving, which are supposed to advance capital formation and long-run growth.

The top statutory marginal rate of tax on income in the US is now 36 per cent. A surtax kicks in for high income persons, pushing the top rate to 39.6 per cent. Payroll taxes for social insurance, with a combined rate of tax of 15.3 per cent, supplement income taxes on money wages, but the payroll tax rate goes down to 2.9 for wages in excess of $65,400, whereas the top marginal rate of 39.6 only applies to individual incomes exceeding $256,500 in 1995.

More relevant to the top marginal rate is the corporate income tax of 35 per cent, which should be included in calculating a total top marginal rate of tax on capital income for very high-income persons. Also, there are state and local personal and corporate income taxes which can push the effective top marginal rate further. Finally, the taxa-tion of nominal capital income can imply higher rates of tax on real capital income.

These figures notwithstanding, less credence is lent to the emphasis on marginal tax rates by orthodox economic theory than might be thought by both advocates and critics of supply-side doctrine. Marginal rates are obviously irrelevant for any income not subject to tax. It turns out that in the US, about 80 per cent of capital assets enjoy some kind of tax preference or exemption. In 1982, of $446 billion in capital income received by households, only $144 billion was included in the tax base.[21] Relatively little capital income is subject to tax under the US personal income tax. Most capital taxation results from the corporate income tax.[22] Another dimension is the extent of personal income subject to offsets of a more general nature – in 1993 over half of personal income was tax-free due to exemptions, deductions, credits, etc.[23]

In the realm of wages and salaries, there are also numerous deductions and other ways in which such income is shielded from tax. The payroll tax of 15.3 per cent is an important addition to the tax burden on labour, but this too can be exaggerated. In the case of social insurance contributions, the tax rate is associated with an implicit positive transfer from government – what should be understood as a marginal *negative* tax rate. Higher earnings under Social Security imply increased benefits in the future, although the effect is not dollar-for-dollar.

What ought we to make of this situation? In a variety of ways, marginal tax rates fell in the 1980s, compared to the 1970s, due to the implementation of indexation in 1984, the granting of ACRS, reduction of statutory rates, the shift in dependence from corporate income tax to the payroll tax, and the slowdown in inflation. What economists call the 'marginal effective tax rate' on capital of all types is markedly lower after 1980.[24] By supply-side doctrine, we had a right to expect an explosion of capital formation. For lack of any such triumph, we could suppose that taxes in general, much less high marginal rates, are not very important. Another point is that from this standpoint, European rates might seem less excessive relative to those of the US.

The thirst for simplicity

Popular discussion of taxes in the US dwells on the burden of compliance and enforcement. Conservative advocates and some economists have suggested huge costs of up to $600 billion, while more highly regarded research by specialists produces estimates of $70 billion.[25]

The simplicity of the flat tax transcends the single rate feature, even for business firms. It derives chiefly from the fact that the base, for all practical purposes, is identical to that of a value-added tax. This is important to the European debate because under the flat tax paradigm, 'simplicity' is implicitly defined as the taxation of consumption and the exemption of capital from tax. Moreover, the taxation of consumption under the flat tax is much less progressive than necessary, even in the framework of the flat tax or of consumption taxes in general. 'Simplicity' is much more than the mundane matter of reducing the costs of compliance and enforcement in the tax code. It implies a fundamental choice in tax policy: *the exemption of capital from taxation, and the attendant concentration of the tax burden on labour or secondary sources.*

The US public thinks the flat tax is filed on a postcard. In fact such a postcard could only be used by employees with no income other than wages and pension disbursements. In order to provide authorities with adequate information, no postcard would be adequate for taxpayers with non-wage income. So the appeal of tax simplification in the US floats in a bubble of illusion.

The popular notion of simplification can be boiled down to the deceptively obvious notion that the fewer rules and the briefer the instructions, the better. The flat tax satisfies this criterion, since the entire flat tax scheme is elaborated in less than ten pages of legislation. For this reason it has been derisively described as a 'miniature internal revenue code'.

The appeal of fewer rules and briefer instructions for the taxpayer is obvious. Less clear is the scope for inequity implied by apparently simple directions for figuring one's taxable income. Where instructions and tax law are brief, discretion as to their interpretation is vested in the taxpayer. The latter can be expected to interpret the law and its rules to his or her advantage. Greater inequities can be expected to result, since persons in similar circumstances could determine different tax liabilities for themselves, depending on their ingenuity and their honesty.

In the case of smaller business entities, such as proprietors and the self-employed, the likelihood of an audit and the enforcement powers of the tax authority would diminish. The lack of rules would be a flagrant invitation to tax evasion. Here again, the meaning of tax simplification for tax reform should be made clear: simplification is a means for facilitating legal and illegal avoidance of taxes by business entities and high income persons. Not only does this provide unfair relief for capital, it also implies arbitrary preferences for the labour of owners of business enterprises.

The genuine scope for tax simplification is also limited because, even if relieved from the need to calculate taxable income under income taxation, business firms will do income accounting in any event for the sake of their owners and shareholders. And transition to a new system would bring huge increases in complexity, since during the transition period the taxpayer would be obliged to comply with two tax systems or some kind of interim, blended system.

Some complexity in the tax code due to deductions is the price for pursuing certain social goals. Calls for simplification may have some political value up to the moment when politicians are called upon to make actual choices which arouse specific constituencies. Some worthwhile reforms, such as the indexation of capital income, the integration of corporate and personal income taxes, or the implementation of a direct, progressive tax on consumption, could entail additional complexity, not less.

Champions of strong dollars and small government

Reductions in inflation benefit some financial interests, notably bondholders. It would seem beneficial to such interests to promote tax reform which is deflationary, including tax increases to reduce fiscal deficits. In the US budget, however, projected growth in deficits is not a result of insufficient tax revenues, but of growth in social insurance expenditures for retirement and especially health care. Tax levels have been stable in the US for the past twenty-five years.

In the US, deficits created during the Reagan Administration by one-shot tax cuts and a defence build-up have been used to urge radical reform – privatisation and devolution – of US social insurance. It is possible that tax cuts causing temporary deficit increases have been motivated by a goal of reducing pressure on deficits in the long term. In the US, conservative politicians have proposed a flat tax with a single rate in the neighborhood of 20 per cent, which would increase the Federal budget deficit by approximately $180 billion per year. Tax cuts of this or any type are promoted by a bond-based US 'deflation lobby.'[26] The interest in deflation parallels the long standing case against the public sector in general. In the late 1970s, US economist and Nobel Laureate Milton Friedman argued that the only way to shrink government is to deny it revenue. This political strategy dovetailed with his view that deficits were not really a problem for interest rates and economic growth, except in the sense that the public sector's decisions about resource use would always be inferior to those of households and business firms.

In practical terms, the dilemma of anti-government conservatives is that once instituted, public expenditure programmes, especially social insurance, tend to be so popular as to defy abolition. The presence of budget deficits, however, lends itself to a portrayal of mismanagement, followed by hysterical premonitions of bankruptcy and national ruin.[27]

For this reason, tax reform which results in tax cuts is the chief strategy of the US right and the contraction of the public sector is their primary motivation in the advocacy of tax reform.

Tax fairness
In the early 1980s, US liberals and progressives were outraged by the hypocrisy of the Reagan Administration. Reagan and other conservatives had lambasted Democrats for fiscal profligacy and then fomented the highest deficits since the World War II. Democrats responded by agitating for deficit reduction, chiefly by means of tax increases. At the national level, tax increases for purposes of deficit reduction were promoted on the grounds that they would be focused on upper-income households or on business firms. This was not a successful political strategy.

One problem with this approach was its failure to contradict conservative economic nostrums about taxes and economic vitality. A second was the inherent unpopularity of deficit reduction as a justification for tax increases. The most positive consequence of this strategy has been that regressive tax changes have been made extremely difficult for conservatives to propose.

For the US public sector, which is relatively small and inadequate to its justifiable missions, the priority in tax reform is improvement in the design of taxes which garners additional revenue. These revenues can be used by public expenditure programmes to eliminate regressive features of tax reforms. For more mature social economies which do not contemplate significant expansions of their public sectors, the priority is less on revenue growth and more on tax reforms that can raise economic efficiency and growth with minimal impact on a progressive distribution of the tax burden.

A constructive, incremental agenda for tax reform

The Tax Reform Act of 1986 and the Clinton tax changes in 1992 provide the most useful guidance for tax reform in Europe. These reforms, particularly TRA86, were consistent with the mainstream consensus of expert opinion in the US.

Loophole closing

Income tax systems are complex in the mundane sense of including a host of deductions and credits devoted to an assortment of social policy goals. These are described as 'tax expenditures' in the US. By law selected agencies of the Federal government are required to estimate the cost of these provisions, which are also described as preferences, loopholes, corporate welfare, socialism for the rich, and industrial policy, depending on the provision in question and the political leanings of the commentator. The idea of tax expenditure reporting is that a budget presentation of the provisions and their costs gives the public and policy-makers information which can inform decisions as to which policies are worthwhile and which not, in light of their costs. Moreover, such devices can be compared more easily to outright expenditure programmes when their costs are reported.

Many US conservatives resist the basic concept of the tax expenditure on crude propaganda grounds. They argue that such an idea presupposes that 'the government is entitled to all of your money'. In fact the concept of a tax expenditure is that, in contrast to a 'clean' tax code stripped of all preferences, the incremental cost of implementing a given preference could be considered an expenditure for a given purpose, no less than an outright expenditure of public revenues. The relevant contrast is not a 100 per cent tax on all income, but an equal-yield tax system with no preferences.

It is possible to go overboard in pursuit of tax reform by loophole-closing. Social goals underlying a given preference might be worthwhile. Certain initiatives in industrial policy might be satisfied most conveniently through tax incentives. Political and economic considerations could argue for universal tax benefits in selected cases.

Labour supply

A high priority for tax reform in the US and Europe is the area of high marginal tax rates on labour faced by the poor and unemployed. Targeted efforts in this regard will be much less costly than broad relief applying to many workers. The chief device in the US is the Earned Income Tax Credit.

Another area for potential scrutiny is payroll taxes. In the US, the first dollar of money wages is subject to the full 15.3 per cent payroll tax. One possibility is to allow a per capita standard deduction which would be pro-rated over the worker's annual wages. More generally, there is the question of how taxes and other policies encourage the use of overtime at the expense of the employment rate. For any given aggregate supply of labour in an economy, some shift in incentives could raise the employment rate and reduce social costs.

Capital taxation

The weight of evidence and opinion in the US runs especially against piecemeal savings and investment incentives. There is also a fair degree of scepticism about the promise of 'wholesale' reform.[28] As things stand, the US personal income tax already provides significant incentives for saving.

One consideration for tax reformers is potentially disparate treatment of corporate and unincorporated sectors. In the US, the benefits of incorporation have become increasingly available to unincorporated business firms, so the rationale for a higher tax burden on corporate income is diminished. A second concern is disparate treatment of equity and debt. The choices of business in how it finances its operations should not be a creature of the tax code. The deductibility of interest in US income taxes encourages leverage and facilitates wholly unproductive tax shelters. A third basic issue is the treatment of inflation. As noted above, inflation causes tax burdens to vary in arbitrary ways. The solution is to index capital income and related deductions for inflation. Finally, business firms, capital gains, wealth, estates, and gifts can all be devices to shelter capital *and labour* income from taxation. To preclude such tax avoidance, all of these entities should be subject to tax.

Under income taxation, the rationale for taxing business firms is straightforward. Business firms may be seen as mere intermediaries for the generation and payment of capital income to their owners, but a tax on the business entity itself is the best way of ensuring that such income is reported and subject to tax. Capital gains are nothing but a type of income, so the rationale for taxing capital gains is obvious, especially in light of the well-known practice of converting labour income to capital gains for high-wage workers. Taxation of wealth, even for a zero net revenue yield, is a way of enhancing taxpayers' reporting of total personal income. For very low rates, wealth taxes probably have negligible effects on incentives and significant effects on the distribution of income. Taxing bequests and gifts could be justified as the taxation of income to the heir or recipient, or as a way of ensuring an accurate, final disposition of the income tax owed by the decedent.

In a consumption tax context, the rationale for business taxation is similar to that of the income tax. Taxing capital gains under a consumption tax is straightforward: a deduction is allowed at time of purchase for a taxable asset, and the full proceeds of sale or transfer of said asset (the latter through bequest or gift) are subject to tax. A wealth tax confined to the very rich does contradict the framework of the consumption tax, but it has the added rationale that it provides a powerful tool to redress excesses of maldistribution of wealth caused by consumption taxation. Finally, the taxation of *transfers* of wealth – bequests or gifts – is fully compatible with the concept of a 'lifetime income tax',[29] which may be described as a consumption tax which defines bequests and gifts as a form of consumption.

The failure to effectively tax business firms, capital gains, wealth, bequests, and gifts is a major handicap of European tax systems, whether the goal is to tax income or consumption.

Tax harmonisation

The task of tax harmonisation in Europe is vastly different than for the US. In the US federal system, the bulk of revenue is already collected by the central government, which might seem to make harmonisation easier, except for the fact that by our constitution and tradition US states have significant sovereign powers to resist schemes for national uniformity. Nevertheless, US taxes as a whole are already harmonised in the form of the Federal tax system. About two-thirds of tax revenue in the US is collected by the national government, a degree of implicit 'harmonisation' which the European Union could barely hope to emulate.

Beyond the Federal tax system, the US can offer little in the way of positive examples in the vein of harmonisation. In fact, the prevailing view among public officials, if not economists, is that competition among states is a positive feature of US federalism. We can offer the negative evidence of the costs of state level tax incentives, in the form of diseconomical programmes to attract employers, and more generally in terms of the relatively reduced size of the public sector in the US, compared to Europe. At the same time, the diversity of US state tax systems does not seem to have limited the level of state-local revenue relative to GDP. In the EU, prospective member nations retain sovereignty and there is no central tax authority or system as yet. This poses a greater challenge to Europe. On the positive side, as noted above, it may be easier to strike up agreements on some basic tax instruments that matter most for coordination, such as the VAT.

Conclusion

The impact of changes in tax structure has turned out to be much less significant than expected by economists.[30] As economic medicine, therefore, it is probably grossly overblown. At the same time, there is plenty of work to do in a constructive vein.

The tax debate in the US has degenerated to the point where no serious proposal can get a fair hearing. A good case in point has been the flat tax. Although the flat tax has numerous, grave flaws, the public was not treated to a substantive evaluation of it – for good or for ill – in the US in 1996. Both advocates and critics of the tax distorted its nature for the sake of political gain.

In the US the tax debate is most victimised by its intertwining with conservative goals of shrinking the public sector and reducing taxes on the wealthy. No progress is likely in such a polarised political atmosphere. It may be hoped that Europe will not fall prey to similar forces who favour a radical devolution and privatisation of the public sector, including the conversion of public social insurance to the equivalent of US 'welfare' and charity. Important initiatives in tax reform, such as those enumerated above, can be business-friendly without necessarily being labour-unfriendly. Such initiatives will typically fail to arouse much popular support. There is an opportunity here for social democrats to achieve related or even unrelated goals as their price for supporting reform.

Given the limited importance of tax structure for economic progress, it pays to keep in mind avenues that are potentially more fruitful. These include first and foremost a more expansionary fiscal and monetary policy for the developing European Union. Second, there is the area of union-wide industrial and trade policy. Third, there is the importance of environmentally-motivated programmes of taxation, expenditure, and regulation. Fourth, there are the uses of workplace reorganisation as a means to simultaneously improve productivity and employee well-being. Finally, there is the field of federal expenditure policy. Entailed here are measures to relieve chronic or cyclical downturns in specific regions of Europe. Also available is the tool of fiscal equalisation for the purpose of alleviating the effects of tax differentials on the location decisions of business firms or households. Finally, social benefits may be geographically related to labour mobility.

In closing, there is plenty to do in the EU outside the field of tax reform. We have tried to show that in the US, the promise of tax reform has been grossly inflated and distorted by extraneous political considerations. Much time, money, and wood pulp have been sacrificed to the obsessions of 'the tax decade' in the US, and very little can be invoked to show for it. The elevation of tax reform as a major tool for economic resurgence is founded on politics, not economics.

Notes

1. C. Eugene Steuerle, *The Tax Decade: How Taxes Came to Dominate the Public Agenda*, The Urban Institute, Washington DC 1992.
2. In 1980 and 1982 real GDP growth was negative, while it was positive in 1981. The NBER defines the three year period as one recession. 1981 is a poor choice of year to date the peak of a business cycle because growth was much lower than years prior to 1980 or after 1982. Including 1980 in either the '1980s' or '1970s' makes a significant difference in comparing the periods, which is one reason why conservative commentaries require a post-1980 period to render a positive judgement about supply-side economics.
3. Jane Gravelle, *The Economic Effects of Taxing Capital Income*, The MIT Press, Cambridge 1994.
4. Max B. Sawicky and Dean Baker, *Been There, Done That, Didn't Work: The Dole Economic Plan*, Economic Policy Institute, EPI Issue Brief 114, August 5, 1996.
5. Joel Slemrod (ed), 'Professional Opinions About Tax Policy: 1994 and 1934', *National Tax Journal*, Symposium on Professional Opinions About Tax Policy, Vol.XLVIII, No. 1, pp21–147, March 1995.
6. Slemrod, 1995, *op.cit.*
7. Henry J. Aaron and William G. Gale, *Economic Effects of Fundamental Tax Reform*, The Brookings Institution, Washington DC 1996.
8. Steuerle, 1992, *op.cit.*
9. *Ibid.*
10. Henry J. Aaron, 'Lessons for Tax Reform', in Joel Slemrod (ed), *Do Taxes Matter? The Impact of the Tax Reform Act of 1986*, The MIT Press, Cambridge 1990.

11. Burtless and Bosworth 1992.
12. Baker 1996.
13. Barry Bosworth, 'The Debate Over Savings', in Bruce L. Fisher and Robert S. McIntyre (eds), *Growth and Equity: Tax Policy Changes for the 1990s*, Citizens for Tax Justice, Washington DC 1990.
14. Jonathan Skinner and Daniel Feenberg, 'The Impact of the 1986 Tax Reform Act on Personal Saving', in Slemrod (ed), *op.cit.*
15. Barry Bosworth, 'Taxes and the Investment Recovery', in *Brookings Papers on Economic Activity*, 16: 1–38, 1985.
16. Alan J. Auerbach and Kevin Hassett, 'Investment, Tax Policy and the Tax Reform Act of 1986', in Slemrod 1990, *op.cit.*
17. Steve Fazzari, 'Investment and US Fiscal Policy in the 1990s', Economic Policy Institute, 1993.
18. Stueurle 1990.
19. Timothy Bartik, *Who Benefits from State and Local Economic Development Policies?*, The Upjohn Institute, Kalamazoo, MI 1991.
20. Robert E. Hall and Alvin Rabushk, *The Flat Tax* (2nd ed), The Hoover Institution, Stanford, CA 1995.
21. Steuerle, 1992, *op.cit.*
22. *Ibid.*
23. Joel Slemrod and Jon Bakija, *Citizens Guide to the Great Debate Over Tax Reform*, The MIT Press, Cambridge, MA 1996.
24. Gravelle, 1994, *op.cit*; Slemrod and Bakija, 1996, *op.cit.*
25. Slemrod and Bakija, *op.cit.*
26. Max B. Sawicky, 'Up From Deficit Reduction', Economy Policy Institute, 1994.
27. Harry Figgie Jr. and Gerald J. Swanason, *Bankruptcy 1995: The Coming Collapse of America and How to Stop It*, Little, Brown, Boston, MA 1993; Peter G. Peterson, *Facing Up: How to Rescue the Economy from Crushing Debt and Restore the American Dream*, Simon and Schuster, New York 1993.
28. Aaron and Gale, 1996, *op.cit.*
29. Aaron and Galper 1984.
30. Aaron, 1990, *op.cit.*

The role of trade unions in an interdependent world

Bill Jordan

In this contribution I would like to focus on seven features of the changing international scene that impact directly on the role of trade unions, in the civil society of developing, transition and industrialised countries.

The reality of interdependence
One of the features of the international trade union movement today is that we are firmly based in an approach to economic and social development based on the reality of interdependence in a global market economy. Any other basis for our work would be futile and be seized upon by the critics of trade unions as an example of an inability to adapt and innovate. Interdependence is a word full of meaning for the ICFTU – in fact full of many meanings: interdependence across national boundaries, between the powerful forces of competition and co-operation, between unions and employers. These are just a few of the aspects of the concept which are part of the reality we are living in. Taken all together they reinforce the importance of building international trade union solidarity.

Building international solidarity
The international trade union movement is built on the natural human sentiment of solidarity; of men and women working together to move forward together out of a combination of self interest and a desire to

help others. This is not old-fashioned romanticism irrelevant to the new hard-faced world of the market, but a political resource we can foster and grow, through serious work that concentrates on bringing people together and building trust and respect.

What makes unions different from other organisations of civil society?

If you ask a stranger 'who are you', they will often answer by telling you their occupation as well their name. People's sense of identity and personal esteem is intimately bound up with what they do for a living. If you become unemployed or if you become trapped in a job that is degrading and debilitating, that vital sense of self respect is destroyed. The work experience is clearly more than just a means of earning a livelihood and escaping from poverty, vital as that is. It is also the main way people participate in civil society.

The market can achieve many things but it cannot build social cohesion. That is a product of the institutions and relationships, both public and private, that constitute civil society. And it seems to me that the institutions and relationships that are developed around the workplace are an essential determinant of both economic progress and social justice. Of course, they have to be constantly adapted, and will reflect the particular experience of different countries, regions and industries; but the universal fact – and it is the key to our past and future strength – is that the workplace is where human values meet the market.

The workplace in the context of a global market

National trade unions are increasingly looking to the ICFTU, the ITS, TUAC and the ETUC for help in their day to day work, because liberalisation of trade and capital markets is moving ahead so fast that global pressures are penetrating into areas of policy which have hitherto been thought of, by and large, as only of national concern. This applies especially to the process of job creation and work relations.

Robert Reich has posed the problem well as the 'diabolical dilemma' of having to choose between high unemployment or increasing social inequality. Escaping from this impossible political choice was the main reason for the decision to hold the Copenhagen Social Summit. And the conclusion of 117 heads of state in March 1995 was that without international action to promote social justice we cannot expect to achieve economic and political stability. As well as being the moral course of action, social development based on full employment is productive.

Elements of consensus on a new basis for full employment in a global context

The 1996 ILO conference made considerable progress on the implications of increased international interdependence for employment policies. The 'Conclusions on Employment Policies in a Global Context' are an agreed tripartite statement based on the premise that maintaining low inflation and financial stability is not only compatible with much higher levels of employment, but also that the stimulation of productive employment is essential to the realisation of the potential benefits of trade and capital market liberalisation.

The five points which ICFTU pressed on the ILO in Geneva, with some success, were: (a) effective co-ordination of fiscal and monetary policies, especially amongst the world's largest economies; (b) a renewed effort to agree and follow concerted policies by governments and the social partners for employment growth with low inflation; (c) that trade and investment liberalisation has created new strong competitive pressures that inhibit a resumption of inflation and thus enlarge the potential for lower real interest rates and higher and sustained levels of growth; (d) that because resistance to change stems from fear and insecurity, policies must aim to increase the speed of adaptation by balancing flexibility and security in employment; and (e) workers, individually, and society, as a whole, need a broad base of skills and the ability to learn throughout working life.

I have to admit, though, that we still need to convince policymakers, including our friends in government, that a faster pace of growth will not lead to higher inflation.

The significance of sound industrial relations

Increased competition and the severe consequences of a deterioration in national financial conditions place a heavy pressure on systems for collective bargaining and the redistribution of income through government budgets. All countries should therefore place high priority on improving the functioning of their industrial relations systems and the mechanisms for tripartite consultation and agreement on economic and social development strategies. A sound industrial relations system founded on respect for the basic ILO labour standards, endorsed by the Copenhagen Summit, and more recently by the Singapore WTO Ministerial Meeting, is a significant component of the enabling environment needed for full employment.

Inflation and devaluation were escape routes for governments and countries that failed to resolve social conflicts – governments, unions and employers have all been parties to the deception of awarding people more money and then allowing its value to depreciate through inflation. But even that temporary escape route is no longer available because liberalisation of trade and of capital markets has imposed a high price on countries that do not achieve price stability. Governments of all colours know that a persistent high public deficit is very costly to finance now that there are no captive savings markets on which finance ministries can sell government bonds.

Sound money and strong trade unions

The new stronger international pressures of competition and financial stability mean that the national institutions for identifying and resolving conflicts, within which free trade unions are very important, have to become stronger and more effective. Otherwise, rather than being seen as a potential source of growth and prosperity, globalisation will appear to many as a restraint on their aspirations for justice and a decent life. This could lead to isolationism, protectionism and ultimately to violence, which could spill over national boundaries into international conflicts.

Trade unions' basic role is thus even more important in this new age. Our job is to articulate grievances and negotiate with employers and governments to find solutions. The Copenhagen Social Summit commitment on basic workers rights is thus very important because it recognises at the highest level our role at the workplace and in the global market.

Many, but not all, problems can be worked out directly between unions and employers. In a increasingly competitive world few employers have the market power to pass on increased labour costs to consumers through price rises. Therefore collective bargaining is focusing more and more on how unions and employers can co-operate to improve productivity and thus both profits and pay. This is a positive development but means in turn that the mechanisms for information exchange, consultation and bargaining have to be improved, so that all concerned see the costs and benefits of the various options available. Such processes work better than macho management because they engage and commit the parties to making them work.

Similar arguments apply to the making of the national budget. The broader the degree of political and social support for the tax and expenditure policies voted by parliaments, the more likely is it that governments will be able to avoid the penalties of financial instability. Tripartite economic and social councils and social pacts are a reinforcement to the democratic process and help governments, employers and unions to follow polices that are convergent and consistent.

Conclusion

There are important signs that governments are aware that market liberalisation does not produce social cohesion. And, furthermore, that in a global market, governments and the international institutions need to increase their co-operation on social policy, and review the way international trade and financial policies impact on society. A blind faith that deregulation will get prices right and that, to use the old phrase, 'a rising tide lifts all boats' is not a policy. Most importantly it will not lead to full employment, without which the resources to tackle, social inequality will be inadequate, ultimately threatening the survival of democracy and the creation of an open world market.

Nevertheless, making our 'alternatives' into the new 'orthodoxy' poses many challenges for trade unions. I am optimistic that we can develop our role, mainly because of the profound impact of globalisation on the workplace. It seems to me that the issue discussed in this book, of how to combine social justice with economic flexibility, will lead to a focus on the workplace. We must rebalance, in the new environment of a global market, the forces of competition and the age old search for human dignity. Within the construct of civil society, trade unions are uniquely qualified for a task that is the foundation for welfare, security and economic performance.

What can civil society do?

Linda Tarr-Whelan

The challenge of creating a healthy civil society in our times is different from that of other eras. No easier. Nor more difficult. But different. There are new realities and rules. Past solutions are great for nostalgia and nostrums: 'a chicken in every pot' was a powerful metaphor in days gone by, but has no resonance today. Leadership for today's civil society requires new thinking and symbols. Old institutions are declining in influence and power. New ones are taking their place.

Three intertwined changes in the society and economy, which are increasing in influence, are reviewed in this paper: the leadership role of women in society; the rise of the third or non-governmental (nonprofit or voluntary) sector; and the rapid development of entrepreneurship, with small business occupying a larger and larger share of jobs, creativity and the economy. They point to new dynamics for civil society.

No longer can the dialogue centre around the old dichotomy of the government as the answer posited against the market as the answer. In current American politics both have recently been discarded by the public in their simplistic terms. Too often the public only equates government with taxes, bureaucracy and unnecessary regulation. And the market smacks of excesses, greed and downsizing. President Clinton recognised the obvious when he said, 'the era of big government is over'. Thus, large or comprehensive solutions, like health care reform in the early 1990s, are easy targets for specialised corporate interests like insurance companies, when the necessary public support is missing. Likewise, the icon of 'no government' has even been finally rejected by the Congressional GOP, the most conservative force for that model. After closing the federal government down to make their case, in the closing days of the last Congress, Republican leaders found salvation with the voters through compromises on increased funding for education and minimum wage increases.

The change in the realities of people's lives is not yet reflected in the political debate, except, perhaps to some degree, in the Presidential debate of 1996. Democrats are caught in a web of defending programmes and policies without an overarching vision or shared values. The New Democrats are united in their shared deficit-reduction hawkishness. Populists aim their criticism at corporate excesses and focus on increasing union strength. On the Republican side, social conservatives war with supply-siders and tax reducers.

The framework of progressive majorities was exemplified by the women's vote. Bill Clinton spoke to the central issue of politics – family security – and garnered a gender gap of 25 per cent. Offering low-cost, pragmatic strategies to meet immediate family and community needs that women voters believe are important to the fabric of society, he tapped the new progressive majority across party lines. 'Soccer moms', suburban mothers with children, largely Republican or Independent, provided Clinton votes in large numbers and then moved back to GOP Congressional candidates.

The Clinton campaign was an exception. All too often our usual political debates seem to be caught in a time machine. Employers and unions are seen as the central players – often the only players – with national governments on the sidelines. In the United States, however, the picture is certainly much more complex. Stereotypes of 'captains of industry' and 'powerful unions', as balancing economic or political forces to determine welfare, security and economic performance, are completely outdated.

What is missing is a reality check on the major transitions in the economy. Groups of employers, large and small, now have vastly different political and economic agendas, and are represented by different organisations. According to the Bureau of the Census, in 1993 large firms (over 500 employees) employed less than half of US workers (46.9 per cent of payroll); firms with less than 100 employees employed 32 per cent of the workforce, with the majority of businesses in this latter category having less than 20 workers. Sectoral changes are well known. However, a very different picture emerges for the challenges faced by the civil society when sectoral changes are combined with the diminished sizes of firms in terms of employment. Immediately post

World War II, in 1950, civilian employment in the US was 40.9 per cent goods-producing and 58.1 per cent service-producing: in 1996 the goods-producing employment was 20.3 per cent and service-producing was 79.7 per cent. Other changes include the increase in self-employment and the growth of the non-profit sector which now employs 8 per cent of workers. Strategies for social welfare policy which fail to take these trends into account will have little effect on workers and their families.

There are changes on the labour side as well. Today's unions do not operate from a position of strength. Unfortunately, they represent only a small fraction of American workers. The new leadership of the AFL-CIO under President John Sweeney offers a new vision, of 'America needs a raise', and organising and political activism to revitalise the power of labour. There is a long way to go. In 1996, according to the Department of Labour, 14.5 per cent of full-time workers belonged to unions or associations which were like unions. The tilt toward male-dominated occupations is still evident since 16.9 per cent of male workers and 12 per cent of female workers are union members. In the service sector, where most women work, only 6 per cent of workers are unionised (many of them by John Sweeney's home union, the Service Employees International Union). Black men have the highest union membership rates of 22 per cent.

The strength of the American labour movement is in the public sector. Teaching remains the occupation with the highest percentage of unionisation. The public sector, which employs 18.3 per cent of American workers, has the highest unionisation penetration rates, with better than 1:3 workers in unions (37.7 per cent). The only comparable sector on the private side is transportation and utilities with 26.5 per cent. Manufacturing is 17.2 per cent.

The popular conception of the influential players in economic discussions – the wealthy white men who are the CEOs of the Fortune 500 – is still true. But now it is short-sighted. That circle is still virtually all men. According to *Catalyst*, only five Fortune 500 firms are headed by women. On the employment side, however, these 'captains of industry' are no longer commanding the growth sector for jobs. A look at where American workers are employed changes the picture. Women-owned businesses now employ one in four US workers – 130 per cent more than the Fortune 500 does worldwide. The National Foundation for Women Business Owners reports that, in 1996, 8 million women-owned businesses employed over 18.5 million people and accounted for $2.28 trillion in sales.

The altered dynamics of the economic power centres – business and labour alike – are particularly compelling given the increasing devolution of federal responsibility and dollars to state and local governments. The focus of decision-making is shifting from the central government in Washington, DC to fifty state houses dominated by locally powerful corporate interests which are poorly constrained by weak unions and other members of the progressive coalition. In only a handful of industrial states are unions strong enough to be a realistic social balance. Washington-based interest groups of the left, built in vertical silos to mirror the social programmes of the New Deal, are only tangentially connected to state decision-makers and processes.

Geopolitical changes also affect the decision-making of the now mythical balancing powers of labour and business. Internationalisation has brought foreign policy and domestic policy into the same arena. Competition is being redefined by multi-lateral international trade agreements such as NAFTA and GATT, the movement of capital and goods by multinational conglomerates and the globalisation of capital and information. Magnified by the falling boundaries of influence and competition between and among nations, pressures from outside nations make domestic decisions only part of the equation in determining social welfare policy. In the United States this is also true for the fifty states which compete fiercely with each other for the 'best business climate' – an analysis by business which means low taxes and public services, poor worker protections and little environmental regulation. Turning around the 'race to the bottom' among states, as indeed among nations, requires new strategies and an understanding that social change occurs horizontally across the nation, not simply vertically by virtue of federal programmes.

The international spotlight is on cost-saving by governments. Ideas move quickly across borders. For example, 'welfare reform' (sometimes termed 'welfare deform') first began to move across the states in the 1980s. Couched in terms of taking 'people off welfare', the policies were aimed at ending the entitlement of single mothers, who were 87.9 per cent of AFDC recipients in 1994, and sending them to work. By the time the issue was debated last year it was clearly more complex. Income support is short and conditional. The ethic is work for parents no matter what. Now the challenge is for civil society – in partnership with government – to create jobs, provide health care coverage, transportation and educational opportunity. It is a new challenge for a democracy to meet the needs of the poorest without tax-supported transfer payments as the base. And the political support for transfers is clearly in tatters – except for the elderly who outvote their proportion of the population.

The United States welfare example will be watched carefully by other countries. Initial figures on the decrease in the welfare rolls will look very rosy. That is due to the base year which has been used, 1994, when the welfare rolls were up, and the economy was softer with less jobs. It is true that welfare rolls in most states are dropping sharply, due to a number of factors, but most impressively, the relatively low unemployment rate. The welfare reform strategy for single mothers with low skills and heavy responsibilities might work to some extent at 5 per cent unemployment, it won't work with 10 per cent unemployment. But, regardless of the real efficacy of welfare reform, the US model will be pushed in other countries, in order to 'be competitive'. While illustrative, welfare reform is only one example of the decrease in social protections.

Now, in the face of concerted conservative budget and tax policies, propaganda and politics, the changing economy and a seeming lack of pressure from the electorate has resulted in the dismantling of the social compact of the last fifty to sixty years. What will take its place? Unemployment policies, social security and retirement, safety net programmes for health, housing and income are under siege or marginalised. Income disparities remain or grow between whites and workers of colour; women and men. Protections are few, insecurities for families are many. Where are the answers?

The programmes of the New Deal were designed for a different age. Men worked and women stayed home (unless they were widows). That is the basic framework of Social Security. For women, nearly half the total workforce (46 per cent), the old model doesn't work very well. It shows up in the extreme poverty of elderly women living alone. Most married working women (who earn lower average pay than their husbands) receive Social Security payments as a spouse and do not receive retirement benefits commensurate with their contribution. Their own income doesn't count to increase social security benefits. This is one example of how old visions of the world put blinders in place that leave families in dire straits. Another example is the common political compromise in the United States, which exempts employers of less than 50 employees from coverage of laws regarding health, minimum wage and other labour standards. The power of the small business lobby is great. In some rural states, like Vermont and Wyoming, only 5 per cent of the employers are covered by the worker protection laws. Women have a different view. In CPA's *Women's Voices* research, a sizeable majority of women believe that all employers regardless of size should provide basic benefits, with men taking the opposite view.

Women's Voices showed that across party, race and class the key issue is family protection. Women believe that partnerships and collaboration are necessary for solutions. They are much more supportive of a role for government than men and resist the dismantling of social programmes. Family and work must be equally important. Strong and healthy families and communities should be the framework for changing the focus and dialogue from old metaphors and symbols to the twenty-first century role of civil society, government, employers and unions.

Health care is an example of a problem needing attention for virtually every family and community. More than 40 million Americans (including 1:7 full-time workers) are without health coverage. With the exception of Medicare for elderly citizens, insurance coverage for health care is tied to employment. But there are no real conditions on employers. As more and more workers are in small firms, coverage rates diminish. Companies which simply compete on the quarterly bottom line are seldom interested in healthy employees, and cut corners and coverage for short-term profits. In the last ten years the percentage of full-time employees covered by health plans in medium and large firms has declined from 96 per cent to 78 per cent. There has been an even greater decline in the coverage of the dependants of workers. Major governmental reform was not successful. Now the challenge is to harness market-based strategies to effect change, and build the political support it will take to achieve universal access.

On the other side of the coin, many support programmes of intense interest to women workers are given short shift by the leaders of liberal or progressive movements. Child care and elder care are often seen as fringe or 'soft' issues, or as not important to the economy, yet they are of central importance in a world where every parent is a worker. The burden of double employment at home and in the workplace still falls on women. The health of the civil society requires a new balancing of needs and responsibilities among a larger group of players than the traditional view of government, employers and unions.

There is new leadership among women following the United Nations Fourth World Conference on Women in Beijing, China in

September, 1995. The lesson of the Conference was to 'see the world through women's eyes'. It brought home a new transformational vision to the 50,000 participants and instituted an expansive agenda for the world's governments and non-governmental organisations to achieve women's equality in the world.

There were new cultural shifts. The non-governmental sector was seen as being as important as government in solving societal problems. There was a powerful shift away from the catalogue of needs and demands that women brought to the meeting. Instead, the exchange moved from a vision of women needing care – as victims, beneficiaries or supplicants – to women as equal political and economic actors, decision-makers and leaders. No matter how poor or beset with obstacles, women began to see themselves as partners, not victims. As leaders, not beneficiaries. Political and economic participation and empowerment are clearly related.

Women are beginning to bring talent, resources and different life experiences to the political process in greater numbers. As women take up equal roles as partners in decision making in the twenty-first century the paradigm for governing must be different. The times are different. There is the challenge of governing in a time of public anxiety and cynicism. Families and children are insecure and at risk. Peace must be defined in a post-cold war world. Work and family must be re-balanced within the context of a new economy. Public policy and accountability in a state-centred post-New Deal era is an opportunity for common ground.

The *Women's Voices* research over the last five years makes a strong case that women, across party, race and class lines share values that are in short supply in civil society – supporting prevention rather than crisis management, community-building and collective responsibility as well as individual responsibility, stakeholding not just share-holding, family economic security not just economic statistics.

With growing political and economic clout, women's ideas which strengthen the fabric of society are moving from the margins to the mainstream. Family and Medical Leave, signed into law in 1993, languished for nine years in Congress. It was labeled 'bad for business' and was vetoed twice by President Bush. In 1996, *Business Week*, hardly a feminist journal, lauded the best family-friendly businesses on its cover recently, as examples of best business practice.

Other trends are apparent. There is a tremendous pressure behind entrepreneurial growth. Women are abandoning corporate life for the uncertainty of self-employment. Numerous studies and stories have told the picture. Tired of banging their heads on the 'glass ceiling' or being trapped by the 'sticky floor', women have turned in time cards and business cards for the chance to see how far their skills and talents will take them. Many want to balance family and work in a more realistic fashion. The trend is enormous and part of the powerful engine of growth in jobs in America.

The traditional roles for women have been in caregiving, both in the home and in the workplace. Those roles are leading to service delivery entrepeneurial growth in the non-profit as well as the profit-making sectors. As government downsizes and more and more services are delivered at the community level this trend offers new jobs and opportunities for women. It also raises the potential spectre of low wages and low benefits. It is a challenge for civil society that caregiving is always at the bottom of the economic ladder.

We need a new social compact which is not based on old myths but on realities for families. Women must play a central role as we move toward the next century. Our shared destiny across the cultural divides of gender, race and class must lead to 'unlikely allies' among all three sectors – government, business and labour, and the voluntary or non-governmental sectors. The new roles of government must include broker, catalyst, and standard setter. Public investment must be leveraged with private sector investment. Sustainability of change requires political participation and empowerment with shared responsibility and accountability. This is a long term vision for civil society in a new era.

NGOs and trade unions: a useful collaboration?

Giampiero Alhadeff

The acronym NGO covers a wide variety of organisations and is unusual as a description, in that it defines an organisation in terms of what it is not. We may all have an image, often different images, of what an NGO is. The term itself is open to wide interpretation and is often used to define organisations which have little in common except the fact that they are not part of government.

And yet collective names for the kind of organisations we are talking about are difficult to agree on. Terms such as Not for Profit, charitable organisations, or Third Sector are used in different countries, but often the definitions are either inaccurate or too restrictive and are therefore abandoned.

The variety of types of organisations and associations involved is at the same time the strength and the weakness of this sector. Even the European Union's efforts to create a statute which might be applicable throughout the Union has stalled. But there are some positive developments. The European Commission in a recent document argues for the need to hold a civil dialogue (with NGOs) alongside the policy dialogue (with national authorities) and the social dialogue (with social partners). In late 1996 NGOs meeting at the UN also confronted the difficulties posed by using different terms and thought that it might be preferable to opt for the term 'civil society organisations'. Clearly a more accurate definition, but hardly one that is more intelligible or accessible to a non-specialist public. Doubtless in time they will become known as CSOs and eventually everyone will once again know what is being referred to.

Whilst recognising the need to adopt a new name defining us in terms of what we are and what we represent, I will for the purposes of this discussion, and until we reach a wider consensus on a new name, continue to use the acronym NGO.

In spite of the confusion over names and definitions, and in spite of the fact that there are no accurate global (or in some cases national) records, one thing is certain: the number of existing NGOs runs into millions and they represent many millions of citizens. Citizens who, contrary to neo-liberal economic models, give their time, energy and resources, freely and willingly for the public good. Citizens who, often for no personal financial gain and sometimes for a financial loss, give of themselves in order to improve the community they live, in or perhaps the world they belong to.

SOLIDAR is the alliance of NGOs linked to trade unions and to democratic socialist parties. We are one of thirty networks of NGOs operating in Brussels. And yet we represent 6 million such citizens and supporters and members with an expenditure of over 2 billion ECUs.

NGOs play an important part in the world's civil society. Consider only that if one excludes the World Bank and the IMF, more development aid is being delivered by NGOs than by the whole of the UN system. But it is not just a question of numbers. NGOs are crucial in civil society because they reach large sectors of like minded individuals and groups who may not be involved in a trade union, or a political party. To the trade union movement they are crucial allies because NGOs reach groups which are either not unionised or ignorant of their rights. In the United Kingdom, KALAYAAN, one of our affiliated members, in collaboration with the Transport and General Workers Union, managed to unionise migrant women domestic workers, a group which is understandably difficult to organise.

Trade unions have much to gain from a collaboration with NGOs, because NGOs are used to both thinking and acting globally. They were quick to spot the uses of the fax and then of e-mail and of the Internet and they have been reaching across borders, disseminating new ideas, breeding protest and mobilising citizens for change. Concepts relating to gender equality, to human rights and to the environment, have been used to mobilise citizens from Amsterdam to Johannesburg.

Beyond mobilising citizens, NGOs have skills, resources and know-how. At the Rio World Environment Summit, they set the agenda for the conference and at the conference itself NGOs served on national delegations, often acting as cross-national conduits for negotiations. One small NGO was asked to lead the delegation from a small Pacific Island. In this way, an NGO with abundant skills and detailed knowledge of the issues, but hardly enough resources to deploy a team of two people at the Summit, was able to reach deep into the negotiations and the decision making. This level of intervention, with similar results, was achieved by some NGOs at the Vienna Human Rights Summit, the Copenhagen Social Summit and the Beijing Women's Summit. NGOs have the flexibility which allows them to take forward this type of action with areas of success.

It is not surprising therefore that NGOs now enjoy good levels of influence in the UN system, with the European institutions, and with many governments around the world. They are an important sector to collaborate with and moreover they share many of the same concerns as the trade union movement and are working for the same outcomes. For example a number of NGOs are involved in negotiating Codes of Practices and are active in the negotiations concerning child labour.

It is therefore important for trade unions to make alliances with NGOs, but they should also do so with a level of caution. Not all NGOs share the same ideals, motivations or levels of accountability. The trade union movement knows about representation and accountability. This is not universally so in NGOs. There is a debate within the NGO world, with many of us arguing that democracy and accountability are vital, but the different standards are not always obvious and it is very much up to trade unions wishing to collaborate to check on the accountability and links of NGOs.

In spite of this word of caution, there is enormous potential for collaboration between NGOs and trade unions at a local, national and global level. We have mutual concerns, and in many instances the collaboration is already taking place. But of course it needs to be strengthened and it needs to be formalised.

Two recent instances of collaboration are worthy of note. The Platform of European Social NGOs is a network of European social welfare NGOs. A first formal meeting was held with the ETUC in January 1997 and the beginning of a common programme was agreed. The ETUC and the Platform have agreed to campaign together for the inclusion of a core of fundamental human rights in the New Treaty of the European Union. This is an example of a good collaboration, which is already bearing results.

A second collaboration concerns the ICFTU. At the Singapore

Ministerial Meeting a number of NGOs decided not to support the unions' position to include Core Labour Standards in the WTO rules. They did so even though they shared a concern with the ICFTU for trade union rights, but they generally felt that the WTO was a tool of the rich industrialised countries and should not be strengthened.

This position was not universally held by NGOs, with a significant number deciding that it was important to organise to support the ICFTU position and to prepare for future summits and conferences in which Core Labour Standards are on the agenda. These NGOs, working in partnership with the ICFTU, formed a loose alliance they called the Workers Rights Caucus, whose object was to organise the lobbying activities and the presence of NGOs in relation to the WTO and in support of the ICFTU position. These are interesting and important developments which should be encouraged and followed through both locally and nationally.

The NGOs could also benefit from a closer alliance with the trade unions. Apart from the organisational strengths and the scale and diversity of international trade union activities, the trade unions can make another type of contribution which is equally vital. In one way or another, a large part of the NGO community drew their strength from the socialist and social democratic concepts of equity and justice. The rise of neo–liberal economics and the accompanying crisis of the left have affected them too, and undoubtedly an intellectual vacuum has developed.

Now the tide is turning, and neo-liberalism has been shown to be a sham, and a new language of the left based on fundamental human rights is being articulated by the trade unions and by the left. A debate is taking place to build a new socialism, a socialism deeply rooted in the indivisibility and inalienability of all human rights. It is therefore important that the trade unions and the left also involve the NGOs in this evolving conceptual and practical discussion.

Economic growth and social justice in the global economy: political challenges, policy choices

David Kusnet and Robert Taylor

The quiet crisis

In most industrialised societies, national economies and working people's living standards are in a slow-motion recession. The problem takes different forms in different places. In Western Europe, there is mass unemployment. In Japan, there has been an unusually lengthy and deep recession. And, in the United States, working people's wages have stagnated for twenty years or more.

The problems are social and political, as well as economic. For the first twenty-five years after World War II, in most advanced industrial nations, the social fabric was strengthened and the political system stabilised by the prevalence of secure jobs with rising wages and the promise of an even better life for the next generation. Now, with the erosion of economic security, there are growing strains on family and community life – and a troubling sense that the values of work, loyalty, and responsibility are no longer honoured. And, as government failed to address economic stagnation and social breakdown, people became increasingly alienated from the political process.

This quiet crisis comes after an era of conservative domination in the

United States, Japan, the United Kingdom, Germany, and most other industrialised societies. The market was deified and deregulated, while government was ridiculed and reduced.

Finance capital and corporate management were strengthened, while labour unions and most other citizens' organisations were weakened. Many of these changes resulted from – and even more were attributed to – the need for countries and companies to compete in an unforgiving new global economy. But, at the end of it all, most people feel less prosperous, less secure, less connected with the life of their communities, and less confident that their values are reflected in their nations' economic and political life. That is why people throughout the industrialised nations are asking: Is there a better way? Can we pursue economic growth – and social justice, as well? Can we reconcile the imperatives of the new global marketplace with the time-honoured values of human society?

At last, the right questions are being asked. But there is no certainty that the right answers will emerge.

The new economy – and the new society it has produced – require new policies to promote our timeless goals: sustainable growth, social justice, and stronger communities. The fragmentation that recent social and economic changes have produced makes it more difficult to generate the social solidarity essential to progressive politics and policies.That is why it is so important that progressives once again do what we have done before – analyse problems, offer solutions, and build movements behind them. This work is not easy, but it is necessary. And we must proceed with an understanding of the new economic, social, and political environment.

Political challenges

New world, new workplace

The world and the workplace that produced social democracy in Western Europe and the New Deal in the United States have been forever transformed. And, before we can change our world, we must understand how our world has changed.

For instance, in the United States, the New Deal of the 1930s and 1940s was premised on a society and an economy that have since changed radically. Men worked outside the home, and, when they could afford to, women stayed home – unless they were single or widowed. (To be sure, many working-class women and most African-American women needed to work outside the home.) Most people worked for large corporations that dominated major industries, with little threat from foreign competition. Most worked at jobs that required little formal education and learned the skills they needed from their fathers, their fellow workers, or their employers.

Post-war reconstruction in Europe saw rising productivity in the mass production economy, combined with (and intimately linked to) full employment and the developing welfare state. As in America, this was predominantly full employment for male 'breadwinners', with women staying at home.

And in America in the prosperous years following World War II, workers in the primary labour market could count on relatively stable jobs, with rising wages and secure benefits and pensions. And progressives struggled so that African-Americans, women, and others who had been excluded from the primary labour market, could join the secure industrial economy.

The social gains of the New Deal era were all designed for this society and the economy that produced it. In different ways, Social Security and Aid to Families with Dependent Children presupposed a society where men were the wage-earners and women stayed home with the children. Unemployment insurance assumed that temporarily laid-off workers would eventually be called back to their jobs. The National Labour Relations Act guaranteed workers the right to organise and bargain with their employers. But its procedures assumed that workers would hold full-time jobs with large and stable corporations. And it failed to foresee the ferocity of employer opposition to the workers' right to organise (and, in fact, was amended over the years to allow employers more opportunities to interfere with the election process and intimidate their employees.) Public education from kindergarten to high school – a legacy of earlier periods of social reform – continued to assume that basic skills and the willingness to work would be sufficient for most jobs.

These premises and programmes lifted most working Americans into the middle class. But now, that secure world has been swept away. Secure industrial jobs are a thing of the past, and it is uncertain what will replace them. In 1950, 40 per cent of the workforce in the United States worked in manufacturing, while 58 per cent worked in services. Now, only 20 per cent work in manufacturing, while 79 per cent work in services.

Meanwhile, large corporate employers have also declined. Firms with 500 employees or more – many a far cry from industrial icons such as General Motors or General Electric – employ only 46 per cent of US workers, while firms with fewer than 100 workers employ 32 per cent of the workforce. While optimists once predicted that the primary labour market of secure jobs with large corporations would expand, recent growth instead has been in what was once called the 'secondary' labour market – unstable jobs with low wages, few benefits, and no future. In the United States, the largest employer is neither General Motors nor IBM nor even McDonald's, but Manpower Inc., an agency that supplies women and men as temporary workers. All in all, as many as 37 million Americans are now 'contingent' workers – part-time employees without steady jobs or health or pension benefits. In what may be a taste of the future for other industrialised economies, we are witnessing what has been called 'the temping of America'. The nature of work is also changing within Europe. Most new jobs created in the 1990s have been part-time. Temporary working has accounted for all the increase in employment of men, and just under half the rise for women. The number of people working nights and weekends has grown.

To be sure, many economic changes reflect expanding opportunities. In the European Union women have accounted for the entire growth of the labour force in the last twenty years, and their activity rate stands at 70 per cent for the Union as a whole. Similar trends can be seen across the globe, from Japan to Australia, as well as America, where women now account for almost half the workforce. And eight million businesses owned by women employ over 18.5 million people – one quarter of the US workforce – and account for $2.28 trillion in sales.

These changes – the bad as well as the good – are taking place across the globe. Throughout the OECD, industrial employment and large corporations have declined (in Europe companies employing fewer than 100 workers have been increasing employment by about 250,000 per year, while larger companies have been shedding jobs at about 200,000 a year), the service sector has grown, women shoulder additional responsibilities and enjoy new opportunities, jobs of all kinds require specialised skills, and societies emphasise personal choice and self-development, sometimes to the extent of an extreme individualism. In many societies, economic inequality has increased, and social problems have worsened.

Social solidarity or social breakdown?

In earlier economic crises – particularly the Great Depression of the 1930s – shared hardship generated social solidarity and, eventually, social progress. But the quiet crisis of the 1990s – economic stagnation, social fragmentation, and political alienation – may impede, not encourage, social solidarity.

Ironically, while the new economy brings the nations of the world closer together, it is also dividing societies more than ever before. The fragmentation of society may have gone furthest in the United States, but trends throughout most industrialised countries promote the break-up of society into smaller units. Large companies are outsourcing jobs to smaller firms. Business and much of the middle class are fleeing the cities for the suburbs – sometimes for new 'edge cities' on the outskirts of metropolitan areas. A growing number of professionals 'telecommute' from home to their offices by way of the Internet. Television and instant communications and information retrieval through computer networks all encourage families to 'cocoon' in their homes during their leisure time. All this contributes to the decline in the institutions that comprise civil society – from religious organisations to labour unions, civic, charitable, and political groups.

So does the impact of economic stagnation on much of the working middle class – a squeeze on time as well as money. In an effort to stay even, middle-class families in the US are sending more members into the workforce, working longer hours at their jobs, and taking second or third jobs. Modern communications technologies – cellular phones, pagers, fax machines, and modems – allow people to stay in touch with their colleagues and clients at any time and from any place, creating an expectation that a growing number of professionals are always 'on call'. Global commerce, too, creates a demand for some employees at every level to work at unusual hours or around the clock. Even among the very wealthy who set the tone for those who aspire to their status, extreme work hours – conspicuous productivity as well as conspicuous consumption – characterise their well-publicised styles of living and working.

All this upsets the balance among work, family, and community. Spending more and more time on their jobs, men and women of the working middle class have less time to spend with their families and in their communities. This contributes to a sense of beleaguered virtue among the hardpressed, hardworking middle class – and a lack of sympathy for those who are unable to work and especially for those who are seen as unwilling to work. Thus, much of the demand for often punitive reform of the welfare system results from the fact that fewer middle-class women can afford to stay home with their children and, therefore, resent a programme that provides even subsistence support for single mothers who do not work outside the home.

While there is pride in hard work, there is also ambivalence, even guilt, about the long hours spent away from families and children. People are alarmed about the impact of an increasingly violent, tawdry, and materialistic popular culture upon their children, and worry whether they have the time to teach them the difference between right and wrong. Across the economic spectrum, the fragmentation of society leaves problems in its wake. With the decline in manufacturing employment and the flight of good-paying jobs from the cities, there are entire communities where, as the sociologist William Julius Wilson writes, 'work has disappeared'. Not only jobs have been lost but also the hopes and habits produced by the expectation of finding work. For the past thirty years or more, family break-up, violent crime, and drug abuse all have tended to increase not only in the inner cities but throughout society. (Recently, there has been a welcome downturn in violent crime, but some observers attribute it to demographic trends and warn it will be temporary.)

The result has been a politics of moral panic, rooted in real fears of social breakdown and moral collapse. In the United States, for instance, movements as varied as the Religious Right, a smaller but increasingly active Religious Left, the ostensibly apolitical Promise Keepers (men who hold mass meetings where they pledge to behave responsibly towards their families), and the Million Man March (which was organised by the controversial Minister Louis Farrakhan but attracted wide support among African-Americans) – all address the yearning for certainty and community in the midst of social and economic change.

In the industrialised countries, these social and economic anxieties contribute to racial, religious, and ethnic tensions. Often, social problems are stereotyped as caused by, or confined to, vulnerable minorities. Immigrants are seen simultaneously as competitors for jobs and as freeloaders unwilling to work. Globalisation in all its forms – immigration, foreign direct investment, shifts in business location and jobs, trade agreements and international economic agencies – give rise not only to economic anxiety and social antagonism but to crises of national identity. These feelings are exploited by right-wing populist movements, such as Patrick Buchanan's presidential campaigns in the United States, the National Front in France, and the Freedom Party in Austria. These movements must be challenged, and the anxieties that feed them must be addressed. For progressives, the challenge is to meld economic and social concerns. Issues of work, family, community, and national identity dominate public debate, and we must be prepared to answer them.

Tale of two stories

Corporate interests and conservative politicians throughout the world have offered remarkably similar explanations for the economic and social problems associated with the new economy: global competition requires advanced nations to cut wages and social programmes. New technologies bid up the salaries for skilled workers and drive down wages for everyone else – or cause large-scale unemployment in economies where wages do not fall. Deregulation and de-unionisation are needed to adjust to this ultra-competitive economy. It's a harsh new world out there, and we all had better tighten our belts and pull up our socks. Or so we are told.

So prevalent is this fear of globalisation that it has paralysed many on the centre-left, who no longer believe governments can establish a countervailing force to confront what is happening in a time of rapid economic and social change.

In fact, there is room for serious debate about the extent and impact of globalisation. But this much is clear: it has further increased the power that financial capital and multinational corporations exert over the rest of society. Capital in all its forms is more mobile than ever – indeed, investment can travel the world with a keystroke on a computer – while working people are tethered to their communities and their countries by ties of family, loyalty, and necessity. Thus, regardless of the impact of international economic competition, globalisation gives capital even more of an advantage over labour, from the bargaining table to the corridors of political power. It has used that advantage to cut wages and social benefits. And it has an all-purpose alibi: 'The global economy made us do it.'

Not surprisingly, right-wing populists – from Patrick Buchanan in the United States to Jean-Marie Le Pen in France – have an equally simple answer: 'Stop the world economy – we want to get off.'

In most advanced societies, progressives have a more complicated story to tell: the problem is not the global economy, but how corporations and their political allies have responded to the challenge. They have taken the low road in international competition – driving down wages and benefits. Instead, we must challenge our companies, our countries, and the European community and emerging trading blocs in North America and in East Asia and the Pacific, to compete by taking the high road – investing in working people's skills, improving the quality of the goods they produce and the services they provide, and including everyone in the gains of a growing economy.

The centre-left needs to take the offensive and recognise it can still exercise pressure and influence to shape events. Most of all, progressives need to make the case for institutions strong enough to challenge the power, and change the priorities, of multinational corporations. These institutions include labour unions, activist governments, and international agreements and agencies capable of enforcing standards for workers' rights and environmental protection.

Encouraging signs have begun to emerge of a credible and coherent progressive agenda to humanise globalisation. Established institutions such as the World Bank and the International Monetary Fund have not shown much sympathy or understanding for the social consequences of global trade, investment and capital market flows in the past; but even they appear to be indicating a new concern about human rights as the world's economic system moves to guarantee the rights of investors, intellectual property and environmental standards. The renewed interest being shown in the strategic role of the state in policy-making is indicative of a change in the direction of the global debate. The case for more effective public regulation at international level looks likely to grow with the 1997 World Bank development report on corporate governance.

Moves to establish greater international coordination in developing macro-economic strategies of expansion may remain less in evidence, but even here there are signs of an increasing concern for more cooperative frameworks for global action. Through well-established bodies such as the International Labour Organisation and the Organisation for Economic Cooperation and Development, a new balance may be possible, which can reconcile the demands imposed by the globalising economy for greater competitiveness, efficiency and productivity and those for more social equity and cohesion, stability and democratic rights. Working with these institutions, progressives can promote a new concept of corporate responsibility that extends not only to their shareholders but also to their stakeholders – their employees, their communities, and their consumers. The harmonising of economic and political objectives in the social market economy should lie at the heart of the new progressive-left agenda.

New unionism

Strong union movements helped forge the post-war social contract that offered working people improved living standards and a stronger voice, from their workplaces to the political process. But now, most national trade union movements across the world – from Japan to the United States – are in decline. Even more seriously, a growing number of employees are no longer protected in their pay and conditions by collectively negotiated agreements. As a result, working people have suffered severe losses in their wages, benefits, and job security, as well as in the influence and respect they enjoyed in their countries' economic, social, and political life.

What can be done?
Trade unions must modernise by adapting their structures to more flexible workplaces and labour markets. They have to recognise and respond in a positive way to new conditions: the more individualistic demands of workers, the rapid increase in the number of small-scale enterprises; and the fragmented private services sector with its greater diversity of employment relationships – part-time and temporary jobs as well as self-employed workers and those working on limited contracts. Trade unions will have to grow more as service providers which meet the vocational and professional requirements of workers in a world without jobs for life. They will have to campaign for wide framework agreements that set down minimum standards. They must also develop mutual insurance functions as friendly societies in the provision of a range of services to supplement those provided by welfare states. Trade unions must widen their practical functions to satisfy the particular concerns of women workers, the low paid and the socially excluded.

This will not be easy anywhere. But trade unions should not forget that, in modernising, they need to reassert their basic core values. They must remain voluntary and collective associations of working people –

free from both state and employer control. As democratic organisations they should be concerned to extend and defend the rights of workers as citizens in the wider society.

Already, in response to this challenge, labour movements in many industrialised societies have been transforming themselves in an effort to organise working women and men in the new economy. Progressives support these efforts, understanding that independent and active labour movements are indispensable institutions in a free society. Indeed the quiet crisis of our own times teaches this truth as surely as did the extreme hardship of the Great Depression.

During the 1930s, the advanced societies learned that, unless working people were paid well enough to afford to buy the products they made, economies would be plunged into depression. That is why countries such as the United States set public policies that guaranteed workers the right to organise and bargain with their employers. It was understood that unions serve a public purpose: to compel corporations to share their profits with their employees. Indeed, for the first three decades after World War II, unionised companies set the pace for the entire economy, lifting wages and benefits for non-union workers as well.

Now, in the new global economy, unions are still essential as a counterweight to corporate power, and as a mechanism to ensure that working people share in the gains of growing productivity. But unions are increasingly essential for other reasons as well.

They are seeking new ways to help working people win a stronger voice in their companies, so they can improve the quality of the goods they produce and the services they provide. In the new economy, small differences in quality spell success or failure in the ultra-competitive global marketplace. Unions can play an important part by giving voice to workers' recommendations for improving the quality of their goods and services, and by offering workers a sense of security, that their ideas and efforts will be used to improve their pay and opportunities, not to eliminate their jobs. In the new social contract that unions seek and progressives support, working people will share power, as well as profits, with their companies.

Before unions can forge and enforce a new social contract, they need to rebuild their strength. In most industrialised countries, labour movements have lost members, power, and prestige for many of the same reasons: the loss of jobs in manufacturing, the shrinking of government, the emergence of new industries, the increasing hostility of employers, and, until recently, the unions' own institutional inertia.

That is why the national labour federations in the United States, the United Kingdom, Australia, the Netherlands, and many other advanced countries are embarking upon remarkably similar programmes of renewal and revitalisation.

The process of renewal begins with an honest admission that unions have lagged behind the pace of change in their societies, their workplaces, and the workforce itself. Acting upon this admission, many labour federations and their member unions are devoting more resources to organising workers outside their ranks. Often they are targeting the very workers whom employers have underpaid and unions have overlooked: women, racial and ethnic minorities, recent immigrants, young people, and workers in clerical, health care, and service sector jobs. In addition, labour federations and their member unions are expanding the services they offer, to include job training and educational programmes, credit cards and other consumer services, and advice on issues from naturalisation to taxes. Many of the most dramatic changes are coming in the United States, where union membership has declined to 15 per cent of the entire work force, and to only 10 per cent in the private sector. In October 1995, in the first contested election in its history, the national labour federation, the AFL-CIO, elected a slate of insurgent candidates as its new leaders. The federation is now earmarking 30 per cent of its budget for organising, and challenging national unions and their locals to devote a similar share of their resources to recruitment. And the AFL-CIO has expanded its Organising Institute, which recruits and trains new organisers for national unions.

Similarly, the Trades Union Congress in Great Britain has launched a national discussion of 'the new unionism'. The TUC is expanding its organising efforts, with a special focus on working women and on part-time employees, who now comprise a quarter of the nation's workforce. The Australian Council of Trade Unions has established a special 'recruitment and organising fund' and is fielding a 'flying squad' of almost 200 young organisers. And, in the Netherlands, the Trade Union Confederation (FNV) has already pioneered such innovations and gained 250,000 members – a 20 per cent increase – over the past ten years.

As unions rebuild their membership strength, they can be expected to push for a voice in corporate decision-making, from the workplace to multinational investment strategies. This, too, is part of 'the new unionism'.

Progressives should promote public policies that help working

236

people attain a stronger voice, in their jobs and throughout society, by encouraging the growth of strong and vibrant unions. Here governments can set an example of worker empowerment and labour-management cooperation in the way that they structure their own agencies and treat their own employees. And, through the power of national leaders to focus public attention and shape public opinion, governments can call attention to the need for working people to have the power to do their jobs better and improve the quality of goods and services. To be sure, conditions, policies and legal structures surrounding employee relations differ from country to country. But, in every society, progressives should support labour relations policies that effectively guarantee working people the right to organise unions and bargain with their employers. To bring labour relations policies into the modern era, part-time employees, white-collar and professional employees, and workers in health care, government, and the service sector should all enjoy the same rights as the workers in full-time industrial and craft jobs who predominated earlier in the century. And the scope of bargaining should be expanded to include decision-making, from the organisation of the workplace to the shaping of corporate priorities, as well as traditional issues such as wages, hours, benefits, and conditions.

It is no coincidence that the most equitable and affluent societies in the world are those which have free trade unions. Open market economies should not be seen as a threat to the existence of organised labour but, on the contrary, as a precondition for the survival and renewal of trade unionism. The contemporary evidence from Europe, Japan and even North America does not suggest that trade unions are reactionary obstacles to corporate efficiency and national competitiveness. On the contrary, they can be vital organisations in the development of the high road economic and industrial strategies that seek to improve living standards and ensure the growth of successful companies.

For these reasons progressives will continue to assert this simple but powerful truth: working people must be full participants in our nations' economic, social, and political life. And that requires strong and vibrant labour movements to give voice to working people's aspirations.

Still, the challenge for progressives is not to defend old models but to offer new ones. We need to promote public policies that allow societies to balance economic efficiency and social justice – and allow working women and men to balance work, family, and community.

237

Policy choices

Unemployment and social exclusion

Fighting mass unemployment and social exclusion and reducing widening inequalities of income and wealth need to be the highest priorities of the centre-left at the end of the twentieth century. To meet new complex modern realities the old values of solidarity and liberty have to be adapted, not abandoned. This means coming to terms in a positive way with the emergence of the post-industrial society, with the rise of female employment, technological innovation and growing job insecurity, as well as the increase in small and medium-sized private companies in a variegated services sector. Above all it requires recognition of what is needed for the individual to survive and flourish in our more complex and fragmented societies, with the help of enlightened public policy.

The centre-left must at all times be economic realists. They need to accept the need for financial prudence, restrained public spending and a clear limitation on the capacity of the state to increase taxes on labour and capital to improve the public good. But this should not mean accepting the destruction of the welfare state based on universal provision in health and education services for all citizens, funded through a redistributive tax system. Nor should it mean pursuing policies aimed at zero inflation or balanced budgets if this endangers social cohesion and inclusion.

An economic agenda for action should aim to secure a wide consensus for coordinated growth, for, after all, sustainable economic expansion remains the best way to reduce unemployment. Public policy at global and national level should encourage greater investment, in both the physical and the intangible capital which provide the basis for growth and development, with higher productivity and improved competitiveness underpinning income growth.

The commitment to fair and open trade, with the removal on restrictions to free movement, must be balanced by recognition that this should not result in the worsening social conditions of a zero-or-negative-sum game. Measures to control the excessive speculation of global financial markets should be appraised to see whether they can go some way to moderate or constrain what often seem like irresistible forces without plunging the world into self-defeating protectionism and selfish 'beggar thy neighbour' trade policies.

Tax and public finance

There must be a broader and more focused attitude to tax and spend. This may mean a shift of the burden of taxation off both labour and capital and an increase in taxation to help the environment. Measures will be needed to plug existing tax havens in the global economy through international coordinated action. Coordination will also be needed if there is to be effective taxation of capital – the most mobile tax base of all. This is important both in order to raise revenue and to promote equity. It highlights the importance of international cooperation – and the need to pool sovereignty if sovereignty is not to flow away to faceless financial markets.

Some suggest generalising the experiment with supply-side economics that the United States conducted during the 1980s: lower marginal rates, and taxation of consumption, rather than income. In Western Europe, with its high unemployment rates, there is also discussion of reducing payroll taxes which companies pay on their employees. Still others suggest 'green taxes' designed to discourage pollution or 'consumption taxes' or value-added taxes. In fact, the lessons of the 1980s and 90s in the US and elsewhere suggest that tax revisions are not an economic panacea: firstly, tax structure has limited and uncertain effects on economic performance, including employment; secondly, the most lasting impact of supply-side tax revisions is to increase economic inequality and threaten the sense of national community; thirdly, the gains from transforming taxes on labour into taxes on consumption – or from reducing social benefits and the taxes that finance them – can be illusory; and, fourthly, for all their attractiveness as a way to encourage environmentally responsible behavior, 'green taxes' to the extent that they succeed in this goal, will draw on a diminishing revenue base over the years.

But scepticism about the supply-side reforms practised in the United States and the UK should not blind us to the need for well-designed tax reform, or structural and micro-economic reform more generally. It is, for example, widely accepted that growth alone will not be enough to overcome deep structural and supply-side constraints in many labour markets. The crisis of long-term unemployment will require a more targeted approach, with a new emphasis on training and education. Subsidies and incentives to employers may help to a limited extent in reducing the numbers of those who have been out of work for over twelve months, but the main emphasis should be on a progressive strategy designed to help individuals through active labour market policies to equip themselves more effectively to meet the demands of the economy.

Social partnerships

Individuals left on their own are in no position to meet the challenges of the modern world. To succeed they need the support and participation of strong and autonomous institutions based on principles of social partnership. Workers and citizens find it more difficult to articulate their demands and aspirations with the spread of deregulation, the growth of global corporations and the decline in effective forms of representation. The encouragement of social institutions does not mean a return to the corporatist centralised structures that were popular thirty years ago, but the creation of new associations that provide a means of mediating the dual aims of economic efficiency and social equity that lie at the heart of the new centre–left approach. In Japan and a number of European countries like Ireland and Denmark, national agreements between the state, trade unions and employers have achieved some success at macro-economic level in this direction. The Irish case is a particularly good example of social partnership based on the themes of inclusion, employment and competitiveness. In Germany a serious effort is being made to modernise that country's social market model through flexible agreements. Recently in Austria employers and trade unions have reached a deal on shortening working time that has reinvigorated a traditional relationship. Even in the UK a loose understanding based on social partnership may begin to emerge as trade unions start to see themselves as part of the solution not part of the problem of making the country more efficient and competitive.

However, social partnership is not a soft option but a hard-headed and pragmatic response to globalisation, technological change and mass unemployment. At European Union level, developing framework agreements between the social partners as an alternative to binding legal regulations may encourage a closer cooperation between capital and labour. Despite genuine differences, both sides are searching for common ground in the creation of joint strategies. So far a deal has been reached through dialogue on the introduction of unpaid parental leave. A further advance looks likely on part-time employment.

Fruitful social partnerships are also being forged at enterprise level. The European Union works council directive has required the introduction of employee information and consultation committees in large corporations operating in at least two member states. These promise an important advance in worker representation inside corporate decision-making. Most sizeable companies operating within Europe may have such institutions by the end of the century.

There is even some hope they may find their way into the United States and Japan. The development of the stakeholder company or the human development enterprise could provide an important way forward for the defence and growth of workers' voice. The demand grows for the encouragement of more socially responsible companies based on trust and centred on a social partnership between capital and labour that accepts a mutual bargain of employee flexibility in return for greater workplace security.

The best means to encourage the development of such new kinds of firm, based on decent core employment practices, remains open to debate – negotiations, different forms of incentive or legal regulation might all play a part. What seems clear is that some such institutional reform will be needed to reconcile the financial objectives of the company in developing competitive goods and services with the demands of employees for greater security at work and the protection of their human rights.

Social partnership should also be extended to help in the establishment of dynamic labour market measures through more activist employment services. Here Germany and Sweden provide practical examples of what can be achieved. There is scope for similar developments elsewhere, in the encouragement of training programmes to help workers become more employable, the encouragement of human resource management techniques and a renewed emphasis on research and development and product innovation. These initiatives should be seen as mutual gains agreements, or social pacts that reflect the common needs of the modern enterprise and those of the employee. A pragmatic consensus should be possible to improve productivity and contain costs.

Social partnership should not be seen as a euphemism for the reassertion of unilateral management power. Nor should it assume the subordination of employees to the unquestioned demands of capital. Social partnership means developing a new trust through psychological contracts in the enterprise that seek to reconcile social cohesion and business competitiveness. For the centre-left it requires reaching out to forge closer ties with progressive capital, to encourage companies to recognise that it is as much in their own interests as that of their employees to work together, while recognising they can still have conflicting interests. Social partnership should not be seen as a pact between big capital and big labour but as a modern means of reasserting the democratic values of the citizen. The emphasis must be on diversity and experiment. Encouragement should be given to new forms of economic democracy through share and capital ownership, employee cooperatives and public/private initiatives.

The restoration of civil society

From public policy-makers to social commentators and ordinary citizens, there is increasing interest in 'civil society' – the rich variety of voluntary institutions that thrive in the shadows of national governments and giant, often multinational, corporations.

These institutions range from religious, civic, and charitable institutions to the new breed of women's, environmental, human rights, and other public interest organisations. In these organisations, people can work with their neighbours, serve their communities, develop their talents, and advance their values. Indeed, when people think of what makes a place a 'community', we think of its community life – its churches, charities, civic, athletic, cultural, and educational groups.

The social partnership we propose should not draw artificial lines between business, government, labour, and something called 'civil society'. Voluntary organisations of all kinds, and the levels of government that are closest to the people, should be included so that we can stimulate a revived sense of public purpose and foster social cohesion and equity.

There is a strong need for the restoration of the public interest in reshaping the market economy in a more socially responsible way. It is widely accepted there can be no return to the mid-century era of big government, high public spending and high taxation. The time of employers and trade unions as the only players may be over.

There is also a bias against centralisation. In a growing number of countries the state is no longer seen as part of the solution but part of the problem. Such views are understandable, and the role of the state should be reappraised, with the emphasis on its capacity to act as an enabling force providing the necessary means for people to realise their individual potentialities. This cannot be done if the state is remote or coercive. But nor can it be done if the state is demonised and denied both political legitimacy and economic resources.

In fact, the new synthesis we need must reconcile effective government with encouragement for the growth of more non-governmental organisations, pressure groups and community-based associations as well as single issue bodies. There has to be a greater recognition of the importance of women's voice in the development of civil society. It is also important that common ground is found that can bring the public and the private interest together in the creation of strategic alliances. New ways have to be found of improving political participation and empowerment, with shared responsibilities and accountability.

At a time when government is being cut back and corporations are downsizing, progressives should join those who are exploring how to promote and revive 'civil society'. But we should also bring our own perspectives to this discussion, not least because at present civil society remains fragmented, weak and unorganised.

There are a number of points that need to be considered in any discussion of civil society. Firstly, small community-based institutions are important, but they are not strong enough to serve as counterweights to multinational corporations and global market forces. Activist national governments and strong labour movements are still needed to counter the power of the modern corporation. Indeed, local government – particularly community-based entities such as school boards and public school systems – should be considered as part of civil society, since they are close to the people in their neighbourhoods. So should labour unions, which, after all, are voluntary organisations outside of big business and big government. Indeed, local unions are among the most vibrant community organisations and often work together with other community groups.

Secondly, the strain on civil society results largely from many of the same economic trends that have put a crimp on working people and their living standards. As working women and men put in more time on their jobs, they have less time to spend with their families and in their communities. Thus, civic life suffers from the wage squeeze and the time famine.

Thirdly, women's voices should be heard on the need to balance work, family, and community. While the great majority of women now work outside the home, they also have to work an unpaid 'second shift' inside the home, since most still have primary responsibility for parenting and homemaking. Thus, they are acutely sensitive to the need for improved social services, from child care to health care, whether they are provided by government or by the social service sector. And attention should also be paid to the growing number of small businesses owned by women. Indeed, businesswomen and the organisations that represent them are an important part of civil society.

Modernising the model

Political as well as economic life is being globalised. Increasingly, political leaders justify their own proposals or attack their opponents' by pointing to the supposed successes or failures of similar policies in other countries.

Thus, in recent public debate throughout the industrialised societies, conservatives have conjured up something called 'Eurosclerosis' – persistent unemployment in Western Europe, supposedly caused by an extensive and expensive welfare state, high taxes, and strong unions. Similarly, they have praised an 'American Model' – more accurately, an Anglo-American model – of reduced taxes on corporations and the wealthy, deregulation of business and finance, and de-unionisation of much of the workforce.

Praising or pillorying countries or continents as economic 'models' generates more heat than light. To be sure, progressives – especially those from the USA or UK – should call attention to the failings of an economic model that has generated an enormous transfer of wealth to the most affluent, while producing little or no gain in living standards for the most vulnerable working people (and in America, for working people in general, vulnerable or not). And conservatives can be challenged on social and moral as well as economic grounds: there must be something wrong with an 'American Model' that produces a society where the leading employer is a temporary-help agency, the fastest-growing industry is prison construction, and the fastest-growing occupation is private security guards.

Social renewal should go hand in hand with strong economic performance. But this means an acceptance of change, going with the current of the remarkable pace of technological innovation, and occupational shifts in the labour market away from manufacturing to the enormous variety of private services that are transforming our world. We cannot passively accept current policy prescriptions that either uncritically worship the free market or seek to maintain social programmes designed for an earlier era. There has to be a new dynamic in our approach to the unemployment crisis, to the problems of tax and spend, to the insecurities of the workplace and the labour market and to the dangers of ecological destruction of our environment. We need to see the return of a politics of hope based on the fundamental values of the centre–left: liberty, equality and fraternity. Above all, this means the reassertion of a distinctive and coherent agenda that seeks to find a new and harmonious synthesis between efficiency and social justice, between business performance and democratic accountability, transcending the existing neo-liberal and social market models.

Notes on Contributors

John Evans is General Secretary of the Trade Union Advisory Committee to the OECD (TUAC).

Allan Larsson is Director General of Employment and Social Affairs, European Commission.

Jürgen Hoffmann is Professor at the School of Economics and Politics, Hamburg University.

Sadahiko Inoue is Deputy Director of the Research Institute for the Advancement of Living Standards (RIALS), associated with the Japanese trade union confederation, RENGO.

Fujikau Suzuki is Senior Researcher at RIALS.

Thomas Palley is Deputy Director of the Department of Public Policy at the AFL-CIO.

Guy Standing works for the International Labour Organisation, Geneva. He writes here in a personal capacity.

Bettina Agathonos-Mähr is European representative of the Austrian Confederation of Trade Unions (OGB).

Heiner Gansmann is Professor of Sociology at the Free University of Berlin.

Dan Corry is Senior Economist, IPPR and Editor, *New Economy*.

Eystein Gjelsvik is an economist working for the Norwegian Confederation of Trade Unions (LO).

Max Sawicky is an economist with the Economic Policy Institute, Washington, DC.

Bill Jordan is General Secretary of the International Confederation of Free Trade Unions.

Linda Tarr-Whelan is President and CEO of the Center for Policy Alternatives, Washington, DC.

David Kusnet is Consultant and Visiting Fellow, US Economic Policy Institute.

Robert Taylor is Employment Editor for the *Financial Times*.

Paul Ormerod is chair of Post-Orthodox Economics, London.

Peter Cassells is General Secretary of the Irish Congress of Trade Unions (ICTU).

Giampiero Alhadeff is Secretary General of SOLIDAR.

David Foden is senior researcher at the European Trade Union Institute, Brussels.

Peter Morris is Director of Policy and Research at Unison, London.